THE
CHRISTADELPHIANS

The Christadelphians

WHAT THEY BELIEVE AND PREACH

Harry Tennant

THE CHRISTADELPHIAN
404 SHAFTMOOR LANE
BIRMINGHAM B28 8SZ
ENGLAND

1988

First published 1986

Reprinted 1988

ISBN 0 85189 119 5

Set by Action Typesetting Ltd, Gloucester
Printed and bound in Great Britain by
Billing & Sons Ltd, Worcester

PREFACE

THE apostle Jude, writing to Christian believers in the first century, spoke of the necessity to contend earnestly for "*the faith which was once delivered to the saints.*" It was therefore understood by the early apostles of the Lord Jesus Christ that the Truth — the "*light which lighteth every man that cometh into the world*" — which had been declared in him would soon be clouded by the avarice and self-aggrandisement of men. And so it happened. The pattern established from earliest days, that the darkness of human lust attempts to veil the light of Godly love, has been repeated in all ages. But just as man's ways are unchanging, so is God's Word. For the sincere seeker for truth, it provides the deepest well of knowledge. For the bereft, the surest comfort. For the lonely, the truest companion. For the disturbed mind, calm sanity. It is the port in the storm of life, the fortress in this warring world, the sanctuary and refuge provided by God.

But, as a man undertaking a long and arduous journey once said of the Scriptures to a companion he met on the road, '*How can I understand what I am reading, unless some man should guide me?*', this is how many people feel when they too approach the Bible. The length of the book, the apparent complexity of some of its teaching, the difficulty of its language, all conspire to make many give up before they really commence to understand its basic message. One of the objectives of this book is to provide such a guide. It charts in its pages the essential message: the Gospel (the good news) of Jesus Christ and God's coming kingdom. As is to be expected in a book about Bible teaching, it quotes extensively from the Bible. In fact, there are over twelve hundred separate quotations. These have been printed in full so that the flow for the reader will be undisturbed. They form an impressive testimony to the utter integrity of Scripture. It is apparent that the Bible message, encompassed in the different and individual books of the Bible, written at the hands of men of differing cultural backgrounds, but united in their love of the God of Abraham and Israel, is distinct and coherent.

The author, who has been a Christadelphian all his adult life, has always sought to set forth Scripture's distinct teachings. He has now written compellingly and honestly about the great hope it contains. He invites the reader to open with him the pages of God's Word and see there the Gospel truth. This is a book which will leave few unmoved by the cogency of its reasoning, and the appeal of its exalted language. It is at the same time both a description of a people's faith, and of that on which it is based, *"The word of God's grace."*

October 1986   MICHAEL ASHTON

Versions of the Bible Referred to in this Book

THE author is a staunch supporter of the *Authorised (King James) Version* (A.V.). In his study of the Bible and in his daily reading, he has found it helpful for many years to make use of the *Revised Version* (R.V.) of 1881 as a means of comparison and occasional clarification of some parts of Scripture. More recently, he has become acquainted with the *Revised Standard Version* (R.S.V.), and with the much more recent *New International Version* (N.I.V.).

In order to provide as much help as possible to the reader, especially to anyone not familiar with the Bible in any version, reference is made to all of the versions mentioned in the hope that these will serve to get the message across.

When a version other than the *Authorised Version* is referred to, there is no substantial difference in meaning, but the alternative rendering may be helpful to new readers of the Bible, and, perhaps, to others.

FOREWORD

IN this book the reader is invited to pursue a path through the Word of God whilst examining the faith of a Christadelphian. Some parts of the journey will be over familiar ground to anyone acquainted with the 20th century world, and even more so if there is also some knowledge of the Bible. The chapters which follow deal freely with the things which Christadelphians believe and do, and what their organisation and way of life are like.

The community has borne the name Christadelphian since the latter half of the 19th century. The name is intended to cover three words, Brethren in Christ. Christadelphians are to be found in countries all over the world. They are bound together by a common faith in the Gospel preached by Christ and his apostles in the first century. It was this faith and its appeal to men and women from all walks of life which brought the community into existence.

Christadelphians do not believe that any of their members, past or present, have received any special revelation direct from God. For reasons which the reader will appreciate more and more as he reads on, the Christadelphian faith rests squarely and solely on the Bible as the Word of God.

From time to time some individual members have set forth in writing the content of their common faith for the benefit of any who would care to ponder its truth. One of the earliest books of this kind is *Elpis Israel* (The Hope of Israel) by John Thomas. It was followed 20 years later by *Christendom Astray*, written by Robert Roberts who became well-known as Editor of the community magazine, *The Christadelphian*. A later Editor, John Carter, produced *God's Way*, which appeared after the Second World War. All these books are still available.

It is hoped that this lesser volume will prove to be an encouragement to read the others. Nevertheless the true object is to give honour to the Word of God alone, and to demonstrate the reasonableness of the faith of the Christadelphians on that sure foundation. It is a faith that works.

Contents

1

THE FAIR EARTH

NEVER since the dawn of history has man known as much as he knows today about the planet on which he dwells. Never before has he been so deeply aware of the great unknown beyond the boundaries of his present knowledge. One of the greatest fruits of his achievements is the sense he has gained of the limitlessness of all things great and small.

At the same time there is a growing realisation of the unity of things. There is a basic agreement, a correspondence, among the principles which govern the arrangement and organisation of all things. There are relationships, balances and inter-dependencies which speak more and more of one system of thought behind everything. The world is one.

Moreover, the earth itself within the solar system is part of a vast heavenly array which extends on and on in countless replications and variations, all of which are governed by physical laws such as are found on our tiny globe. Everything, everywhere speaks of intelligent order and consistency, and of a mighty power which is universally and unfailingly present.

The Bible alone matches the world about us with an explanation of the origin of things which is both simple and comprehensive:

"In the beginning God created the heaven and the earth."

(Genesis 1:1)

Out of one God came all that is. Day and night, earth and sky, sea and land, grass and trees, fishes and birds, animals and insects, and, lastly but supremely, man. God is the Unity behind, within

1

and around all. His Word is the wisdom and reason and order in all things. His Spirit is the power by which in wisdom He produced creation and still sustains it.

A Godless beginning would mean a Godless development and a Godless end, whenever and whatever that might be. In such a case man would not know whence he came, why he is here and where he is going. The universe would be without a pilot and without a purpose. There would be no mind to account for the complex unity of all parts of the universe and of everything found in it.

Man would be a prisoner in a cage of unintelligent powers greater than himself, a seeing captive in a blind cosmos. There would be no sure explanations for what and where we are, and inevitably no grounds for hope but simply a wishful groping in the darkness with never the possibility of finding a Hand to hold. Man would be his own "maker", but without power to govern and determine his destiny. He would be like a ship adrift on a vast ocean, always uncertain of finding land or of whether there was any land to find.

In marvellous and lucid contrast to the mindlessness of atheism there are the following words of Scripture:

About God:

> "*Where wast thou when I laid the foundations of the earth?*"

(Job 38:4)

> "*Have ye not known? have ye not heard? hath it not been told you from the beginning? have ye not understood from the foundations of the earth? It is he that sitteth upon the circle of the earth, and the inhabitants thereof are as grasshoppers; that stretcheth out the heavens as a curtain, and spreadeth them out as a tent to dwell in.*"

(Isaiah 40:21 – 22)

> "*Hast thou not known? hast thou not heard that the everlasting God, the Lord, the Creator of the ends of the earth, fainteth not, neither is weary? there is no searching of his understanding.*"

(Isaiah 40:28)

About the earth and its wonders:

> "*He watereth the hills from his chambers:*
> *The earth is satisfied with the fruit of thy works.*
> *He causeth the grass to grow for the cattle,*
> *And herb for the service of man:*

2

That he may bring forth food out of the earth:
And wine that maketh glad the heart of man,
And oil to make his face to shine,
And bread which strengtheneth man's heart.
O Lord, how manifold are thy works!
In wisdom hast thou made them all:
The earth is full of thy riches.
So is this great and wide sea,
Wherein are things innumerable,
Both small and great beasts."

(Psalm 104:13 – 15, 24 – 25)

About the sky and the heavens:

"Stand still, and consider the wondrous works of God.
Dost thou know when God disposed them,
And caused the light of his cloud to shine?
Dost thou know the balancings of the clouds,
The wondrous works of him that is perfect in knowledge?"

(Job 37:14 – 16)

"Canst thou bind the sweet influences of Pleiades,
Or loose the bands of Orion?
Canst thou bring forth Mazzaroth (or, the signs of the Zodiac) in his
*   season?*
Or canst thou guide Arcturus (the Bear) with his sons?"

(Job 38:31 – 32)

"And God said, Let there be lights in the firmament of the heaven to
divide the day from the night; and let them be for signs and for seasons,
and for days, and years: and let them be for lights in the firmament of
heaven to give light upon the earth: and it was so. And God made two
great lights; the greater light to rule the day, and the lesser light to rule the
night: he made the stars also."

(Genesis 1:14 – 16)

"The heavens declare the glory of God;
And the firmament sheweth his handiwork."

(Psalm 19:1)

The Divine Summary:

"God that made the world and all things therein, seeing that he is Lord
of heaven and earth, dwelleth not in temples made with hands; neither is

3

worshipped with men's hands, as though he needed anything, seeing he giveth to all life, and breath, and all things; and hath made of one blood all nations of men for to dwell on all the face of the earth, and hath determined the times before appointed, and the bounds of their habitation; that they should seek the Lord, if haply they might feel after him and find him, though he be not far from every one of us: for in him we live, and move, and have our being."

(Acts 17:24 – 28)

Jesus said:

"I thank thee, O Father, Lord of heaven and earth."

(Matthew 11:25)

The Ultimate Purpose:

"Thou art worthy, O Lord, to receive glory and honour and power: for thou hast created all things, and for thy pleasure they are and were created."

(Revelation 4:11)

"The Lord said . . . As truly as I live, all the earth shall be filled with the glory of the Lord."

(Numbers 14:20 – 21)

Surely no one can read these beautiful words of Scripture without being impressed by their majestic simplicity. They are at the same time both comprehensive and profound. There is instruction and comfort for the ordinary man in the street, and there is sufficient for the educated man of the 20th century. The Unity of things is explained: all come from One God. One wisdom pervades all. One power upholds the heavens, contains the mighty seas, is the fountain of all life, lies behind the power of the atom and the instincts of living creatures, and paints the wing of the butterfly and the sunset sky. The infinitely great and the infinitesimally small are equally the work of His creative power and lie within the ambit of His control.

And the best is yet to be! Creation is not an end in itself. There is more to come. Glory greater than anything yet seen is to fill this planet. God's purpose holds a splendour and a promise in store which all of us can share. Indeed, it is this purpose and our part in it which we propose to examine in the pages that follow.

2

MAN: GOOD OR BAD?

HOW complex a creature is man! Constantly creative, he produces wonders in earth and sea and sky. Man-made probes have penetrated the nearer fringes of the universe and examined the inner recesses of the human body. Man-made devices leave multitudes dead or maimed in times of war, whilst the same scenes of carnage are illumined by acts of heroism and self-giving which draw respect from friend and foe alike.

The pages of history and of daily life are filled with a strange paradox. Man is a bewildering mixture. Thousands are moved by tenderness, care and compassion for their fellows, and devote their lives in constant service without counting the cost. And yet, every day there are acts of brutality and oppression, violence and murder, sometimes involving babes and children or the aged and helpless.

Even the highest brains and the most dedicated of statesmen have taken decisions which have resulted in the destruction of whole cities in a flash of time, taking away young and old, men and women, weak and strong. Those who survived are left with memories of terrifying horror, and often with scars or inner injury which they must bear for the rest of their uncertain lives.

How is it that man, from the same source, brings forth repeatedly things of exquisite beauty and of sickening repulsiveness? Why is the diary of man marked by wonderful steps forward and then by retreat into near bestiality, as though the best had never been? Is it that man is simply an animal who from time to time returns to the savagery of the wild? Or is there some flaw in an otherwise fine vessel, like a crack in a bell or a knot in a fine piece of wood?

Shakespeare, for different purposes, gave a picture of this paradox:

> What a piece of work is man!
> How noble in reason! how infinite in faculty!
> In action how like an angel!
> In form, in moving, how express and admirable!
> In apprehension how like a god!
> The beauty of the world! the paragon of animals!
> And yet, to me, what is this quintessence of dust?
>
> *Hamlet II:ii*

"Quintessence of dust." That is one of the pointers to man's frailty. Despite the grandeur of the mind and the skill of hand, at his end man lies down in the sleep of death and his beauty moulders into dust. He is gone. The great procession from cradle to grave is unrelenting. It has drawn the most poignant verse from poets and music from composers: it fills the pages of books and appears in the dramas of every country, and is captured for the eye on canvas and in stone. The problem of suffering and death has engaged the mind of man throughout the ages. It is all the more puzzling when, as sometimes happens, the worst of men die peacefully in their beds, and the best are victims of intense suffering.

The paradox of man's mixed goodness and evil is mirrored in the world around him as circumstances and nature seem to conspire to increase the enigma of mere existence. How is one to explain the riddle? Is there an explanation which is sufficient to embrace the whole of human life?

Yes, there is. Moreover, the explanation provides real hope, hope of perfect happiness, happiness without flaw and without end.

If we go back to the beginning of things as described in the Bible we are given some foundation principles, a kind of key to unlock the seeming mysteries of what is to follow. In this way we can begin to answer some of our deepest questions and find solutions to some of the most perplexing and persistent problems affecting all of us.

The Bible tells us that everything which God made in the beginning was "good" or "very good". This you will find by reading the first chapter of Genesis. Please read it for yourself.

There is no substitute for Bible reading. The Bible is a marvellous mind-builder. It draws aside the curtain and lets us see the whys and wherefores behind the things which are visible to the eye. Furthermore, the Bible has a special purpose:

> "*The holy Scriptures which are able to make you wise for salvation through faith in Christ Jesus. All Scripture is God-breathed and is useful for teaching, rebuking, correcting, and training in righteousness, so that the man of God may be thoroughly equipped for every good work.*"
> (2 Timothy 3:15 – 17, N.I.V.)

Your reading of Genesis 1 will show that God commenced with that which is "good" — see verses 4, 10, 12, 18, 21, 25. The good God made good things, and when all His work was finished He declared it to be "very good".

The crown of Creation was man. Man was unique. He was made from the lowest of materials, but was wonderfully fashioned and given life by God:

> "*The Lord God formed man of the dust of the ground, and breathed into his nostrils the breath of life; and man became a living soul.*"
> (Genesis 2:7)

"In the image of God"

The Bible tells us something more about man, something which accounts for the uniqueness which differentiates him from the other parts of creation. Man was related directly to his Maker:

> "*God created man in his own image, in the image of God created he him; male and female created he them.*" (Genesis 1:27)

The expressions, "in the image of God" and "after our likeness" (see verse 26 also) are used only about man. At this stage the Bible does not develop all that lies behind these intriguing words, but it is preparing us for the accounts which follow.

From everyday speech we can glean something of the meanings of "image" and "likeness". We speak of a son or daughter being the image of father or mother, and we know what we mean. Sometimes the similarities extend into mannerisms, character and ability, and these likenesses are frequently commented on.

To whom or what is man like? And in whose image was he made? In the first place the Bible, in a later book, says:

> "*Thou madest him a little lower than the angels.*" (Psalm 8:5)

7

In some respects therefore man is like the angels and in others he is presently deficient. Angels frequently appeared to men in Bible times and were described as being like men, though often they shone with glory. See Genesis 18:1,16; 19:1,15,16; Matthew 28:2 – 6 and Mark 16:5 – 7. It is not that angels look like men, but rather that men have something in common with the outward appearance of angels. The subject of angels will come up again later.

But is there any other kind of likeness, beyond that of outward appearance? We believe that there is. Unlike all other creatures, man has a capacity to worship God and to relate to Him and His purpose. He is able to understand what God says to him and to respond. Furthermore, man can pray and he can believe. None of these things is involuntary; each depends on man's willingness. Nevertheless these abilities are latent in all men.

Thus it is that man can be obedient to God and can seek to show Godlikeness – godliness. Besides, man has the gift of speech which enables him to give expression to praise and worship: what he contemplates in his mind can be made known in words. Man alone has this attribute. There are creatures which can imitate sounds – parrots and mynah birds, for example – and occasionally God has given other creatures the gift of intelligible speech (see the serpent in Genesis 3 and Balaam's ass in Numbers 22); but man alone has the combined gift of thought and the ability to express his thought in words. Moreover, it is this faculty of man which God seeks to employ when He reveals Himself by means of the spoken and written word of His prophets.

"A living soul"

Is there any fundamental respect in which man differs from the angels? For example, the Bible tells us that angels cannot die (see Luke 20:34 – 36). Is the same true of man? Look again at the basic Bible teaching:

> "The Lord God formed man of the dust of the ground, and breathed into his nostrils the breath of life; and man became a living soul."
>
> (Genesis 2:7)

The first man consisted of "dust" and "the breath of life". In his entirety he was called "a living soul". Notice that in this verse man is not so much said to *possess* a soul as to *be* one. In total, therefore, man was in the image and likeness of God and consisted of dust and the breath of life. But beyond all this, was man in fact like unto the angels to die no more?

One thing is clear: there is nothing in the creation record to tell us that there was a part of Adam which could not die. Take another look at him in Eden in those days when all was well. Was he at that time subject to the fear of death, the certainty of dying, as is the common lot of all mankind at this present time? The answer is, No. Adam had no fear of that kind and he enjoyed the felicity of life in Eden untrammelled by cares, fears, tears or arduous toil. Indeed, the Bible tells us why this was so, and a little reflection will further our understanding.

In those early days Adam was undeveloped in character. He had potential and freedom of choice, but was spiritually immature. He was not made with built-in perfection of character, nor was he a mere automaton made to run along totally predetermined lines. God then took steps to provide man with the opportunity to develop an image and likeness in the truest sense, a character in which the virtues of God could be found. The method was simple: the man was put to the test. He was given a commandment, the word of God from the Creator to the created:

> "*Of every tree of the garden thou mayest freely eat: but of the tree of the knowledge of good and evil, thou shalt not eat of it: for in the day that thou eatest thereof thou shalt surely die.*" (Genesis 2:16 – 17)

There was a sweet reasonableness about this command. It matched the blessings which man was enjoying. God had made the garden in Eden and had placed man in charge. The garden was "paradise", a word which means "a park" or a "garden". Eden's garden was the finest ever to have existed on earth and it has never been surpassed. Adam's habitat was totally congenial. There was nothing hostile about it and all he had to do was to dress and to keep it (Genesis 2:15). God was the owner and provider: man was the tenant and beneficiary.

But how was Adam to have a truly free choice in his obedience to God? Since God clearly did not want mindless and loveless obedience, but an intelligent willingness, how was this to be made possible? Unlike us, Adam enjoyed a mind which was uncorrupted by evil; there was no taint within and only "goodness" outside.

The Serpent in Eden

The appearing of the serpent in the garden may strike us as very odd. Some have regarded the serpent as the embodiment of evil, a concentrate of wickedness which has arrived from outside the earth. In other words, on such a view, the serpent was the Devil or Satan seeking to wreck God's handiwork. The Genesis record tells us nothing of this kind and to introduce it creates many more problems than it is supposed to solve. What then of the serpent? How are we to regard it?

In the first place, we are told that all the creatures made by God were "very good". Then we are told that the serpent was also a "beast of the field" (Genesis 3:1). Some have questioned whether the words, "the serpent was more subtil than any beast of the field", mean that the serpent was itself one such beast. There would be little point in mentioning the circumstance were we not intended to understand that the serpent was in fact a beast of the field. The conclusion is strengthened by the way in which the Hebrew words have been translated in other versions. For example:

> *"Now the serpent was more subtle than any other wild creature that the Lord God had made."* (R.S.V.)

Moreover, it is very hard to conceive that God would have allowed the invasion of His garden by a living manifestation of wickedness, and had such an intrusion been permitted, should have failed to give Adam the slightest hint of warning. On the other hand, if as the record tells us, the serpent was one of earth's creatures, then Adam would already have been aware of its existence and its propensities because God had showed him all the animals, one by one, and Adam had given them their names (Genesis 2:19).

But the serpent could speak and had powers of observation and reasoning. This makes it unique. Clearly, many animals have the capacity to observe and to sense what is around them, and are able to interpret for their own safety and well-being what they find out. But there is no animal alive today which has the power to converse freely with man. This is no reason for doubting the record of Scripture and, in any case, the description of the serpent given to us by God tells us that the creature was extraordinary.

Apart from the powers of speech and reasoning, the serpent had no supernatural power; and there is nothing in the account in Genesis to warrant any conclusion that the serpent exercised any other influence or had any power to do so. Nevertheless the serpent occupies a significant part in the tragedy of the garden of Eden, and we must conclude that this was foreseen by God.

10

Why then was the serpent made? More especially, why was it allowed access to Eve when such disastrous results were to follow? It is dangerous to philosophise or to conjecture beyond what the Bible tells us; such surmisings usually take us down false tracks laid by merely human thinking.

We can be sure about God. He is all-wise and all-righteous: He is kind and beneficent. He had created man with glorious opportunities and granted him the privilege of being aware of God. Adam was hedged about by countless blessings. He knew the command of God. As yet he knew no evil. In one sense, therefore, there was no true test of his obedience as he stood in idyllic surroundings, unsullied in mind and body.

The serpent provided another point of view for man to contemplate. It was a purely theoretical view, a conjecture without proof or substance. All that the serpent said to Eve in contradiction of her existing knowledge was totally unsubstantiated. The serpent "said", but produced no evidence. It took the facts known to Eve and gave them another interpretation, an altogether spurious and totally unattested interpretation. Instead of death for transgression, there would be life, and there would be glorious, godlike enlightenment and an equality with God.

In all this the serpent did not suggest that anything lay within its own power. It had nothing to give but ideas, and for them it provided not one shred of proof. Its words were either in direct contradiction of what God had said – "Thou shalt not surely die" – or a fabrication of supposed blessings which would follow the partaking of the tree of knowledge of good and evil – "Ye shall be as God, knowing good and evil" (R.V.).

The serpent's preposterous lie, "Thou shalt not surely die", was the key to his persuasiveness. This glittering untruth lay unchallenged in Eve's innocent mind, even though she knew the Word of God. She allowed the insidious ideas to activate her natural, hitherto unadulterated, desires, and foolishly surrendered to selfishness and rebellion. Her desires had previously moved her to live in accordance with God's will, but now she inflamed and corrupted them. She had been deceived. Adam followed at her invitation knowing what he was doing. He carried the major blame and responsibility, because he was the principal part of God's creation and appears to have left his wife in some way vulnerable to the blandishments of the serpent.

11

The New Testament comments on Eve and on Adam tell us the plain truth:

"The serpent beguiled Eve through his subtilty."

(2 Corinthians 11:3)

"Adam was not deceived, but the woman being deceived, was in the transgression." (1 Timothy 2:14)

"By one man sin entered into the world." (Romans 5:12)

Adam and Eve knew that they had sinned and were painfully aware of their defiled consciences. Shame and fear overtook them. Their nakedness became embarrassing, and they provided makeshift coverings for themselves. Neither their fig-leaf girdles nor their hiding place among the trees of the garden was of any avail against the judicial scrutiny of God.

Sin and Death

They were now in a state of sin. Sin is the transgression of God's law; in other words it is lawlessness (1 John 3:4). Moreover, they were now to die: "The wages of sin is death" (Romans 6:23). They had passed from righteousness and peace into sinfulness and strife. Their sin had separated between themselves and God, and the consequences were beginning to make themselves manifest.

As God had clearly stated the original command to Adam, so now He states and pronounces the consequences of their sin. Their protestations that someone else was to blame – Adam blamed Eve and indirectly God Himself, and Eve blamed the serpent – were set aside. Each of them had to carry his own burden. The serpent had no moral responsibility before God, since so far as we know it was not under any command, and in any case had not been made in the likeness and image of God. Nevertheless it was to bear the disfavour of God because of what it had been instrumental in doing. It was to lose some of its advantages and was henceforth to go upon its stomach. Moreover, God said to the serpent:

"I will put enmity between thee and the woman, and between thy seed and her seed; it shall bruise thy head, and thou shalt bruise his heel."

(Genesis 3:15)

In the heart of these words lies a pearl of great price. Within the sounds of enmity and conflict there is a note of hope which will engage our attention a little later in our story. Suffice it to say for the moment that the key to the riddle (for such it must have seemed to Adam and Eve) lies in the word "it" or, as some versions translate the word, "he".

The pronouncements upon Adam and Eve were as follows:

"Unto the woman he said, I will greatly multiply thy sorrow and thy conception; in sorrow shalt thou bring forth children; and thy desire shall be to thy husband, and he shall rule over thee.

And unto Adam he said, Because thou hast hearkened unto the voice of thy wife, and hast eaten of the tree, of which I commanded thee, saying, Thou shalt not eat of it: cursed is the ground for thy sake; in sorrow shalt thou eat of it all the days of thy life; thorns also and thistles shall it bring forth to thee; and thou shalt eat the herb of the field; in the sweat of thy face shalt thou eat bread, till thou return unto the ground . . . for dust thou art, and unto dust shalt thou return."   (Genesis 3:16 – 19)

Shame, sorrow, toil and death had come into the world, and that would be the kind of world in which Adam and Eve's children would live outside the garden of Eden. In the coming pages we shall have to look at the consequences stated above, seek to understand them and find out the full meaning of the Riddle.

3

DEATH: FRIEND OR FOE?

OF all the subjects to excite the talents of writers and composers, love and death, together and separately, must surely rank among the highest. Love and death have a power of their own and have produced some of the most noble characters in real life and in fiction. But it is when we come to the Bible that these two experiences meet in unsurpassed greatness and beauty, a meeting so powerful as to turn sinners into saints, slaves into freemen, and the hopeless into victorious conquerors. Here are the timeless words:

"God so loved the world, that he gave his only begotten Son, that whosoever believeth in him should not perish, but have everlasting life."

(John 3:16)

Christ's own words have a similar greatness:

"Greater love hath no man than this, that a man should lay down his life for his friends." (John 15:13)

Love and death meet in the Lord Jesus Christ in a way which is redemptive. The New Testament rings with this message of hope:

"The Son of God . . . loved me and gave himself for me."

(Galatians 2:20)

It is the greatness of *this* love which makes it transforming for others. It is the difference of *this* death which provides deliverance beyond all imagining. It becomes the source of everlasting life, the

14

wellspring of salvation. This is the confident and glad message of Scripture.

But what about our own death? Is it friend or foe? Is it an end to everything or a doorway to a new existence?

The world is full of ideas on this subject. Everything from complete and permanent annihilation to repeated reincarnation is to be found among the beliefs of men. None of these conjecturings is new. All of them are to be found among pagan beliefs the world over. What is the truth of the matter?

We believe the truth to be clear. It is found in both Old and New Testaments. Let us take the subject step by step, holding God's hand as He leads us along. In the first place, life came from God. Here is the Scripture once more:

> *"The Lord God formed man of the dust of the ground, and breathed into his nostrils the breath of life, and man became a living soul (N.I.V., a living being)."* (Genesis 2:7)

> *"God that made the world and all things therein . . . giveth to all life, and breath, and all things."* (Acts 17:24,25)

Although man was a special and unique creation, he was not alone in having the breath of life or in being a living soul. We are told that when the Flood swept the world in the days of Noah:

> *"All flesh died that moved upon the earth, both of fowl, and of cattle, and of beast, and of everything that creepeth upon the earth, and every man:* **all** *in whose nostrils was the breath of life."* (Genesis 7:21 – 22)

Man's uniqueness lay in his capacity to enjoy a spiritual life, which he greatly corrupted when he turned away from the Word of God in loveless disobedience. He broke the bond between himself and God, and set sin in the place of fellowship. As we have read earlier, one of the consequences of transgression was to become a dying creature, and meanwhile to suffer, as later Scripture puts it in Hebrews 2:14, "fear of death". Why *fear* of death? What is there about death to engender such a feeling? Surely the sentence which God pronounced gave ample reason:

> *"Cursed is the ground for thy sake; in sorrow shalt thou eat of it* **all the days of thy life . . . till thou return unto the ground***; for out of it wast thou taken; for dust thou art,* **and unto dust shalt thou return***."* (Genesis 3:17 – 19)

In this way God set out the physical consequences of Adam's sin. Sin would work itself out in death. Take particular note of those emphasised expressions. There would be an end to life and a dissolution to dust from whence man came. This simple description, returning to dust, is the Bible's frequently used phrase when speaking about the end of life. The process is described also in other words in various parts of Scripture, but the effect is always the same: life ends and man ceases to be. It is for this reason that "fear of death" came into existence. Adam and Eve knew well enough that the serpent had been wrong and that God meant what He had said.

This truth is most unpalatable to all of us and is shunned by many who would prefer to think otherwise. Nevertheless, in countless funeral services, the truth of the Genesis record is re-echoed by the words of the committal: "Dust to dust and ashes to ashes". Lest you should be tempted to cease reading at this point, it can be said with absolute confidence that there is a hope which is greater than death; but it is a hope which at the same time faces up squarely to the Bible teaching about the dead:

> *"For in death there is no remembrance of thee:*
> *In the grave who shall give thee thanks?"* (Psalm 6:5)

> *"Wilt thou shew wonders to the dead?*
> *Shall the dead arise and praise thee?*
> *Shall thy lovingkindness be declared in the grave?*
> *Or thy faithfulness in destruction?*
> *Shall thy wonders be known in the dark?*
> *And thy righteousness in the land of forgetfulness?"* (Psalm 88:10 – 12)

> *"What man is he that liveth, and shall not see death?*
> *Shall he deliver his soul from the hand of the grave?"* (Psalm 89:48)

> *"The dead praise not the Lord,*
> *Neither any that go down into silence."* (Psalm 115:17)

> *"Put not your trust in princes,*
> *Nor in the son of man in whom there is no help.*
> *His breath goeth forth, he returneth to his earth;*
> *In that very day his thoughts perish."* (Psalm 146:3 – 4)

> *"Cease ye from man whose breath is in his nostrils: for wherein is he to*
> *be accounted of?"* (Isaiah 2:22)

This Old Testament picture is complete and could be multiplied many times. Moreover, it is wholly in harmony with the Bible account of creation and with God's sentence on man when he sinned. All the men of God in the pre-Christian era had the same understanding about death, and they never sought to evade the issue by other means.

Of course, there were those who thought differently. These were not the faithful followers of the Word of God. Such men flatly contradicted the sentence of God and believed and persuaded others to believe the serpent's lie: "Thou shalt not surely die." These false teachings misled many people and the teachings were accompanied by practices, much like those to be found today, in which bereaved persons and others sought to make contact with the dead, despite God's clear word that "the dead know not anything" (Ecclesiastes 9:5). These superstitions and those who followed them, or perpetrated them for gain or power over men, were roundly condemned by the prophets:

> "*When men tell you to consult mediums and spiritists, who whisper and mutter, should not a people enquire of their God? Why consult the dead on behalf of the living? To the law and to the testimony! If they do not speak according to this word, they have no light of dawn.*"

> (Isaiah 8:19 – 20, N.I.V.)

The Hope of Resurrection

The idea of surviving death or passing through it in some way or other has taken firm root in the minds of many, including many who would claim to hold the Christian doctrine. The doctrine of the immortality of the soul has prevailed over the Bible doctrine of death, and arising out of that doctrine various related teachings have been developed and are believed. Indeed, some people are convinced that to disbelieve the doctrine of the immortality of the soul is to deny a basic Christian doctrine. We are sure that this is not so. On the contrary, belief in the clear Bible teaching about the unconsciousness of the dead is an essential step to a true understanding of one of the great treasures of the Word of God, the doctrine of resurrection from the dead as the way to everlasting life.

It will surprise some readers to know that nowhere in Scripture are the words "immortal" and "soul" brought together. Immortality is God's own inherent nature, and His alone. Con-

17

sequently the word "immortality" is used in the Bible only to describe God's own existence and the life which will be bestowed on the faithful *after* their resurrection from the dead. Here are *all* of the occurrences of the words "immortal" and "immortality" in our English Version of the Bible (there are more in the Greek Bible, but all of them are consistent with what follows). For convenience, they are grouped to show those which apply to God and those in which immortality is promised to man by God:

About God:

"Now unto the King eternal, immortal, invisible, the only wise God, be honour and glory for ever and ever. Amen." (1 Timothy 1:17)

"The blessed and only Potentate, the King of kings, and Lord of lords, who only hath immortality, dwelling in the light which no man can approach unto; whom no man hath seen, nor can see: to whom be honour and power everlasting. Amen." (1 Timothy 6:15 – 16)

About God's promises to man:

"Our Saviour Jesus Christ, who hath abolished death, and hath brought life and immortality to light through the gospel." (2 Timothy 1:10)

"(God) will render to every man according to his deeds: to them who by patient continuance in well doing seek for glory and honour and immortality, eternal life . . . in the day when God shall judge the secrets of men by Jesus Christ." (Romans 2:6,7,16)

"For this corruptible must put on incorruption, and this mortal must put on immortality. So when this corruptible shall have put on incorruption, and this mortal shall have put on immortality, then shall be brought to pass the saying that is written, Death is swallowed up in victory." (1 Corinthians 15:53 – 54)

It must be evident when we compare that cluster of New Testament verses, the only ones of their kind, with our earlier quotations, that Old and New Testaments meet together in teaching the same truth. The New Testament, too, teaches that death is an end of existence from which there is hope of resurrection to everlasting life for those whose faith and life have been pleasing to God.

However, the doctrine of the immortality of the soul is very resilient, and those who hold it clutch at every possible explanation of Scripture verses to establish their case. Despite the clarity of the following verse, already referred to, the usual rejoinder to the straightforward understanding of it is to say that the verse refers only to Adam's body, but not to his soul. In other words, the real Adam was inside the outer Adam and would survive at death. We have seen that there is absolutely no justification for this view in the Creation record. In any case, even if there were an inner Adam with some kind of separate existence, in this verse God is surely addressing the *real* Adam:

"*. . . till* **thou** *return unto the ground: for out of it wast* **thou** *taken: for dust* **thou** *art, and unto dust shalt* **thou** *return.*"

(Genesis 3:19)

Nevertheless we must look further at the word "soul". It is used hundreds of times in the Bible. Everything which we normally associate with our present existence is clearly attributed to the soul:

"*Every soul that eateth . . .*" (Leviticus 17:15)

"*His soul draweth near unto the grave.*" (Job 33:22)

"*Let me die with the Philistines.*"
(Judges 16:30, where the Hebrew words for "me" are "my soul", as shown in the margin of A.V. Bibles)

"*Deliver my soul from the sword . . .*" (Psalm 22:20)

"*An idle soul shall suffer hunger.*" (Proverbs 19:15)

"*As cold waters to a thirsty soul . . .*" (Proverbs 25:25)

"*My soul shall weep in secret places.*" (Jeremiah 13:17)

"*Every living soul died in the sea*" (Revelation 16:3)

It would be difficult to find more convincing proof that the soul is the living man, the living mortal man. Moreover, from these verses it is clear that the soul can die and be put in the grave, exactly as we would expect from the pronouncement of death upon Adam. Here are two more verses telling precisely the same story:

"*Our soul is bowed down to the dust:*
Our belly cleaveth to the earth." (Psalm 44:25)

"*What man is he that liveth, and shall not see death?*
Shall he deliver his soul from the hand of **the grave***?*" (Psalm 89:48)

Compare the following verses: one is an Old Testament

19

pronouncement and the other is Christ's own comment on himself as Calvary drew near:

> "*The soul that sinneth it shall die.*" (Ezekiel 18:4)

> "*My soul is exceeding sorrowful, even unto death.*"
> (Matthew 26:38)

There is harmony between the Testaments and a common teaching about the soul and about death.

Finally in this connection, the word "soul" is sometimes used to denote man's life, but never to suggest that somehow man himself continues to live after death. Here are two examples, the first a prophetic account of the death of Jesus, and the second taken from one of the Lord's parables:

> "*He (Jesus) hath poured out his **soul** unto death.*" (Isaiah 53:12)

> "*Thou fool, this night thy soul shall be required of thee; then whose shall those things be, which thou hast provided?*" (Luke 12:20)

(The N.I.V. translates the opening of the latter verse as follows: "*You fool! This night your very life will be demanded of you.*")

The heading to this chapter posed the question, Death: Friend or Foe! The Bible answer is undoubtedly, Foe! Indeed, the victorious chapter on resurrection, 1 Corinthians 15, declares, "The last *enemy* that shall be destroyed is death". The enemy can be conquered and the victory is through the Lord Jesus Christ. We shall develop this theme more fully later, but meanwhile here is a selection of Bible verses, arranged in a progression which tells of the way in which "salvation of the soul" can be secured:

> "*None can keep alive his own soul.*" (Psalm 22:29)

> "*The law of the Lord is perfect, **converting** the soul.*"
> (Psalm 19:7)

> "***Receive** with meekness **the engrafted word,** which is able to save your souls.*" (James 1:21)

> "*Them that **believe** to the saving of the soul.*" (Hebrews 10:39)

> "*Let him know, that he which converteth a sinner from the error of his way **shall save a soul from death**, and shall hide a multitude of sins.*" (James 5:20)

20

"Ye have purified your souls in obeying the truth . . . being born again . . . by the word of God." (1 Peter 1:22 – 23)

"God will redeem my soul from the power of the grave."

(Psalm 49:15)

"And many of them that sleep in the dust of the earth shall awake, some to everlasting life, and some to shame and everlasting contempt."

(Daniel 12:2)

". . . heaven, from whence also we look for the Saviour, the Lord Jesus Christ: who shall change our vile body, that it may be fashioned like unto his glorious body." (Philippians 3:20 – 21)

The transformation from a dying body to a glorious body is the change from mortality to immortality, from a living soul to an ever-living soul. This is Bible teaching. It relates directly to what we know about life and death. It affords us redemption from sin and death in the Lord Jesus Christ. The Lord God who created the first man in the beginning, punished him with death when he sinned, and we inherit his fallen and mortal nature. Christ is the Redeemer, the divine antidote to all of man's ills. Salvation begins now in this life as we yield our hearts and minds to God through Christ in the appointed way. Salvation will be completed when Christ returns to earth, raises the sleeping dead and blesses the faithful with immortality, even everlasting life in a glorious body in Christ's kingdom on earth.

4

THE BEGINNING OF THE PROMISES
OF GOD

"PROMISES, promises." The words have an empty and
derisory ring in modern ears. Bitter disappointments
and man's actual avarice have brought about a new way
of thinking. Man wants the future now. He demands instant
satisfaction. This attitude affects everything from sex to politics
among nations. Worse still, man has undermined the value of any
promises he cares to make, and regards it as permissible or, at
least, expedient, to break his word should new circumstances seem
to merit it or, even, should the one who made the promise merely
"feel like it".

By their very nature promises concern the future. In some cases
they depend for their fulfilment on the keeping of conditions by the
giver or the intended beneficiary. Man's promises run the risk of
being deeply affected by the unseen future. Many a man has, by
circumstances entirely outside his control, been unable to keep
promises solemnly made.

Sometimes, of course, promises are made with very little
likelihood of being kept. It has become standard practice to regard
cynically any promises made by politicians at the time of elections.
Voters take everything with a large pinch of salt, and political
leaders can always plead that new circumstances have made it
impossible or highly disadvantageous to keep to their manifestos.

Whether we want to or not, all of us make promises, some
trifling and others substantial. Our vows on marriage are doubtless among the most significant. It is a sad reflection on our society

that these vows are often lightly taken and lightly broken. It is an indictment of Western nations, with all the material advantages they possess, that their way of life is littered with broken marriages and broken hearts, and bewildered children who have been deprived of their right to enjoy an upbringing by the parents who have brought them into the world. These things ought not to be. The truly Christian way creates conditions which are conducive to maximum permanence in marriage and to homes where confidence and godliness abound. This is what God intended.

But what about God's promises? Does God always keep the promises he makes? What kinds of promise are they, and how do they concern us? Are they dependent on man as well as on God, or on God alone, for their fulfilment?

God began to make promises to men as soon as the first sin had been committed. Man's dilemma was matched by God's willingness to help. God's promises sprang out of God's inherent goodness and not out of any obligation or indebtedness to man. The promises were mighty and they were sure. The basic content of the promises was dependent on nothing but God's faithfulness for its fulfilment.

God is not looking into an unknown future, as man is obliged to do, but sees the end of everything from the beginning. God challenges man with this very fact. God declares His ability to speak of the future as certainly as we speak of the present, as the incontrovertible evidence that He is God. This is how the Scripture sets it forth:

> "*Who hath declared this from ancient time? Who hath told it from that time? have not I the Lord? and there is no God else beside me; a just God and a Saviour; there is none beside me.*"   (Isaiah 45:21)

> "*Declaring the end from the beginning, and from ancient times the things that are not yet done, saying, My counsel shall stand, and I will do all my pleasure.*"   (Isaiah 46:10)

These declarations of the Almighty can be tested against the prophecies He has made as recorded in the Bible, and their fulfilment at the appropriate time, in the manner and completely according to what was foretold. There are most amazing examples of this in both Old and New Testaments, and some of these we shall consider for other purposes in due course. The basis of Bible prophecy is God's will and the accurate communication of it well in advance of its fulfilment by means of His holy prophets:

23

> *"And we have the word of the prophets made more certain, and you will do well to pay attention to it, as to a light shining in a dark place, until the day dawns and the morning star rises in your hearts. Above all, you must understand that no prophecy of Scripture came about by the prophet's own interpretation. For prophecy never had its origin in the will of man, but men spoke from God as they were carried along by the Holy Spirit."*
>
> (2 Peter 1:19 – 21, N.I.V.)

Promises are prophecy of a particular kind. They will be fulfilled as surely as every other prophecy of God has been realised at its proper time. Moreover, since Jesus Christ is the basis of salvation and we are dependent upon him, God gave more promises and prophecies about Jesus than about anything or anyone else throughout history. This was done in order to provide assurance for us and to put beyond doubt our hope in the promise of everlasting life. Christ, shortly after his resurrection from the dead, demonstrated for the benefit of his apostles prophecies taken from all parts of the Old Testament concerning himself. The apostles used these illustrations as part of their evidence when they preached the Gospel to Jews and Gentiles:

> *"He (Jesus) said unto them, 'How foolish you are, and how slow of heart to believe all that the prophets have spoken! Did not the Christ have to suffer these things and then enter his glory?' And beginning with Moses and all the Prophets, he explained to them what was said in all the Scriptures concerning himself . . . He told them, 'This is what is written: The Christ will suffer and rise from the dead on the third day, and repentance and forgiveness of sins will be preached in his name'."*
>
> (Luke 24:25 – 27, 46 – 47, N.I.V.)

So Paul, in his preaching of the Gospel, declared:

> *"For I delivered unto you first of all that which I also received, how Christ died for our sins according to the Scriptures; and that he was buried, and that he rose again the third day, according to the Scriptures."*
>
> (1 Corinthians 15:3 – 4)

We can have absolute confidence in the promises of God. God is utterly and always faithful, and there is no variableness or inconsistency in Him:

> *"Know therefore that the Lord thy God, he is God, the faithful God,*

24

which keepeth covenant and mercy with them that love him and keep his commandments to a thousand generations."

(Deuteronomy 7:9)

"God, who has called you into fellowship with his Son Jesus Christ our Lord, is faithful." (1 Corinthians 1:9, N.I.V.)

This is the basis of faith. Sometimes men and women agonise about having faith, as though somehow it would spring up in them without reason or consisted of a leap into the dark. Nothing could be further from the truth. Faith comes from the influence of the Word of God and the irrefutable evidence which it supplies. Faith is:

"Being fully persuaded that, what he had promised, he was able also to perform." (Romans 4:21)

This is the kind of faith which men of old had in God. Without this faith it is impossible to be a follower of Christ. It is the kind of faith which he himself possessed:

"Without faith it is impossible to please him (God); for he that cometh to God must believe that he is, and that he is a rewarder of them that diligently seek him." (Hebrews 11:6)

How else could God give us assurance about the future than by repeatedly making prophecies about it and fulfilling them without fail? God alone can do this and He employs this fact to challenge the men who do not believe and those who seek enchantments and the like to foresee the future.

" 'Present your case,' says the Lord. 'Set forth your arguments,' says Jacob's King. 'Bring in your idols to tell us what is going to happen . . . and know their final outcome. Or declare to us the things to come, tell us what the future holds, so that we may know that you are gods.' "
(Isaiah 41:21 – 23, N.I.V.)

"Keep on, then, with your magic spells and with your many sorceries, which you have laboured at since childhood. Perhaps you will succeed, perhaps you will cause terror. All the counsel you have received has only worn you out! Let your astrologers come forward, those stargazers who make predictions month by month, let them save you from what is coming upon you." (Isaiah 47:12 – 13, N.I.V.)

The challenge still remains. Man is still powerless, even in this age of highly computerised technology, accurately to foretell major world events. He seeks to hedge himself about with all kinds of guesses in an attempt to ward off the worst effects of the unseen future. Millions look at their daily horoscope and titillate themselves with the words of the dabblers in scientific or other guesswork. All of this is futile in determining the future of man.

God knows. God says. God does. God promises and He fulfils. God demonstrates infallibly and calls for faith. God is good and trustworthy. God is kind and merciful. God wishes to save us and will do so if we trust Him. Our future is certain, if we commit ourselves into God's care by believing what He has told us. Christ is the greatest fulfilment of prophecy of all time, and he is God's guarantee to us that we can be saved. *"With God nothing shall be impossible"* (Luke 1:37). To the fainthearted, God says, *"Is anything too hard for me?"* (Jeremiah 32:27).

With our confession of man's helplessness and the assurance of God's goodness and faithfulness, let us take the first of the promises of God (the 'Riddle' referred to earlier). It was spoken in the garden in Eden before Adam and Eve were expelled:

*"I will put enmity between thee (the serpent) and the woman (Eve),
and between thy seed and her seed;
it shall bruise thy head,
and thou shalt bruise his heel."* (Genesis 3:15)

There is an air of mystery about this promise. It speaks of struggle, a struggle that would continue through the generations to come. In the end the serpent's evil would be undone. The Deliverer would strike the mortal blow (to the head) and would himself suffer injury (in the heel).

The Seed of the Woman

Whilst Eve, without further enlightenment, could not fully fathom the meaning of this promise, we know that she had an understanding of it and believed it. She knew that through a descendant of hers (the seed) the tide of evil would be stemmed and its source would be overcome. It is interesting to notice that when her first child was born Eve declared, *"I have gotten a man with the help of the Lord"* (Genesis 4:1, R.V.). It would seem that she was ruminating on the promise of the Coming Seed, the Deliverer. She was mistaken in the person and in the time, but not in the hope.

Ages would have to roll by before the mystery was fully

26

revealed. Meanwhile the faithful would have to believe in the Coming Seed, and God would reinforce their faith with new and more expansive promises as time went by.

It is important to note that this first promise is entirely unconditional. God promised and God will fulfil. The promise rests squarely and only on God Himself. Salvation is the gift of God.

This first promise of God must have been talked about by faithful men. It was the gleam of hope in the darkness. It is probable that Adam's grandson was alive in Noah's time, and Noah's son alive in Abraham's day. Thus the first two thousand years were spanned by no more than six lives. The Edenic promise must have been preserved with remarkable freshness.

One wonders what those men thought about the way in which the promise was cast. Why, for example, was the Deliverer to be called the "seed of the woman", rather than the seed of the man? Perhaps the worthies of old pondered about it, but it was not until Christ the Deliverer came born of a virgin without the aid of man that everything became crystal clear! The Virgin Birth was locked away in this first mystery.

Much as we could linger around the warmth of this first fire of promise, we must needs move on. Adam's descendants inherited two great weaknesses: they were prone to sin and they were destined to die. Sin and death were man's twin enemies. In one way or another they have proved to be the despair of all men. Man's imperfection is evident in everything he undertakes. Perfection always eludes men in whatever field they care to exercise themselves. Sadly, even the best of men must fade and pass away:

> *"For we are strangers before thee,*
> *and sojourners, as were all our fathers:*
> *our days on earth are as a shadow,*
> *and there is none abiding."* (1 Chronicles 29:15)

But without death the world's worst sinners would render the earth an enormous hive of wickedness wherein no vestige of anything good could survive. There is an interesting example of this fact in the early pages of the Bible. As we have noted, man's lifespan in these earliest days was much longer than it is now. This allowed for the growth of the human race. But it allowed too the growth of man's sinfulness. He became ungodly, immoral and violent. Gradually righteousness and godliness were driven away, and

27

there remained but few faithful men. God pleaded with men through the righteous life and faithfulness of Noah, but it was to no avail (we learn this from 2 Peter 2:5). Men were incorrigible. God called Noah and his little family into the ark where the animals had already entered. The ark was large and would have taken all who would come. But there were no others. God's goodness was spurned and man chose the dark road, the road to judgement and death.

God's Covenant with Noah

There was seven days' silence after the door of the ark had been shut by God. And the Flood came and took them all away. The besom of God swept the earth clean, and Noah and his flock came out to the new world. It was at this time that God gave His second promise:

"I will not again curse the ground any more for man's sake; for the imagination of man's heart is evil from his youth; neither will I again smite any more every living thing, as I have done. While the earth remaineth, seedtime and harvest, and cold and heat, and summer and winter, and day and night shall not cease." (Genesis 8:21 – 22)

"And God said, This (the rainbow) is the token of the covenant which I make between me and you and every living creature that is with you, for perpetual generations: I do set my bow in the cloud, and it shall be for a token of a covenant between me and the earth."

(Genesis 9:12 – 13)

By these promises the assurance was given that the world would remain and be provided for. The rainbow would be the sign of God's goodness and blessing. Once again the promise was unconditional. It was a covenant made by God alone. Whilst it did not explicitly expand the first promise of God, it ensured the arena for its fulfilment. The earth would remain and in later times the Lord Jesus would teach us to pray:

" Thy kingdom come.
Thy will be done in earth, as it is in heaven." (Matthew 6:10)

As we follow our story through Scripture we shall find more evidence of the faithfulness of God in fulfilling His promises.

5

GOD'S COVENANT WITH ABRAHAM

FROM Noah and his wife, through their sons, Shem, Ham and Japheth, the earth was populated after the Flood. As the descendants of Noah increased in number, so did world wickedness. It was as though the Flood had never been and the covenant of God with the earth did not exist. There seems to be little doubt that idolatry was rife. It is certain that man was trusting in himself and not in God.

In the vast plains of the Mesopotamian region men came together to build a city and a tower. They used bricks and bitumen as men did for centuries afterwards. The object of their building was Self and not God:

> *"Go to, let us build us a city and a tower, whose top may reach unto heaven; and let us make us a name, lest we be scattered abroad upon the face of the whole earth."* (Genesis 11:4)

There was a strange irony in this situation. The people were united. Sadly, they were united in man and his sin, and not in God and His righteousness. This new activity threatened once again to put out God's light, and to destroy the living hope in His promises. God acted. What He did may seem to contribute to man's problems. In a measure it did. God confounded the speech of man so that instant communication between the groups was not possible. Sin could not travel like a forest fire. The firebreaks of language helped to contain it or, at least to prevent the consolidation of the whole world in sin which would have made the survival of the righteous well nigh impossible. So *"the Lord scattered them abroad from thence upon the face of all the earth: and they left off to build the city"* (Genesis 11:8).

By this unique means God prepared the way for the time when He would give the greatest promises He had yet made to someone chosen to receive them. These promises have suffered from neglect over the centuries. Happily, they have been an essential part of the Christadelphian faith from the beginning. We believe them to be crucial to an understanding of the purpose of God. Let us look at their setting and their content.

Around the year 2000 BC there lived at Ur of the Chaldees in Mesopotamia a man whose name was Abram. Later on his name was changed to Abraham, and for simplicity's sake that is the name we shall use. The most remarkable aspect of this man's life was his faith in God, although he lived in a city where moon worship was the predominant cult.

In the 19th century there were men of learning who denied the existence of Ur of the Chaldees. They knew of no such place and therefore it had never existed! This is not an acceptable approach to Scripture. What the Bible says is true and we must be prepared to accept it. We may from time to time have problems such as, for example, those 19th century men experienced when they knew of no place corresponding to Ur of the Bible. They should nevertheless have trusted the Bible. It is trustworthy and proves itself to be so time and time again. Archaeologists have researched many sites in Mesopotamia and are now confident in the location of Ur. Its size, way of life, sophistication and skills, and its idolatry have been brought to light. Museums in many places hold some artefacts from Ur, and some of them are now world famous.

Abraham's life in Ur was to come to an end and he was to say farewell to everything, never to return. God had chosen him for a mighty purpose whose fulfilment is to be found in Christ and the kingdom of God. The following is the first promise which God gave to Abraham:

> *"Get thee out of thy country,*
> *and from thy kindred, and from thy father's house,*
> *unto a land that I will shew thee:*
> *and I will make of thee a great nation,*
> *and I will bless thee, and make thy name great;*
> *and thou shalt be a blessing:*
> *and I will bless them that bless thee,*

and curse him that curseth thee:
and in thee shall all families of the earth be blessed."

(Genesis 12:1 – 3)

Those promises should be read again and again. They are detailed, unique and wonderful. In their fulfilment lies the fulfilment of the first great promise which we have already considered. Look at the vital elements of the promise made to Abraham:

(a) There is a *land* involved in the promise. The Bible leaves us in no doubt at all that the land is the land of Israel, formerly known as the land of Canaan (please read Acts 7:3 – 5 and Hebrews 11:8 – 9).

(b) There is a *nation* to come from the promise. In the first place the nation was the nation of Israel (see, for example, Exodus 2:24 – 25) which later on was called the nation of the Jews. But, more significantly, there is an even greater nation intended by the promise. It consists of the host of spiritual believers of all nationalities who trust in the promises made to Abraham knowing that these are made sure in the Lord Jesus Christ (see 1 Peter 2:9 – 19 and Galatians 3:7).

(c) Abraham himself is to be blessed and his name is to be great. So great is this man that God deigned to call Himself the God of Abraham. His name is mentioned more than seventy times in the *New* Testament, often by the Lord Jesus Christ, and this is more than any other Old Testament character.

(d) *All* nations are to be blessed in Abraham. Above all, this refers to the blessings which come through the Lord Jesus Christ, the seed of Abraham, by which all men, regardless of race, may be blessed with salvation (see Galatians 3:26 – 29 and Revelation 5:9 – 10). There is a secondary meaning to this aspect of the promise. When Christ reigns as King on earth, all nations will experience the blessings of his beneficence.

The Promised Land

It will be observed that most of the developments took place after Abraham's death. How do we know that he personally will be caught up in their fulfilment and will then enjoy the blessings they contain? We can be sure of this because the promises were expanded to Abraham himself in subsequent revelations (he was a

31

prophet according to Genesis 20:7). Here is one such expansion, made at a time when Abraham was alone in the land of Canaan:

"Lift up now thine eyes, and look from the place where thou art northward, and southward, and eastward, and westward: for all the land which thou seest, to thee will I give it, and to thy seed for ever."
(Genesis 13:14 – 15)

In these words, the land of Canaan was promised to Abraham personally. There is no doubt about it because we have the confirmation in the New Testament:

"God . . . removed him (Abraham) into this land, wherein ye now dwell. And he gave him none inheritance in it, no, not so much as to set his foot on: yet he promised that he would give it to him . . ."
(Acts 7:4 – 5)

"By faith Abraham, when he was called to go out into a place which he should after receive for an inheritance, obeyed . . . by faith he sojourned in the land of promise, as in a strange country, dwelling in tabernacles with Isaac and Jacob, the heirs with him of the same promise . . . these all, having obtained a good report through faith, received not the promise: God having provided some better thing for us, that they without us should not be made perfect."
(Hebrews 11:8 – 9, 39 – 40)

God's word could not have made it more clear that the promise was made, that it concerned the land of Israel which Abraham was to inherit. But he has not yet done so. He is dead not having received the promise. There is only one possible conclusion to draw: the inheritance is yet future. Moreover, it is an *eternal* inheritance. Therefore, Abraham must live again on earth in an eternal age in order to receive the blessing. And he will!

The authority for this is none other than the Lord Jesus Christ himself who declared that Abraham will surely be raised from the dead (Matthew 22:31 – 32). When Christ returns to earth Abraham will receive from him the gift of everlasting life. He will then enter his inheritance, centred in Israel but extending over all the earth (Romans 4:13). For this reason Christ declared:

" Ye (disbelieving Jews) shall see Abraham, and Isaac, and Jacob, and all the prophets, in the kingdom of God . . . and they shall come from the east, and from the west, and from the north, and from the south, and shall sit down in the kingdom of God."
(Luke 13:28 – 29)

Abraham was 75 years old when he first came into the land of Canaan in which he sojourned as an alien. He was still childless years later, and he pleaded with God concerning the coming of his seed. God responded by telling Abraham to look at the stars:

"Look now toward heaven, and tell the stars, if thou be able to number them: and he said unto him, So shall thy seed be."   (Genesis 15:5)

This reiteration of the promise evoked a response from Abraham:

"He believed in the Lord, and he counted it to him for righteousness."
(Genesis 15:6)

Faith is not a vague hope or a blind, unknowing trust. It is absolute confidence in God's promises and their fulfilment. Trust God; He never fails. Righteousness is that relationship in which a man stands with God, once he knows that he has confessed his total inability to save himself and yet believes implicitly that God will fulfil all His promises. This is shown forth supremely in the Lord Jesus Christ in whom God's salvation is both promised and made secure.

There was still more for Abraham to learn. God repeated His promise to him:

"I am the Lord that brought thee out of Ur of the Chaldees, to give thee this land to inherit it."   (Genesis 15:17)

Abraham asked: "Whereby shall I know that I shall inherit it?" The answer was surprising and instructive. Abraham was commanded to prepare sacrifices ordained by God, but he was not to offer them. Abraham waited and guarded the sacrifices he had laid out before God. As the sun set, a deep sleep came over him, and he felt himself being engulfed in a dreadful darkness. It was then that God spoke to him. This is recorded in Genesis 15:13 – 20 where God lays out in advance the history of Abraham's descendants for centuries ahead. By this time the sun had set. Abraham saw fire, and a flaming torch passing between the pieces of the sacrifice. It was not uncommon in those days when a binding covenant was made between them that the contracting parties prepared sacrifices and met under their solemn oath at a point midway between the pieces (we read of this also in Jeremiah 34:18 – 19). But Abraham's experience was different. There was, as it were, only one party to the covenant, and that was God Himself as symbolised by the flaming torch.

*"In the same day **God** made a covenant with Abram."*

(Genesis 15:18)

The promises were sure because they depended only upon God for their realisation. This vision was God's assurance to His servant. At the same time Abraham was taught the lesson that fulfilment was a long way ahead. It would be after Abraham had died. Abraham would inherit the land only by resurrection from the dead.

Abraham continued his sojourn in the land of Canaan. Still he was childless, 24 years after his coming down into the land. He and his wife Sarai (later called Sarah) were past hope of having a child. Sarah was barren. At this time Abraham was 99 years old and Sarah was about 90. Is anything too hard for the Lord? God spoke again to Abraham and renewed the promises with the utmost clarity:

"My covenant is with thee, and thou shalt be a father of many nations . . . I will establish my covenant between me and thee . . . for an everlasting covenant, to be a God unto thee . . . I will give unto thee . . . all the land of Canaan, for an everlasting possession."

(Genesis 17:4 – 8)

It was at that time that God introduced the rite of circumcision which has remained with Jews ever since. And God said Sarah would have a child! At this news both Abraham and Sarah were filled with wonder, but they believed God:

"He (Abraham) staggered not at the promise of God through unbelief; but was strong in faith, giving glory to God; and being fully persuaded that, what he had promised, he was able also to perform."

(Romans 4:20 – 21)

"Through faith also Sara herself received strength to conceive seed, and was delivered of a child when she was past age, because she judged him faithful who had promised." (Hebrews 11:11)

In this way Isaac was born, the second of the great patriarchs. Abraham was now approaching his final and greatest test. Isaac was precious to him because all the promises of God seemed to centre around this child. God said so: *"In Isaac shall thy seed be called"* (Genesis 21:12).

Can we imagine the feelings of Abraham when God asked him to take his son to an appointed place and offer him for a sacrifice?

Every parental instinct would be pained. Moreover, what would become of the promises of God? We know what Abraham did and what he thought; the Bible tells us. He went to do what God had asked and he was certain that he would come back with his son alive:

> *"By faith Abraham, when he was tried, offered up Isaac: and he that had received the promises offered up his only begotten son, of whom it was said, That in Isaac shall thy seed be called: accounting that God was able to raise him up, even from the dead; from whence also he received him in a figure."* (Hebrews 11:17 – 19)

God was proving Abraham to the limit. In a sense, God was asking Abraham whose son Isaac was, to whom did he really belong? There was only one answer: he was God's. God did not wish for Isaac's death (indeed, he did not die), but he wanted Abraham's mature and full faith made evident by his willingness to give Isaac back to God. It was then that Abraham was given the final promises:

> *"By myself have I sworn, saith the Lord, for because thou hast done this thing, and hast not withheld thy son, thine only son: that in blessing I will bless thee, and in multiplying I will multiply thy seed as the stars of the heaven, and as the sand which is upon the sea shore; and thy seed shall possess the gate of his enemies; and in thy seed shall all the nations of the earth be blessed."* (Genesis 22:16 – 18)

The Promised Seed

Amongst Abraham's numerous and blessed seed there would be one particular seed, one person. This is made plain by the words, *"Thy seed shall possess the gate of **his** enemies"* (verse 17). Abraham, who believed the first promise made in Eden, would recognise the similarities between what was said to him and what lay in that first promise. His seed would conquer the enemy. The Deliverer would come through his line and yet, as God had taught him repeatedly, the work would be of God.

We are not left in doubt as to Abraham's deepest thoughts and keenest vision, for Jesus tells us:

> *"Abraham rejoiced to see my day:*
> *he saw it, and was glad."* (John 8:56)

Through the pain of his experience, when he took "his only

35

begotten son" to the appointed place, which turned out to be where Jerusalem and the temple stood in later years, Abraham perceived that deliverance would come because "*God will provide himself a lamb*" (Genesis 22:8). At last he had the picture complete: inheritance would come through salvation by faith, and salvation would come through a redemptive sacrifice provided by the Lord God Himself. Sacrifice and offerings were to hold an important part in the worship which God would ordain for Israel. We reserve comment on this and its meaning until a more appropriate point in the narrative.

There would be another "only begotten son" who would come to Jerusalem and would be offered; for God would not spare His only begotten Son, but would give him up for us all.

The promises made to Abraham were renewed to Isaac (Genesis 26:2 – 8) and to his son Jacob (Genesis 28:3 – 4, 15). The covenant made with Abraham is one by which all true believers may benefit by belief and baptism through the work of the Lord Jesus Christ. There are more promises to come as the Scripture unfolds, but all of the future promises of God rest upon these foundation Abrahamic promises by which all nations will be blessed in Christ.

6

WHO IS KING?

THIS is an important question. The answer will lead us into an understanding of a great Biblical theme, namely, the Kingdom of God. In the beginning, when creation was new, there was peace, harmony and glory to God. God was King. His dominion was everywhere. His rule governed the heavens, His law ran through the earth and all His creatures, and the earth was at rest.

When Adam and Eve sinned they rebelled against God the King. As we have seen, the consequences were disastrous for man. But God too was affected by the flouting of His law and usurpation of His authority. Man had broken the peace of God.

The peace of God is the basis of all true peace; its loss meant that enmity came into the world through sin. It is for this reason that it is useless for man to seek a remedy for earth's wars without recognising that (as one of earth's politicians once said), peace is indivisible. There can be no lasting peace among men without true peace with God. As we shall see, this is the basis of the victory of Christ in whom all things will be brought into subjection to God.

Of course, despite Adam's sin, God was still the King. *"The earth is the Lord's, and the fulness thereof"* (Psalm 24:1); *"The Lord is a great God, and a great King"* (Psalm 95:3). Earth, sea and sky are His, and all creation lies in His hand. There is no other god. Adam's sin had not affected this aspect of the rule of God. Its meaning lay deeper. Adam had disputed the Lord's authority over him. He had challenged God and raised the standard of rebellion on God's earth.

37

God's sovereignty determined and administered the punishment for this defiance. Man was delivered into the dominion of sin and death, as he himself had chosen. This is clearly expressed in the New Testament:

> "*Jews and Gentiles* . . . **are all under sin** . . . *Their feet are swift to shed blood: destruction and misery are in their ways: and the way of peace have they not known: there is no fear of God before their eyes.*"
>
> (Romans 3:9,15 – 17)

> "*Sin hath **reigned** unto death.*" (Romans 5:21)

Man, having refused the goodness of God, was now subject to His severity.

This explains why man cannot find permanent remedies for his major ills. He has marred the image of God in himself and seeks to solve his problems by means of ideas devised in the kingdom of sin and death. They are always doomed to failure. Even the greatest acts of compassion and charity, or the works of major social reform, merely alleviate but never remove the cause of the evils they seek to remedy. For example, untold effort has been expended in seeking to solve the scourge of war among men. But the basic problem is not war and peace among men, it lies much deeper than that. The problem is man himself. Man is sinful. Remove sin and the way is open to paradise restored. How this is done is the subject of this book.

"Thy kingdom come"

The pointer is clear enough in the Lord's prayer:

> "*Hallowed be thy name.*
> *Thy kingdom come, thy will be done in earth,*
> *as it is in heaven.*" (Matthew 6:10)

The restoration of the kingdom of God on earth can come about only by the "hallowing" of God's name and the doing of His will on earth. Man alone can never achieve this. Without help from God man will remain in his shackles. The story of the Gospel is the glad tidings of the kingdom of God and the name of Jesus Christ. Christ is God's answer to man's need, and through him the blessings of Eden, and more, will be restored to this torn planet adrift from God. Christ alone has totally hallowed the name of God on earth and completely done His will. Therefore, in him lies the ultimate answer to man's distress as we shall discover as the story unfolds in these pages.

Whilst earth herself must wait for the day of deliverance at the return of Christ, individual men and women can find the way of peace and become heirs of the kingdom that is to come:

> *"Therefore being justified by faith, we have peace with God through our Lord Jesus Christ."* (Romans 5:1)

The terms of surrender for rebels in the kingdom of sin and death are plainly stated in the words of God the King in the Scripture. God dictates the terms and He does so with understanding, mercy and righteousness. It is worse than useless for man to devise his own remedy, once again to sew fig leaves together, as it were, to cover his shameful sin.

There is a simple principle enunciated in the Bible:

> *"I will be sanctified in them that come nigh me, and before all the people I will be glorified."* (Leviticus 10:3)

The first-time reader may have problems over words like "hallowed" and "sanctified" and, even over the word "name" in the expression, "Hallowed be thy name". Perhaps a few words of explanation would be helpful. Let us start with "thy name" and work onwards from there.

"Thy name" is God's name. God's name is not simply a means of identification as are the names of men. God's name, or more correctly His *names*, are revelations about Himself and His purpose. In other words, the names describe divine attributes, the divine purpose and the divine promises.

Therefore, to respect, honour or hallow (which word means to set apart, to sanctify or believe to be holy) is to express one's belief in the attributes of God and in His purpose, and to have a desire to be related to these things. In other words those who use the name(s) of God are expected to share the things the name stands for as the following verses will demonstrate:

> *"Thou shalt not take the name of the Lord thy God in vain."* (Exodus 20:7)

> *"Ye shall not swear by my name falsely."* (Leviticus 19:12)

> *"Observe to do all the words of this law ... that thou mayest fear this glorious and fearful name, the Lord thy God."* (Deuteronomy 28:58)

39

"They that know thy name will put their trust in thee."

(Psalm 9:10)

"He leadeth me in the paths of righteousness for his name's sake."

(Psalm 23:3)

"The Lord knoweth them that are his: and, Let every one that nameth the name of the Lord depart from unrighteousness."

(2 Timothy 2:19, R.V.)

The same principles apply to the name of Christ. Everyone who takes to himself the name of Christ must seek to be Christlike.

The meanings of some of the titles of Christ are obvious and require little explanation. For example, when the Lord Jesus Christ is called the Good Shepherd or the Light of the World, we soon grasp the meaning. But there are names, as distinct from titles, which hold secrets in themselves and are a kind of spiritual shorthand. Take the names "Jesus" and "Christ": what do they mean?

It is common to say that "Jesus" means "Saviour". Whilst this is a part of the truth, it is not the whole truth. The fuller meaning is, "The Lord saves" or, more precisely, "Jah saves", where "Jah" is a short, emphatic version of the Old Testament name for God, "Yahweh". The word "Jesus" is Greek and its Hebrew Old Testament counterpart is "Joshua". Therefore, whilst it is true that Jesus is Saviour, the complete truth is that God is the Saviour who provided Jesus to save us.

The word "Christ" is the New Testament equivalent of "Messiah" in the Old Testament. Both words mean "Anointed". Christ is God's anointed. He is God's anointed Prophet, Priest and King. At his baptism *"God anointed Jesus of Nazareth with the Holy Spirit and with power"* (Acts 10:38). At his resurrection, Christ was "anointed with the oil of gladness" above his fellows. As prophet he lived and proclaimed the Gospel; as priest he is the intercessor for faithful prayer; as king he will be revealed on earth as the anointed of the Lord.

There are a number of names of God in the Bible, but we select two for special reference: God Almighty or the Almighty God, and the LORD God. God Almighty is the English translation of two Hebrew words, El Shaddai (which can be found in the margins of some Bibles). El is a singular noun for God and it carries the meaning of power, powerful one. Shaddai is plural and means simply mighty ones or, perhaps, mighty one; it is associated with fruitfulness. But the way in which God Almighty is used in the Bible indicates to us that more than power and powerful ones is intended. The power is used to ensure the fulfilment of the promises and judgements of God, and is associated with the exercise of God's power in mercy to bring blessings and fruitfulness. The ultimate concept is the Fatherhood of God whereby He begets His spiritual children and promises them an eternal inheritance. Useful Scriptures to ponder are: Genesis 17:1 – 2; 28:3 – 4; 35:11 – 13; 2 Corinthians 1:3 – 4; 6:17 – 18; Revelation 15:3 – 4; 21:22.

Much has been written and conjectured about the word LORD. It represents four Hebrew letters YHWH which when vocalised become in English the word Jehovah or Yahweh, the latter being the more probably correct. In our English Bibles it is represented by LORD (though the practice is not followed in this book) and, occasionally, by Jehovah or Jah. The word occurs from the earliest chapters of the Bible but it receives special prominence at the time when Moses is selected by God to lead the new-born nation of Israel out of their bondage in Egypt. Yahweh is not the name for a mere tribal god as some would have us believe.

There is nothing of the occult or mysterious about the Name. It is derived from a simple verb which is translated in our Bibles as I AM (Exodus 3:14). Those two simple words refer supremely to the absolutely self-existent God. But God is ever-existent and the margins of some Bibles indicate that "I AM" may also be translated as "I will be". This latter translation blends with God's own explanation of the Name as "my name for ever". LORD is a noun derived from the word "I will be" and carries the meaning "He who will be".

Moreover, Yahweh also comprehends within itself all of the divine attributes (see Exodus 34:6 – 7) and because it is used when giving every major promise (see Genesis 3:14 – 15; 8:21 – 22; 12:1 – 3,7; 13:14 – 15; 15:18; 22:15 – 18; 26:2 – 4; 28:13 – 15; 1 Chronicles 17:7 – 14; Psalm 110; Isaiah 9:6 – 7; 53:1 – 12, etc.) Yahweh is the covenant name by which the believer was bound to the promises and inheritance of everlasting life in the coming kingdom of God. Take, for instance, the following example:

> "They that feared the LORD spake often one to another: and the LORD hearkened, and heard it, and a book of remembrance was written before him for them that feared the LORD, and that thought upon his name. And they shall be mine, saith the LORD of hosts, in that day when I make up my jewels."
> (Malachi 3:16 – 17)

41

What then is the meaning of 'LORD God'? The word *elohim* translated literally means: powerful ones. Elohim is used for God Himself, for His angels, for judges appointed by Him and, in one case, for the people of Israel who received the word from God. Briefly, *elohim* is used for God or for special people empowered or authorised by Him. 'LORD God' could therefore be translated as "He who will be powerful ones". This is helpful when we learn from the Lord Jesus Christ that Exodus 3:15 is, in fact, God's promise to give everlasting life to the faithful by resurrection from the dead (see Matthew 22:31 – 32 and Luke 13:28 – 29). The faithful will then indeed be "sons of power", as one hymn writer described the children of the resurrection.

The first stage in the fulfilment of this wonderful promise was the resurrection of the Lord Jesus Christ. The next stage will be the resurrection at his second coming (about which more will be said later in this book). The promises which God made under His ancient name Yahweh began their great fulfilment when God became known in fulness as Father by the birth of His son of the virgin Mary.

Therefore, when we pray: "Our Father, which art in heaven, hallowed be thy name. Thy kingdom come. Thy will be done on earth as it is in heaven", we are in fact praying for the fulfilment of all that lies in the Old Testament name of the LORD made resplendent in the Fatherhood of God in Christ and in the Sonship of the Son of the Father.

It was this trust in His name and the hallowing of it in daily life which the Lord God sought in man whom He had created and, particularly, in those who had survived the Flood and were now spreading abroad upon the face of the earth after the confusion of tongues at Babel. There was, however, little hope that a godly remnant would survive in a sea of wickedness. Sooner or later they would have been engulfed and have disappeared.

Therefore, God took special measures to ensure the preservation of His Word in the earth. The process was both unique and marvellous. It was an illustration of that which made the apostle Paul exclaim with wonder and adoration when he came to know the truth in Jesus: " *O the depth of the riches both of the wisdom and knowledge of God! how unsearchable are his judgements, and his ways past finding out!*" (Romans 11:33).

There was little in the initial steps to indicate how effective God's special measures would be in preserving His Word in the earth. He chose the man Abraham, whom we have already considered, and then promised that the welfare of his seed would always be the concern of God Himself.

In practice this worked out in a remarkable way. Abraham's descendants were the children of Israel, later known as the Jews, and He gave to them His revealed Word in written form as He had never before made it known. The Jews became the recipients and custodians of the Word of God. For this reason, they bore special responsibilities. God made it abundantly plain to them that He would directly intervene in the nation's affairs to bring blessings for obedience and cursings for disobedience towards Him. It was as though God had made an outpost for Himself amongst men, this time in a nation which bore the torch of His Word and the nucleus of the blessings for the whole world.

Israel were entrusted with the deposit of God's Word. God promised them that they would never be destroyed as a people and so His Word would remain:

> *"(Israel) to whom pertaineth the adoption, and the glory, and the covenants, and the giving of the law, and the service of God, and the promises; whose are the fathers, and of whom as concerning the flesh Christ came."* (Romans 9:4 – 5)

There are in the world as many ideas about God's dealing with the Jews as there are nations, and these ideas continue to exercise the minds of men in the 20th century. There is no nation on earth which has provoked more reaction and thought than this seemingly insignificant people. We hope to look at some aspects of this intriguing subject later. Meanwhile we would emphasise that it was God's choice to work out His plan in this way. Left to man there would have been nothing but overwhelming darkness.

From this we conclude that it is the best way for the good things God has in mind. God was not seeking to destroy hope, but to preserve it; not to obliterate man, but to deliver a remnant for eternal happiness in the earth made all-glorious.

From time to time men have suggested that the degree of privilege seemingly accorded to the descendants of Abraham must mean a corresponding degree of unfairness to the rest of the world. This reasoning has a fatal flaw in it. It assumes that if God had left it to mankind at large to preserve His Word, all would have been well. This is not so. God had already done that twice in world history, and it had resulted in the consolidated wickedness of man which is destructive of God's Word and ways. Hence the Flood and the Tower of Babel, as already discussed. Therefore, God chose the method of making a nation the custodians of His Word and taking special steps to preserve the nation to ensure the survival of His Word.

Another objection has been raised at different times; this, too, is based on a false premise. If, as the Bible tells us, the Jews were chosen as God's people, why does He persist in that choice even when the Jews have proved themselves unworthy of Him? In response to this we must first get rid of the self-righteousness which may lie behind the question. The suggestion is that had God chosen some other nation, they would have done better than the Jews. There is no proof for this whatsoever. Indeed, knowing man's sinfulness, it should be evident that any other nation would have gone its own wilful way as did the Jews.

No, it was not the goodness of the Jews which determined God's choice; it was His grace. Moreover, it was not that God wished to create an exclusive élite, but rather that the chosen people should have been the means of bringing God's blessings to everyone: "In thee shall all families of the earth be blessed." They were to be the gateway through whom all could come to learn of God. It was the Jews who turned inwards and used their exclusiveness to the disadvantage of others. Even so, in the end, through them by the Lord Jesus Christ, God threw open the gates of salvation to all who would enter.

Under the direction and protection of God the children of Israel were brought out of Egypt under the leadership of Moses. They had journeyed to Egypt hundreds of years earlier at a time of famine, when they were very few in number. This was the beginning of nationhood for a formerly captive and oppressed people. Moses spoke to them the word from God and thereby provided the spiritual basis for law and order. In due course, by the inspiration of God, Moses wrote what we now know as the first five books of the Bible, the Pentateuch, in which we have a record of God's commands and dealings with men from the days of creation until the day when Moses said farewell to his people on the borders of the land of Canaan.

Meanwhile in the wilderness there had been set up under Moses' tutelage, and by direct command and revelation of God, a system of worship which was to persist until the days of the Lord Jesus Christ, and some of whose essential elements remain in the

Gospel and practice of the Lord himself. The tent-like structure of the Tabernacle with its linen-walled courtyard, its ordinances and priesthood, became the focus of religious life. Indeed, it was the focus of *all* life, because the laws of God governed every aspect of life, and would have brought Israel untold good had they sought to follow them. The principles of law and order, of neighbourliness, of land inheritance and of a joyful spiritual life with regular feasts of gladness and praise would have made them outstandingly blessed. The blessings would have issued forth in blessings for all peoples.

Even when, later on, in the settled conditions of the land, the tabernacle was replaced by a solid temple, the same principles and worship were continued. It is not that church and state were in partnership, as happens in some western countries; the people were the state and they were the congregation of the Lord. Civil and spiritual life were twin aspects of one existence. It was the law of the Lord which should have governed everything. The land was His, the laws were His, the people were His, and, though they did not confess it, He was their King. They were, however imperfectly, a kingdom of God; indeed, they were *the* kingdom of God since there was no other nation under such governance.

The Throne of David

When in the days of David and Solomon the kingdom reached its zenith and the old system of judges had been replaced by a visible king, it was made explicit that the order was known to God as His kingdom:

> "*The Lord . . . hath chosen Solomon my son to sit upon* **the throne of the kingdom of the Lord** *over Israel.*"　(1 Chronicles 28:5)

Not only had a visible king been added, there was also a capital city chosen by God, Jerusalem. The earthly monarch ruled for God.

There were two major weaknesses in this kingdom — the people and the earthly king. These two shared a common weakness; human frailty. For this reason this phase of the kingdom of God could not endure. Sin and death reigned even in the kingdom of God. Human rebellion raised its head many times, and the true worship of God became polluted with manifold idolatry.

Early in its history the nation had been divided into two kingdoms. One was in the north with its capital in Samaria. It had the allegiance of ten tribes and was variously known as Israel,

45

Ephraim and Samaria. The other kingdom was in the south and was known as Judah. It had two tribes, but it retained the capital city, Jerusalem, and with it the temple.

In both kingdoms the Lord pleaded with His people to forsake other gods and return to Him. His prophets witnessed, exhorted and warned, without intermission. The northern kingdom never had a righteous king, and its worship was entirely idolatrous with a wicked and false priesthood. Finally, when there was no remedy, God according to His Word gave them into the hands of the Assyrians who took them captive and transported them into their empire. As a nation they never returned.

Meanwhile, down south, Judah fared somewhat better. Some of their kings were good and sometimes they worshipped acceptably. But in the end the corruption took over. God warned them and reminded them what had happened to their sister kingdom in the north: all to no avail. Whilst the armies of Babylon were in the process of invasion and destruction, God caused His prophet Ezekiel to deliver this denunciation to Judah's last king, Zedekiah:

> "*And thou, profane wicked prince of Israel, whose day is come, when iniquity shall have an end, thus saith the Lord God: Remove the diadem, and take off the crown: this shall not be the same: exalt him that is low, and abase him that is high. I will overturn, overturn, overturn it: and it shall be no more, until he come whose right it is; and I will give it him.*"
> (Ezekiel 21:25 – 27)

Here, as the kingdom was dying and the people were being transported to Babylon in wave after wave, the words of doom contained a kernel of hope. Who would come to fulfil those bright words: "Until he come whose right it is"? Who indeed?

Zedekiah, the last king of Israel, saw his sons killed before him and then his eyes were put out. Jerusalem was destroyed, its walls were broken down and its temple burned. The captives arrived in Babylon clutching to their breasts the precious books of the revelation of God, even those books which had foretold their departure into captivity as a punishment for unfaithfulness and persistent, obstinate rebellion. The prophet who saw it said:

> "*How doth the city sit solitary, that was full of people!*
> *How is she become as a widow!*
> *She that was great among the nations, and princess among the provinces.*
> *How is she become tributary!*

46

How hath the Lord covered the daughter of Zion with a cloud in his anger, and cast down from heaven unto the earth the beauty of Israel . . . !

Behold, and see if there be any sorrow like unto my sorrow, which is done unto me . . ." (Lamentations 1:1, 2:1 and 1:12)

7

WHO WILL BE KING?

IF the Israelite kingdom of God was doomed to failure by virtue of human sinfulness, how can anything better emerge? Does the solution lie in the intriguing words, "He whose right it is"? The words were spoken to the dissolute king Zedekiah at the end of his kingdom. If the words were in isolation we should be left to conjecture and consequently to some doubt about their meaning. It so happens, however, that the words, "whose right it is", are themselves an echo of an ancient Scriptural promise, one which is part of the golden thread running through the Bible.

It will be recalled that Abraham's grandson Jacob had twelve sons whose names were given to the twelve tribes descended from them. Jacob died in Egypt, but prior to that event he called his twelve sons together and pronounced blessings on them. There is no doubt that these blessings were inspired prophecies from God outlining something of the future for each of the tribes. Amongst these blessings is the following promise specific to the tribe of Judah:

> "*The sceptre will not depart from Judah, nor the ruler's staff from between his feet, until he come **to whom it belongs** and the obedience of the nations is his.*" (Genesis 49:10, N.I.V.)

"He whose right it is" and "To whom it belongs" have a similar ring about them. Each speaks of a king to come. The Genesis prophecy says that the promised One will be of the tribe of Judah. The words of the Ezekiel prophecy were addressed to a king of Judah. Who will this royal personage be? How can it be said that

48

WHO WILL BE KING?

he has the right to reign? What can be meant by the words, "obedience of the nations"? The key lies in God's words about the crown: "I will give it him". The king will reign by divine appointment.

One cannot read these things or reflect seriously upon them without sensing that they are of great importance for Israel and for the nations. They remind us about the promises made to Abraham. Those promises, too, involve both the seed of Abraham and the Gentile nations. We quote once more the words of the last promise which God made to Abraham:

> "*Thy seed shall possess the gate of his enemies; and in thy seed shall all the nations of the earth be blessed.*" (Genesis 22:17 – 18)

Is this seed of Abraham the same person as "He whose right it is", the one "to whom it belongs"? We can place these questions in the context of a Royal Promise made to David the king, which places the issues beyond doubt. Here is the background to that Royal Promise. David knew that he was ruling for God. He had a keen sense of service in this respect, and above all he wanted to see the true worship of God flourish in the kingdom. By this time David had built himself a cedar house in Jerusalem and, seemingly conscience-stricken, wanted to build a permanent home for the tabernacle worship by housing the ark of the covenant in a solid structure. The king was restrained from pursuing this work, commendable though it seemed to be, by words from the prophet of the Lord, amongst which are found the following:

> "*I will raise up thy seed after thee, which shall be of thy sons; and I will establish his kingdom. He shall build me an house, and I will establish his throne for ever* . . . *I will settle him in my house and in my kingdom for ever: and his throne shall be established for ever more.*" (1 Chronicles 17:11 – 14)

This is God's covenant with David and corresponds in importance with the one made to Abraham. In fact, together they form the total covenant because they encompass the grand purpose of God, described in the New Testament as "the things concerning the kingdom of God and the name of Jesus Christ".

We now have the following elements in these promises concerning the king:

He will . . .

49

possess the gate of his enemies;
bring blessings to all nations.   (Genesis 22:17,18)

be the one to whom it belongs.   (Genesis 49:10)

be of the seed of David.   (2 Samuel 7:12)

reign over God's kingdom.   (1 Chronicles 17:14)

be "the one whose right it is."   (Ezekiel 21:27)

Furthermore, we know that this victorious king had not arrived up to the time that Zedekiah was deposed by God and went into captivity. He was still to come. The hope of the coming King was cherished by the captives in Babylon. Faithful men ruminated on the promises of God and longed for their fulfilment. Amongst these men of hope was the well-known prophet Daniel. Not so well-known is a remarkable God-given dream in which Daniel was involved as interpreter. The dream was a vision of major history in advance. The circumstances in which it arose were as follows.

About six centuries before Christ Nebuchadnezzar was king in Babylon, and his glory and empire were widespread. He was wondering what would happen to his vast realms after his death. His sleep was disturbed by a most vivid dream which so impressed him that he believed it held meaning for him. Next morning he assembled his magicians, enchanters, sorcerers and astrologers, and set them an impossible task. He told them he had had a powerful dream but had forgotten what it was about. Would they tell him the dream? and also the interpretation? The wise men were is disarray. The king's demands left them no scope for their usual fanciful embroidery on ideas already presented to them. He had told them nothing, and threatened them with death if they failed in their task!

The dream and its consequences were of God. He had created the perfect illustration of man's powerlessness to recall the unknown past or delineate the unknown future. The wisdom of the wise had been brought to nothing.

Among the wise men was Daniel. He had been directed into their ranks when he was taken captive. Daniel approached the commander of the king's guard and asked for a stay of execution. Meanwhile he and his three Jewish companions sought the help of the Lord in prayer, and to Daniel was revealed both the knowledge of the dream and its meaning. These were then made known by

Daniel in the presence of the king whose astonishment must have increased as he listened to the lucid description of the dream and its interpretation piece by piece.

Nebuchadnezzar's Dream

The king in his dream had seen a bright, metallic and awesome statue of a man. The head was golden, the arms and chest were silver, the lower body and thighs were brass, the legs were iron, and the feet were a mixture of iron and clay. Into this static scene was injected major drama. A stone from the mountain side hurtled through the air, as though not humanly projected, and smote the statue on its feet.

The statue fell to the ground and was broken to pieces. The stone then ground all the pieces to powder which was blown away by the wind. The stone alone was left. It grew and grew until it filled the whole earth.

No wonder that Nebuchadnezzar felt that the dream had a meaning! Daniel proceeded to reveal the meaning of the Image and the Stone as God had revealed it to him. Briefly stated, the dream was a panorama of world history right up to the time when the kingdom of God will be established on earth. And it ends like this:

> "*In the days of these kings shall the God of heaven set up a kingdom, which shall never be destroyed; and the kingdom shall not be left to other people, but it shall break in pieces and consume all these kingdoms, and it shall stand for ever.*" (Daniel 2:44)

The grand sweep of history was relative to the land of Israel and the nations around her, particularly the empires which held sway over the Middle East. Three parts of the image are interpreted within the book itself: the head of gold represented Babylon (Daniel 2:31), the arms and chest of silver represented the Medo-Persian empire (Daniel 8:20), and the lower body and thighs portrayed the Grecian Empire of Alexander the Great (Daniel 8:21). It follows that the legs must have symbolised the next empire, the one which followed the Greeks. This must be the Roman Empire, the significance of which for the western world would be hard to over-estimate. Perhaps the legs represented the eastern and western parts of the empire. What then of the feet of iron and clay?

When Rome had gone there was no succeeding empire which

covered the same extent of territory. Empires there were from time to time, but none approached Rome in importance or in the wide extent of its territories. Indeed, we can conclude from the dream that no succeeding empire is intended by God.

However, in passing, it must be noted that although the parts of the image are successive, according to the interpretation, they also represent in total, "the kingdoms of men". It may well be that in some way, undisclosed in the dream, they will have some kind of coherence at the time when the stone smites them. We shall examine this thought later in the chapter.

Nebuchadnezzar must have been delighted to have his dream reconstructed by Daniel and to look down the corridor of future time by means of the interpretation. There was, however, an aspect of the dream which, though clearly of major significance, had not been fully developed by Daniel. What or who did the Stone represent?

In the dream the stone was the powerful means whereby the kingdom of God on earth was to be established. Let us say at once that the Stone is Christ. We know this because Christ applies that title to himself. In the last week of his life, when he was being pressed on every side by Jewish rulers intent on his destruction, Christ uttered a parable telling of the forthcoming overthrow of the Jewish vassal state because of their repeated rejection of the Word of God. The rulers perceived the meaning of the parable and vehemently opposed it. Christ then asked them the devastating question:

*"Did ye never read in the scriptures: **The stone** which the builders rejected, the same is become the head of the corner: this is the Lord's doing, and it is marvellous in our eyes?"* (Matthew 21:42; Psalm 118:22 – 23)

The rulers were the supposed builders of Israel, but they could not fit Christ into their structure. Christ was telling them that it was the structure which would fall, but the Stone they were rejecting would be the cornerstone of God's work! Christ is the Stone.

Christ was the Stone prepared "without hands" (as we read in Daniel 2:34). Truly, he came from the mountain of humanity, but he was "cut out without hands", since he had no human father; he was the Son of God. More than that: he was raised from the dead by the same divine power and granted the gift of immortality from the Father. Furthermore, when he returns to this earth, as he assuredly will, the time will be of God's choosing:

52

"He (Jesus) must remain in heaven until the time comes for God to restore everything, as he promised long ago through his holy prophets."

(Acts 3:21, N.I.V.)

Christ the King

That is the time when God will restore His kingdom on earth. There is no clearer teaching in the whole of the Bible than that which tells us about God's world-wide Kingdom to be established on earth with Christ as the King. This has been the hope of faithful men throughout the ages. Look at this small, yet impressive, selection of Scriptures on this theme:

"He that ruleth over men must be just, ruling in the fear of God. And he shall be as the light of the morning, when the sun riseth, even a morning without clouds; as the tender grass springing out of the earth by clear shining after rain. Although my house (said David) be not so with God; yet he hath made with me an everlasting covenant, ordered in all things, and sure: for this is all my salvation, and all my desire."

(2 Samuel 23:3 – 5)

"He shall cry unto me, Thou art my father, my God, and the rock of my salvation. Also I will make him my firstborn, higher than the kings of the earth."

(Psalm 89:26 – 27)

"He shall judge thy people with righteousness, and thy poor with judgment . . . he shall save the children of the needy, and shall break in pieces the oppressor . . . In his days shall the righteous flourish; and abundance of peace so long as the moon endureth. . . . Yea, all kings shall fall down before him: all nations shall serve him . . . His name shall endure for ever: his name shall be continued as long as the sun: and men shall be blessed in him; all nations shall call him blessed."

(from Psalm 72)

"For unto us a child is born, unto us a son is given: and the government shall be upon his shoulder: and his name shall be called Wonderful, Counsellor, The mighty God, The everlasting Father, The Prince of Peace. Of the increase of his government and peace there shall be no end, **upon the throne of David**, *and upon his kingdom, to order it, and to establish it with judgment and with justice from henceforth even for ever. The zeal of the Lord of hosts will perform this."*

(Isaiah 9:6 – 7)

"Then the moon shall be confounded, and the sun ashamed, when the Lord of hosts shall reign in mount Zion, and in Jerusalem, and before his ancients gloriously."

(Isaiah 24:23)

"For out of Zion shall go forth the law, and the word of the Lord from Jerusalem. And he shall judge among the nations, and shall rebuke many people: and they shall beat their swords into plowshares, and their spears into pruninghooks: nation shall not lift up sword against nation, neither shall they learn war any more." (Isaiah 2:3 – 4)

"At that time they shall call Jerusalem **the throne of the Lord;** *and all the nations shall be gathered unto it, to the name of the Lord, to Jerusalem."* (Jeremiah 3:17)

"Behold, the days come, saith the Lord, that **I will raise unto David** *a righteous Branch, and a King shall reign and prosper, and shall execute judgment and justice in the earth. In his days Judah shall be saved, and Israel shall dwell safely: and this is the name whereby he shall be called,* **The Lord our righteousness."** (Jeremiah 23:5 – 6)

"And the Lord shall be king over all the earth: in that day shall there be one Lord, and his name one." (Zechariah 14:9)

"Fear not, Mary . . . thou shalt . . . bring forth a son and shalt call his name **Jesus.** *He shall be great, and shall be called the Son of the Highest: and* **the Lord God shall give unto him the throne of his father David***: and he shall reign over the house of Jacob for ever; and of his kingdom there shall be no end."* (Luke 1:30 – 33)

"For the Son of man shall come in the glory of his Father with his angels; and then he shall reward every man according to his works." (Matthew 16:27)

"When the Son of man shall come in his glory, and all the holy angels with him, then shall he sit on the throne of his glory." (Matthew 25:31)

"The Lord Jesus shall be revealed from heaven with his mighty angels, in flaming fire taking vengeance on them that know not God, and that obey not the gospel of our Lord Jesus Christ: who shall be punished with everlasting destruction from the presence of the Lord, and from the glory of his power; when he shall come to be glorified in his saints, and to be admired in all them that believe." (2 Thessalonians 1:7 – 10)

"For thou wast slain, and hast redeemed us to God by thy blood out of every kindred, and tongue, and people, and nation: and hast made us kings and priests: and we shall reign on the earth." (Revelation 5:9 – 10)

"Blessed and holy is he that hath part in the first resurrection: on such the second death hath no power, but they shall be priests of God and of Christ, and shall reign with him a thousand years."

(Revelation 20:6)

"And the seventh angel sounded; and there followed great voices in heaven, and they said, The kingdom of the world is become the kingdom of our Lord, and of his Christ: and he shall reign for ever and ever . . . We give thee thanks, O Lord God, the Almighty, which art and which wast; because thou hast taken thy great power, and didst reign. And the nations were wroth, and thy wrath came, and the time of the dead to be judged, and the time to give their reward to thy servants the prophets, and to the saints, and to them that fear thy name, the small and the great; and to destroy them that destroy the earth."

(Revelation 11:15 – 18, R.V.)

These Scriptures will bear reading and re-reading. They bring together so much of the prophetic promises of God, particularly those given to Abraham and to David. Christ is God's appointed king. God will give him the throne of David in Jerusalem; and on his return to earth Christ will reign over the Kingdom of God on earth at the time when the resurrection and judgement will take place. Those who receive immortality at the hands of the Lord Jesus Christ as Judge will reign with him in his Father's Kingdom on earth.

Moreover, from the same Scriptures we know that the initiation of this Kingdom will be at a time of world trouble. Christ's irresistible and righteous power will rebuke the wicked and remove the oppression among earth's multitudes. The Stone will smite the kingdoms of men in order to end the old world order and bring in the majesty and blessings of God to a world of sin and suffering.

8

WHAT WILL THE KINGDOM OF GOD BE LIKE?

GOD has revealed a great deal about the coming Kingdom. A thrilling picture of world-wide peace and divine care can be constructed from the many hundreds of verses in Scripture on this subject. First, however, we must look at the principles upon which the kingdom will be established.

Christ in glorious power will be the world ruler. He himself spoke about this on a number of occasions:

> "*Ye shall see the Son of man sitting on the right hand of power, and coming in the clouds of heaven.*" (Matthew 26:64)

> "*Ye which have followed me, in the regeneration when the Son of man shall sit in the throne of his glory, ye also shall sit upon twelve thrones, judging the twelve tribes of Israel.*" (Matthew 19:28)

The associates with Christ in administering world government will be the saints, that is, the faithful of all ages. These will be gathered, the living and the dead, and after the day of judgement they will receive the gift of immortality. This is how Scripture puts it:

> "*In Christ shall all be made alive . . . but every man in his own order . . . they that are Christ's **at his coming**. . . . We shall not all sleep, but we shall all be changed . . . the dead shall be raised . . . this corruptible must put on incorruption, and this mortal must put on immortality.*"

> (1 Corinthians 15:22 – 23, 51 – 53)

56

"I (Paul) endure all things for the elects' sakes, that they may also obtain the salvation which is in Christ Jesus with eternal glory. It is a faithful saying: For if we be dead with him, we shall also live with him: if we suffer, we shall also reign with him."   (2 Timothy 2:10 – 12)

"But the saints of the most High shall take the kingdom, and possess the kingdom for ever, even for ever and ever . . . And the kingdom . . . **under the whole heaven,** *shall be given to the people of the saints of the most High, whose kingdom is an everlasting kingdom, and all dominions shall serve and obey him."*   (Daniel 7:18,27)

"They lived and reigned with Christ a thousand years."
(Revelation 20:4)

The laws of the Kingdom on earth will be unique. They will not consist of legislation enacted by man for man, whether democratically or otherwise, but of divine laws whose purpose will be to lead the nations to live in a right relationship with God, and thereby have a proper relationship between man and man. It was this arrangement which Adam and Eve rejected in Eden's garden, thereby bringing misery upon themselves and sorrows for all their descendants. The same kind of arrangement was provided for Israel when they left Egypt and, more especially, when they settled in the land of promise. They too failed to observe and preserve that which was designed for their lasting good.

In the Kingdom of the new age, however, the government will be invincible and incorruptible, because it will be exercised by Christ and his beloved servants. Together they will teach the nations the ways of God, and provide authoritative power to ensure that national obedience will be forthcoming. Listen to the word of God:

"With righteousness shall he judge the poor,
and reprove with equity for the meek of the earth:
and he shall smite the earth with the rod of his mouth,
and with the breath of his lips shall he slay the wicked.
And righteousness shall be the girdle of his loins . . .
for the earth shall be full of the knowledge of the Lord,
as the waters cover the sea."   (Isaiah 11:4 – 5,9)

"The lofty looks of man shall be humbled, and the haughtiness of men shall be bowed down, and the Lord alone shall be exalted in that day."
(Isaiah 2:11)

> *"Then judgment shall dwell in the wilderness, and righteousness remain in the fruitful field. And the work of righteousness shall be peace; and the effect of righteousness quietness and assurance for ever."*
>
> (Isaiah 32:16 – 17)

> *"And many people shall go and say, Come ye, and let us go up to the mountain of the Lord, to the house of the God of Jacob; and he will teach us of his ways, and we will walk in his paths . . ."* (Isaiah 2:3)

But where do the nations come from to be subjects in the Kingdom of God? The answer lies in the events which take place when Christ returns. At that time the world will consist of two kinds of people: those who are taken away to the judgement seat of Christ for individual judgement, and those who will not so appear personally before Christ. The basis for this distinction will be discussed later under the headings of resurrection and judgement. Those who are not taken away will be involved in the man-made havoc and tribulation which will envelop the world at that time. Those who survive that time of chastisement will become the subjects of the Kingdom of God. They are the mortal inhabitants of that age.

This world-wide population will become one empire under one King and his princes, and will be governed by the good, beneficent laws of God. This will be in marvellous and blessed contrast to the oppression, failure, starvation and exploitation which have blighted the existence of many for so long.

What place will the Jews have in the kingdom? God will vindicate Himself in His former dealings with that strange people, and they in turn will be brought to acknowledge Christ the Rejected as Christ the King.

The Jews and Israel

At the present time the Jews are being regathered, at least in part, to their ancient land. Under God's hand they have established the State of Israel with a population of roughly three million. But they are not basically God-fearing, and they remain obstinate in their rejection of Christ as their looked for Messiah. Consequently the State of Israel rests upon the skills of the Jewish people and not on the laws of God. It is not in any way the Kingdom of God at the present time. As we shall have occasion to say when considering the survival of the Jews, the existing State of Israel is doomed to suffer tragically in a major invasion of their land. They will be crippled and hopeless. All their inventiveness, persistence, privations, military prowess and national courage will lie in ruins. It will look as though all has been in vain (see for example, Ezekiel 38 and Zechariah 14).

What will happen then?

The returned Christ will be revealed to the crushed and hopeless people. The invaders are destroyed (as described in Ezekiel 38 and in Zechariah 14:1 – 4). The defeated Jews will be brought face to face with reality, not just the reality of invasion, but the stunning realisation that Christ is their Deliverer (Zechariah 12:7 – 13). Only by these humiliating and overwhelming experiences will one of the seemingly impossible prophecies be brought to a wonderful fulfilment. The words that stood over the Cross for all to read will be shown to be true:

"THIS IS JESUS THE KING OF THE JEWS."

(Matthew 27:37)

The repentant Jews will weep for shame. Out of the ashes of the broken State of Israel will arise a better and more worthy inheritance. The repentant (though still mortal) Jews will be at the centre of the Kingdom of God and will live in the land promised to Abraham which Christ will give them. The Jewish population dispersed throughout the world will be brought home and, if similarly repentant, will be caused to dwell in Israel under the rulership of the twelve apostles as promised to them at the Last Supper (Luke 22:28 – 29).

The vicissitudes of the Jews will be over and anti-semitism will have gone for ever. And the almost sterile Judaism on which many of the Jews have sought to survive will be cleared away by the law of Christ and the principles of his reign.

But what of the Arabs, who have regarded Israel as their enemy on account of the usurpation of the "rights" of the Palestinians, and have been dispossessed by the State of Israel? The Arabs have never been a united people and have never ceased to fulfil an ancient prophecy which foretold their endless quarrelling among themselves (Genesis 16:11 – 12). When the great invasion of the land of Israel takes place the Arabs are not expected to play a major part, except for Libya and Ethiopia (whose population is a mixture of Semitic and negroid races with a corresponding mixture of religions). At least one Arab power, probably Saudi Arabia, will be amongst those who ineffectually challenge the invaders (these details are to be found in Ezekiel 38 and Daniel 11). Egypt will

59

certainly not be amongst the invaders. How then will the Arabs fare in the kingdom of God?

Saudi Arabia appears to be amongst the willing and suppliant kingdoms to become subjects of the Kingdom of God (Psalm 72:10,15). Egypt receives special mention and has a blessed relationship with Israel at that time. In fact, there will be a highway which will run from Egypt, through Israel, to Syria and beyond:

> *"In that day shall there be a highway out of Egypt to Assyria, and the Assyrian shall come to Egypt, and the Egyptians into Assyria, and the Egyptians shall serve (worship) with the Assyrians. In that day shall Israel be the third with Egypt and with Assyria, even a blessing in the midst of the land: whom the Lord of hosts shall bless, saying, Blessed be Egypt my people, and Assyria the work of my hands, and Israel mine inheritance."* (Isaiah 19:23 – 24)

This unexpected harmony of nationhood and peace among former inveterate enemies will lie at the heart of the Kingdom of God, and will be symbolic of what will happen throughout the world, for *"nation shall not lift up sword against nation, neither shall they learn war any more"* (Isaiah 2:4). As the Psalmist has prophesied, there will be *"abundance of peace so long as the moon endureth"* (Psalm 72:7).

The rivalries among the Arabs will end and their lands will be blessed and become fertile and luxuriant everywhere.

The elimination of world armaments and the economic strain which their cost incurs, to say nothing of the scourge of war itself, will provide ample opportunity for true prosperity and for the generous agricultural pursuits which will characterise the new age. The curse of thorns and thistles, imposed as a consequence of Adam's sin, will be lifted and the whole earth will become exceedingly fruitful. All malnutrition and near starvation will be banished for all mankind:

> *"There shall be an handful of corn in the earth upon the top of the mountains; the fruit thereof shall shake like Lebanon."*
> (Psalm 72:16)

> *"Behold, the days come, saith the Lord, that the plowman shall overtake the reaper, and the treader of grapes him that soweth seed; and the mountains shall drop sweet wine."* (Amos 9:13)

> *"And it shall come to pass in that day, that the mountains shall drop down new wine, and the hills shall flow with milk."* (Joel 3:18)

"The wilderness and the solitary place shall be glad . . . and the desert shall rejoice, and blossom as the rose. It shall blossom abundantly, and rejoice even with joy and singing: the glory of Lebanon shall be given unto it, the excellency of Carmel and Sharon." (Isaiah 35:1 – 2)

Whether it will arise from the new way of life, peaceful and unoppressed, free from all the offences with which our present civilisation abounds; or whether it will be direct blessing from God, we do not know, but the Scriptures strongly suggest that mortal man will live much longer in those golden days than in this present age of evil, pressure and uncertainty:

"There shall yet old men and old women dwell in the streets of Jerusalem, and every man with his staff in his hand for very age." (Zechariah 8:4)

"There shall be no more thence an infant of days, nor an old man that hath not filled his days: for the child shall die an hundred years old; but the sinner being an hundred years old shall be accursed." (Isaiah 65:20)

How will the problems created by the barriers of language be coped with by the new administration? How appropriate it would be in the Kingdom to have all men worship in one language, and for the constraints of a polyglot world to disappear! There is a hint of this in Scripture, sufficient to give rise to the hope that in the world-wide kingdom there will also be a world-wide language:

"For then will I turn to the people a pure language, that they may all call upon the name of the Lord, to serve him with one consent." (Zephaniah 3:9)

There would be a particular delight in having one language in view of the unity of worship of the Coming Age. All the divisions of religion, including those which lie within Christendom, will disappear in the truth which then will be known by all. It will not be the ecumenism which many at present strive for, but the dissemination of the truth of God by Christ and his government to all the world which will bring about unity and harmony. Moreover there will be a striking centre-piece to the worship of God in Christ's reign.

Jerusalem — The World's Capital

There will be one world capital: Jerusalem in its glory. In the closing chapters of the prophecy recorded by Ezekiel there is a description of a magnificent temple to be erected in Israel which all nations will visit from time to time by way of pilgrimage, to render praise to God in the place where He sets up His throne; and to enjoy the richness of communal worship with a variety of ordained ritual remarkably reminiscent of the old worship of the Jews, yet modified in the prophecy to show that by the time the vision becomes reality Jesus the Christ will have once and for all died for our sins and risen to live for ever. Here are some of the Scriptures telling about this temple worship:

> *"At that time they shall call Jerusalem the throne of the Lord; and all the nations shall be gathered unto it, to the name of the Lord, to Jerusalem: neither shall they walk any more after the imagination of their evil heart."* (Jeremiah 3:17)

> *"And it shall come to pass in the last days, that the mountain of the Lord's house shall be established in the top of the mountains, and shall be exalted above the hills; and all nations shall flow unto it."* (Isaiah 2:2)

> *"And it shall come to pass, that from one new moon to another, and from one sabbath to another, shall all flesh come to worship before me, saith the Lord."* (Isaiah 66:23)

> *"Likewise the people of the land shall worship at the door of this gate before the Lord in the sabbaths and in the new moons."* (Ezekiel 46:3)

Such are some of the experiences, beauties and delights of the Promised Age. Everything will blend in perfect harmony as though Eden were restored and made world-wide. In the land of Israel there will be some topographical changes brought about by a mighty earthquake at the time of Christ's intervention against the northern invader (see Ezekiel 38:20 and Zechariah 14:4 – 10). From the centre of the new temple, there will flow a perpetual and pure river, part of which will run into the Mediterranean Sea, and part to the Dead Sea whose waters will be made fresh and life-bearing. Deserts will be made to blossom. The whole picture is one of idyllic conditions in which there will be no fear of man by man. Instead, man will be able to address himself to the fruitful pursuits of a peaceful and spiritual existence under a benevolent and all-

wise government exercising guidance in the true principles
life.

Some Scriptures seem to indicate that the miraculous healing
powers shown by the Lord and his disciples in the first century will
be available in the Kingdom, perhaps through the ministration of
the saints (the faithful believers now made immortal) in all parts of
the world. Thus we read:

> *"The wilderness and the solitary place shall be glad for them; and the
> desert shall rejoice, and blossom as the rose. It shall blossom abundantly,
> and rejoice even with joy and singing: the glory of Lebanon shall be given
> unto it, the excellency of Carmel and Sharon, they shall see the glory of
> the Lord, and the excellency of our God. Strengthen ye the weak hands,
> and confirm the feeble knees. Say to them that are of a fearful heart, Be
> strong, fear not: behold, your God will come with vengeance, even God
> with a recompense; he will come and save you. Then the eyes of the blind
> shall be opened, and the ears of the deaf shall be unstopped. Then shall
> the lame man leap as an hart, and the tongue of the dumb sing: for in the
> wilderness shall waters break out, and streams in the desert. And the
> parched ground shall become a pool, and the thirsty land springs of
> water."* (Isaiah 35:1 – 7)

The blessings of the Age to Come are almost boundless. Almost?
Will there be anything to mar the unprecedented joy and peace
under Christ? How could there be? Yet, there is in fact one
remaining problem, the final hurdle to be surmounted. Indeed,
one of the reasons for the millennium is to bring a harvest, a second
harvest of men and women to immortality.

During the thousand years men and women, other than the
glorified saints, will be mortal. They will still be capable of sin and
of death, even though these may be modified by the conditions of
that age. The discipline and blessings of the Kingdom will greatly
restrain the innate sinfulness of man. Christ's rule will remove all
the calculated and open rebelliousness among the nations. Man's
instinct for social evil and for political or other power over his
fellows will not be allowed to develop.

The Millennium

But this restraint is not the same thing as a totally willing response
from the heart of the individual men and women. In other words,
true faith and true love must flow freely from the heart and not by
any kind of constraint or mere fear of punishment. Faith does not

come simply by experiencing untold blessings or by seeing the evidence of God's work among men. It lies deeper than that, although such things may be conducive to the growth of faith. Faith comes from a willing belief in God's principles and God's promises. As always, *"Faith comes by hearing, and hearing by the word of God"* (Romans 10:17). This will be equally true in the age to come. There will be a process of selection in progress throughout the millennium whereby those who truly believe in the principles of the Kingdom and hope for the promise of eternal life will live a life of faith.

Others may resent the rule of Christ and the constraints which his righteousness imposes. It may at first be hard to imagine that anyone would wish to have conditions other than they will then be. But we forget what happened in Eden, and we forget also that there were people who saw Jesus raise Lazarus from the tomb, indeed they saw Lazarus actually emerge from the tomb, and yet did not have true faith in Jesus: they went and told the Pharisees in a spirit of jealousy or resentment (John 11:45 – 46). Therefore, it should not come as a surprise that at the end of the thousand years the rulership and authority of Christ will be openly challenged. It will be the final act of rebellion, the last upthrust of human wickedness, inexcusable and reprehensible. The overthrow of the rebellion will bring down the curtain on the Age of Blessing. As at the inception of the Kingdom, there will be a resurrection and judgement. The faithful of that Age will join Christ and the saints in immortality. The unfaithful will perish for ever.

Thus will God accomplish His great purpose. Sin and death will have been abolished. Death, the final enemy, will have finished its dark work and will be removed from the face of the earth. The earth will be peopled by all-glorious and immortal saints. Then will be fulfilled in entirety the prayer of the Lord:

> *"Thy will be done in earth,*
> *as it is in heaven."* (Matthew 6:10)

Or, as it is put in one of the Psalms:

> *"O Lord our Lord,*
> *How excellent is thy name in all the earth!"* (Psalm 8:1,9)

This wonderful consummation is described as a final act of submission to God by Christ and the saints:

64

"Then cometh the end, when he shall have delivered up the kingdom to God, even the Father; when he shall have put down all rule, and all authority and power. For he must reign, till he hath put all enemies under his feet. The last enemy that shall be destroyed is death."

(1 Corinthians 15:24 – 26)

What lies beyond the thousand years? That is still a secret. Doubtless there are wonders and treasures of wisdom and knowledge which the Father has meanwhile reserved to Himself in order to make them known at the appropriate time. All that there will be is summed up in a few words:

"So that God may be all and in all."

(1 Corinthians 15:28, N.I.V.)

9

HOW CAN THIS BE?

BUT why should Paradise on earth be restored? The promises are clear enough; and no one who reads them can reasonably doubt that the purpose of God is to fill the earth with every conceivable blessing to the glory of His Name. But why? Or, more to the point, *how* can this be?

After all, if the original garden in Eden was blighted as a consequence of man's sin, why should Paradise be restored when sin still remains a cardinal factor in the affairs of the human race? Is it simply that as time has passed God has relented and is now prepared to overlook what He once condemned? Such a view would reflect seriously on the nature and righteousness of God, and would suggest capriciousness or variableness in His person so as to leave us in grave doubt as to His steadfastness and integrity. The reason for the coming glory must lie deeper, in something much more satisfying to our minds and perfectly consistent with God's declared abhorrence of sin. As with every question vital to our understanding of salvation, the Bible provides an answer so complete and wonderful as to fill us with admiration for the wisdom and mercy of the Lord God.

From the pages of the Bible, we know that the root cause of all earth's distresses is sin. When Adam opened the door of his heart to sin, he opened the world to sin's consequences. The enormity of his transgression became apparent to him when he was driven from the garden bearing in himself the infirmity of mortality with its proneness to sin. All his children have shared that inheritance, and its evil effects have spread upon the face of all the earth, like the thorns and thistles which sprang up from a hitherto entirely fruitful earth.

These facts are the starting point for our consideration: perfect blessedness on earth is the conclusion of the whole matter. Between these two significant conditions, there lies that which binds them together and provides the divine answer to man's plight and helplessness. The provision for all man's need is the Lord Jesus Christ, the Son of God. Between Eden's Paradise and the Paradise of Eden restored, there stands another Garden, known as Gethsemane in which Christ agonised in prayer on the night before his crucifixion:

> *"Then cometh Jesus with them unto a place called Gethsemane, and saith unto the disciples, Sit ye here, while I go and pray yonder . . . And he went a little farther, and fell on his face, and prayed, saying, O my Father, if it be possible, let this cup pass from me: nevertheless not as I will, but as thou wilt . . . He went away again the second time, and prayed, saying, O my Father, if this cup may not pass away from me, except I drink it, thy will be done."* (Matthew 26:36 – 42)

Herein lies the crux of man's dilemma and God's salvation for him: *"Not as I will, but as thou wilt."* This confrontation of wills had occurred in other men, but never had anyone emerged sinless from life's conflict. Gethsemane was different. Unlike all who had gone before, Christ did not *"fall short of the glory of God"* (Romans 3:23). When he was led from the Garden to his shameful trial, Christ was the altogether sinless Son of God.

Gethsemane was the culmination of a lifelong fight against sin. At every stage Jesus was victorious. Even when surrounded by those who were his enemies he had issued the challenge: *"Can any of you prove me guilty of sin?"* (John 8:46, N.I.V.). There was no response and there could be none. Christ was righteous and altogether godly. This integrity of character was known to all. Pilate's wife knew about it and at the trial of Jesus she caused a letter to be put into her husband's hands, which read: *"Have thou nothing to do with that righteous man"* (Matthew 27:19, R.V.). Equally remarkable was the declaration of the Roman centurion at the foot of the cross. He had witnessed the manner of the Lord's death and had heard the words which he spake from that cruel tree. The centurion's spontaneous tribute was: *"Certainly this was a righteous man"* (Luke 23:47).

The Sinless Son of God

Christ who had been sinless in his living remained sinless in his dying. He died in an act of total surrender to the holy will of his Father. It was a determined refusal to follow the steps of Adam the rebel; as though all that had been stolen by the first man was being returned in humility and love. Christ who had consistently destroyed the urges to sin arising from our nature which he fully shared, renounced at the end the spirit of self-preservation which is so strong in all of us, and in his total sacrifice prayed:

> *"Father, into thy hands I commit my spirit!"*
> (Luke 23:46, N.I.V.)

Thus ended the 33 years of the mortal life of Jesus of Nazareth. No life like his had ever been lived: no death like his had ever been died. In Christ the attributes of God had been revealed in the frailty of human flesh; the qualities of the Divine Name had been lived out in human nature:

> *"The Lord, The Lord God, merciful and gracious, longsuffering, and abundant in goodness and truth, keeping mercy for thousands, forgiving iniquity and transgression and sin . . ."* (Exodus 34:6 – 7)

The New Testament declares the same wonderful truth:

> *"And the Word was made flesh, and dwelt among us (and we beheld his glory, the glory as of the only begotten of the Father), full of grace and truth."* (John 1:14)

> *"Jesus saith unto him, Have I been so long time with you, and yet hast thou not known me, Philip? he that hath seen me hath seen the Father."* (John 14:9)

> *"For God, who commanded the light to shine out of darkness, hath shined in our hearts, to give the light of the knowledge of the glory of God in the face of Jesus Christ."* (2 Corinthians 4:6)

It is clear that what God had planned when He made the first man *"in the image of God"* (Genesis 1:27), He fully achieved for the first time in His only begotten Son:

> *"Christ, who is the image of God."* (2 Corinthians 4:4)

> *"His Son . . . being the brightness of his glory, and the express image of his person."* (Hebrews 1:2 – 3)

Christ's gracious words were his Father's words: his deeds of compassion came from God: his seeking of the lost sheep of the house of Israel was the seeking of the Father for man whom He had made. *"God was in Christ, reconciling the world unto himself"* (2 Corinthians 5:19). All of this was accomplished despite the fact that Christ *"was tempted in all points like as we are"* (Hebrews 2:15). But that same verse of Scripture ends in a note of triumph: *"Yet without sin"*.

Without sin. This is what God asked Adam to be, and he failed. Adam brought sin into God's first garden and marred the image of God which he should have glorified. Christ brought righteousness into man's sinful world and showed perfectly what God is like. As Adam lost Eden's paradise and caused all his progeny to be born outside where sin and death reign, so Christ prepared the sinless way for the restoration of Eden's blessings and for the redemption of a new people for God.

There are two deep mysteries at the heart of this great work of restoration. Men have puzzled over them from the earliest centuries of the Christian era. The two mysteries are inextricably related. To interpret one of them wrongly makes it impossible to understand the other. Rightly to grasp the first makes the way clear for the comprehension of the second. The mysteries are these: how is the Lord Jesus Christ our redeemer? And, was Jesus God or man, a mixture of both, or both at once?

We consider first our redemption in Christ, and then the Sonship of our Saviour. Let us think reverently, pausing in our reading to remember that what we reflect upon is not theoretical theology. It was lived out by the Lord Jesus, even to laying down his life at his Father's pleasure.

10

THE LORD WHO BOUGHT ME

THE redemption of man by Christ Jesus has been tearfully contemplated, angrily debated, reduced to mathematical equations, abandoned as incomprehensible, and, sometimes, made a matter of scorn. Some have thought that the Lord Jesus succeeded in placating a fiercely angry Deity and caused Him to turn His face toward us when hitherto He had been wrathful and unforgiving. Others have regarded redemption like a system of weights, pulleys and strings by which the redemption of man was, as it were, mechanically contrived. Yet others have taken it as a spiritual business transaction whereby the inestimable value of Christ's blood was paid to a being known as the Devil in order to secure the release of sinners from his evil grasp. Some have found it helpful to look upon Christ's death as substitutionary: that is, that Christ went to the cross instead of us, paying in this way the price for our personal sins. And some have regarded his death as a tragedy, an accident of wicked circumstances, and in no way *of itself* redemptive.

What is the truth? How can one find a way through this maze of speculation? As in everything else, there is only one sure way, and that is to let the Bible do the teaching and guiding, and to submit humbly to the discipline of this instruction.

Let us start by dismissing the notion that Jesus was pleading on bended knee to a God whose anger had caused Him to turn His face away from us. The secret of the cross is love, the love of God and the love of His Son. Whatever else we may have to consider, let us lay down this foundation: The motivating force for redemption is love:

"For God so loved the world, that he gave his only begotten Son, that whosoever believeth in him should not perish, but have everlasting life."
(John 3:16)

"But God commendeth his love toward us, in that, while we were yet sinners, Christ died for us." (Romans 5:8)

"The Son of God who loved me, and gave himself for me."
(Galatians 2:20)

Love is the reason for redemption. Love flowed first from God, and therefore from the Son whom He sent into the world. Love cannot be and must not be reduced to law or considered in terms of rights and earnings. Love is above and beyond all considerations. Love owes nothing to any goodness or merit in us. Love comes from God who is "merciful and gracious".

Forgiveness of Sins

The second secret of the cross is that it is the source of the forgiveness of sins. It is not a debt settled by due payment. It is not a substitutionary offering whereby someone is paid a price so that others might then go free. No, the cross is a means of *forgiveness*, and forgiveness is an act of grace and not of rights or earnings by the settlement of a debt. Therefore, our understanding of the redemptive work of Jesus our Lord must allow for the full expression of the love of God and His forgiveness.

The blessings of love and forgiveness flow to us through the channel of faith in the message of the Gospel of Christ and by God's acceptance of us through Jesus. Forgiveness comes to the believer when he personally seeks and asks for it in the way appointed by God. Forgiveness is certain: but it is not automatic. There is forgiveness with God, but it is not bestowed on men without their knowledge and co-operation. Such a thing would be true if redemption were the erasure of a debt, or a substitutionary transaction which had totally removed the necessity for us to seek forgiveness.

The Bible approach is much simpler and much more satisfying. Forgiveness comes to the man who believes the Gospel, repents and is baptized in the name of Christ. The following Scriptures make this perfectly clear:

"Then Peter said unto them, Repent, and be baptized every one of you in the name of Jesus Christ for the remission of sins." (Acts 2:38)

71

> *"Repent ye therefore, and be converted, that your sins may be blotted out."* (Acts 3:19)

> *"And now why tarriest thou? arise, and be baptized, and wash away thy sins, calling on the name of the Lord."* (Acts 22:16)

> *"Know ye not, that so many of us as were baptized into Jesus Christ were baptized into his death? Therefore we are buried with him by baptism into death . . . But now being made free from sin, and become servants to God, ye have your fruit unto holiness, and the end everlasting life. For the wages of sin is death; but the gift of God is eternal life through Jesus Christ our Lord."* (Romans 6:3 – 4, 22 – 23)

> *"I am crucified with Christ: nevertheless I live; yet not I, but Christ liveth in me: and the life which I now live in the flesh I live by the faith of the Son of God, who loved me, and gave himself for me."* (Galatians 2:20)

These Scriptures are clear and consistent. The wondrous benefits from the saving work of Jesus flow to us and are effective for us when we come in faith, repentant, and join Jesus in his death by baptism into his name. We shall consider baptism more fully later on; at this point we are concerned to establish the link between the sinner and the Saviour by means which have baptism as an essential element.

We can now consider the question so vital to each one of us: What is it that has made the death of Jesus the means whereby we can be forgiven and saved? We are unbelievably weak and marked by a lifetime's bondage to sin; and he is altogether holy and righteous and true and sinless. What possible bridge or link could there be between Christ and ourselves?

Herein is a marvellous thing. The Gospel makes plain that Christ is the bridge builder between God and man. He is the seeker for the lost sheep, the physician for the sick. Christ is the light for those in darkness, life for the dead:

> *"I am the door of the sheep . . . by me if any man enter in, he shall be saved . . . I am the good shepherd: the good shepherd giveth his life for the sheep."* (John 10:7,9,11)

Language could not be more comforting or reassuring. Jesus is the door to life for *"any man"* — *"whosoever"* as it says elsewhere in the Bible. When we pass through the door we enter into the fold of the sheep. No other shepherd can promise us everlasting life: no other shepherd has made good his word by sealing it with his life's blood.

In the light of these words of consolation and promise we are again constrained to ask, "But how can this thing be?" How is it that Christ is so effective? Other men have given their lives for their fellows or for some cause which they held more dear than their own lives. Wherein is Jesus different?

The Lamb of God

There is a most interesting lead in the words "sheep" and "shepherd". We can perhaps understand why Jesus should be called the Good Shepherd. Why should he then be also called the Lamb of God? In this lies the heart of our redemption. He who is the shepherd was also the lamb: he shared the life of the sheep and knows the need for a shepherd. If we move from this figurative language and seek to express the thoughts in straightforward words, we shall not find any clearer than these:

> *"Since therefore the children (those whom Jesus came to save) share in flesh and blood, he (Jesus) himself likewise partook of the same nature . . ."* (Hebrews 2:14, R.S.V.)

Although truly the Son of God, Jesus was flesh and blood. Long ago there were men who found this objectionable and invented ideas which helped them to get round the implications of the statement that Jesus was flesh and blood. These men said that these things only *seemed* to be, but were not so in fact. This will not do, not simply because such a theory has no Biblical foundation, but also because it completely undermines the whole work, indeed the very possibility, of redemption.

If, as the Bible says, Jesus shared flesh and blood, was he truly tempted as we are? Did he truly die as we do? Certainly. These are the true meeting points between Christ and those he came to save. By sharing all these things, he was indeed like unto us. If there was no sharing, then he was something "other than" we are. But the Bible tells us that it was precisely in these things that Jesus was "of us".

Take, for example, the matter of temptation. The Bible provides us with ample teaching on this subject in respect of the Lord Jesus himself:

> *"Wherefore **in all things** it behoved him to be made **like unto his**

73

> **brethren**, *that he might be a merciful and faithful high priest . . . For in that* **he himself** *hath suffered* **being tempted**, *he is able to succour them that are tempted."* (Hebrews 2:17 – 18)

> *"For we have not an high priest which cannot be touched with the feeling of our infirmities; but was* **in all points tempted like as we are**, *yet without sin."* (Hebrews 4:15)

> *Jesus "kneeled down, and prayed, saying, Father, if thou be willing, remove this cup from me: nevertheless not my will, but thine, be done . . . And being in an agony he prayed more earnestly: and his sweat was as it were great drops of blood falling down to the ground."* (Luke 22:42,44)

And most starkly of all, the Scripture says:

> *"For he (God) hath made him to be sin for us, who knew no sin."* (2 Corinthians 5:21)

Therefore, we conclude that it is not only that Jesus was called a sinner at his trial by his enemies or that he was "numbered with the transgressors" when he was crucified between two thieves, but more particularly that he shared the very nature which had made a sinner out of every other man who had borne it. It is for this reason that the nature we bear is called "sinful flesh" or more briefly, "sin" (Romans 7:20 and 8:4). The source of our temptations, in simple Bible shorthand, is itself called "sinful" or "sin", even though we are in no way blamed for possessing the nature we bear. Christ was "made sin" for us by sharing our human nature and, though sinless, by being treated as a sinner by sinful men. He "knew no sin" because he never sinned, but not because he was never tempted.

In order to bind sin and take it captive, Jesus met it on its own ground, human nature. Thus his victory was both true and unique. True in that he overcame sin though tempted precisely as we are; and unique in that he is the only one who has been totally sinless even though tempted. Christ did not demonstrate righteousness and holiness in a detached way; he brought his sinless life to God in this earthen vessel of human nature. This wonderful circumstance was a marvel of faith and righteousness, a real conquest of sin, and a perfect offering to God:

> *"God sending his own Son in the likeness of sinful flesh and as a sin offering . . . condemned sin in the flesh."* (Romans 8:3, R.S.V.)

It is by this means that our redemption does not involve a weakening of the righteousness of God, but instead both supports and demonstrates it. By means of Jesus, God declares at the same time and in the same nature the ugliness of sin and the perfection of righteousness. By being sinless in this mortal house, Jesus condemned sin in what had hitherto been its undisputed property.

Moreover, as the house was kept sinless, so the way was prepared for it to be changed from mortal to immortal, from dying to deathless. Sin and death are parts of one problem; the one is the result of the other; from Adam's sin sprang death. The Lord Jesus broke the power of sin and opened the doors to endless life. As he broke sin by his victory over the nature he bore so he broke death by entering into its cold chamber to emerge victorious.

Jesus shared totally the weakness of our mortality, its toil and tears, its suffering and its death. None of these experiences merely "seemed to be so": it truly was. He faced and endured the agony of mental and physical pain. He saw that the path chosen for him by his Father led to and through the dark portals of death, and he went in believing in his resurrection to life eternal. Here are a few brief Scriptures which tell us something of these things:

> "*Jesus . . .* **being wearied** *with his journey . . . sat thus on the well.*" (John 4:6)

> "*Jesus* **wept.**" (John 11:35)

> "*Now is* **my soul troubled***; and what shall I say? Father, save me from this hour: but for this cause came I unto this hour. Father glorify thy name.*" (John 12:27)

> "*But when they came to* **Jesus***, and saw that he* **was dead** *already, they brake not his legs: but one of the soldiers with a spear pierced his side, and forthwith came there out blood and water.*" (John 19:33 – 34)

> "*Jesus the author and finisher of our faith . . .* **endured the cross***, despising* **the shame** *. . . consider him that* **endured such contradiction of sinners against himself.**" (Hebrews 12:2 – 4)

> "*Who in the days of his flesh, when he had offered up prayers and supplications with strong crying and tears unto him that was able to* **save him from death** *. . .*" (Hebrews 5:7)

Surely, there is no room for doubt about the reality of each of these elements of the suffering and dying of the Lord? As sin and death are real for us, so they were for him as enemies to be conquered in true combat.

It is for this reason that the victory was real. He truly conquered sin and death, and brought *"life and immortality to light through the gospel"* (2 Timothy 1:10).

The death of Jesus was altogether unlike any other death, not in its reality but in the circumstances surrounding it. Man dies because of his mortal inheritance from Adam and Eve. Simply put, human nature dies of itself. However, men and women compound this natural condition by adding personal sins to their mortality, thereby making it doubly plain that the wages of sin is death. For Jesus it was different. Certainly he died because he was mortal and surrendered willingly to death's embrace. But he was in no way personally worthy of death. He was a righteous man. Perhaps it is for this reason that some have mistakenly been led to think that Christ's death was a grievous misfortune in an otherwise God-planned life. This is not so.

Calvary

The death of Jesus was an integral part, the keystone, of the bridge of redemption. It was an act whereby temptation was totally destroyed and sin finally condemned; it was the ultimate sacrifice of self, the final repudiation of the self-will of human nature. Look carefully at the following Scriptures and note how the will of God and the voluntary submission of Christ meet at Calvary. Calvary's death was the supreme act of obedience, the sacrifice of the Lamb of God, without spot and without blemish, as the perfect offering to God:

> *"From that time forth began Jesus to shew unto his disciples, how that he **must** go unto Jerusalem, and suffer many things of the elders and chief priests and scribes, and be killed, and be raised again the third day."*
> (Matthew 16:21)

> *"The reason my Father loves me is that I lay down my life — only to take it up again. No-one takes it from me, but I lay it down of my own accord. I have authority to lay it down and authority to take it up again. This command I received of my Father."* (John 10:17 – 18, N.I.V.)

> *"Jesus of Nazareth, a man approved of God among you by miracles and wonders and signs, which God did by him in the midst of you, as ye*

yourselves also know: him, being delivered by the determinate counsel and foreknowledge of God, ye have taken, and by wicked hands have crucified and slain." (Acts 2:22 – 23)

"The redemption that is in Christ Jesus: whom God hath set forth to be a propitiation through faith in his blood." (Romans 3:24 – 25)

"For I delivered unto you first of all that which I also received, how that Christ died for our sins according to the scriptures; and that he was buried, and that he rose again the third day according to the scriptures." (1 Corinthians 15:3 – 4)

"All things are of God, who hath reconciled us to himself by Jesus Christ." (2 Corinthians 5:18)

"He humbled himself, and became obedient unto death, even the death of the cross. Wherefore God also hath highly exalted him ..." (Philippians 2:8 – 9)

"Then said I (Jesus), Lo, I come (in the volume of the book it is written of me) to do thy will, O God ... by the which will we are sanctified through the offering of the body of Jesus Christ once for all." (Hebrews 10:7,10)

"The volume of the book" describes the Old Testament Word of God. That Word held many promises and prefigurings of the Christ who would come. The animal sacrifices offered under the law given through Moses spoke of Jesus in a way which became plain only when he came and lived and died. The faithful Israelite in those days before Christ was commanded by God to bring "a lamb without blemish" as an offering. No doubt he would perceive in the lamb's perfection a stark contrast with his own sinfulness, and in its death he would acknowledge the relationship between sin and death. But he little knew that the Messiah would bring himself, sinless, to supersede all sacrifice and offering by the perfect sacrifice of a perfect human life:

"This man, after he had offered one sacrifice for sins for ever, sat down on the right hand of God." (Hebrews 10:12)

The sacrifices of old time, whilst teaching necessary lessons and allowing the offerer practical expression of his repentance and his desire to have fellowship with God, were lacking in one essential respect. There was no actual link between the offerer and his sacrifice and, much more importantly, the sacrifice could not get

77

rid of sin. It was for this reason that the sacrifices were repeated over and over again, and sin was rememberd but never removed. In this way man's plight and need were emphasised and graphically presented, and the sacrifices themselves pointed forward to something better, to the day when God would provide the one and only way whereby man's sins could be forgiven:

> *"But this man (Jesus), after he had offered* **one** *sacrifice for sins* **for ever**, *sat down on the right hand of God."* (Hebrews 10:12)

> *"Christ . . . through* **his own blood**, *entered in* **once for all** *into the holy place, having obtained* **eternal** *redemption."*
> (Hebrews 9:12, R.V.)

Unlike the animal sacrifices, Jesus had a real link with those he came to save. He was one of us even though God was his Father. As the Old Testament had put it long ago, he was from among his brethren (Deuteronomy 18:15) and in that sense he was a sheep from the flock. Yet he did not act like one of us, for *"all we like sheep have gone astray"* (Isaiah 53:6), whilst of him it was said: *"Who did no sin, neither was guile found in his mouth"* (1 Peter 2:22). He was indeed the spotless lamb, the sinless one among sinners. In him and in him alone there actually existed a bridge between God and man. In sinlessness and redemptive purpose, he and his Father were one.

The death of Jesus was a declaration of the righteousness of God. Jesus repudiated the sinful pull of the flesh, even to the extent of taking it to the tree by crucifixion, and exalted the will of his Father above all else. By this means the living way to God was opened for ever by His Son's blood. The life of man had been offered to God in perfection by Jesus Christ the Righteous.

> *"As sin hath reigned unto death, even so might grace reign through righteousness unto eternal life by Jesus Christ our Lord."*
> (Romans 5:21)

Close by the place where Jesus had died there was a garden in which there was a rock-hewn tomb which had never been used. As darkness approached and the sabbath drew on, two men, Joseph and Nicodemus who were not hitherto openly professed disciples of Jesus, now declared themselves unequivocally to be his friends and followers. Hastily they gave the Lord they loved a decent burial. They little knew, as they rolled a great stone across the mouth of the tomb, that they had played a small part in setting the scene for the greatest dénouement in all history.

The Empty Tomb

Within the new tomb lay the body of a man who had been totally sinless. Death seemed to have triumphed over him as surely as over anyone else. But this man whose blood had sealed the everlasting covenant lay at the heart of a mighty question: If death is for sinners, how can a righteous man be held by it? God who keeps covenant and mercy, and in whose ways there is no unrighteousness, "*brought again from the dead that great shepherd of the sheep by the blood of the everlasting covenant*" (Hebrews 13:20). Or, as it is put elsewhere in Scripture:

"*But God raised him from the dead, freeing him from the agony of death, because it was impossible for death to keep its hold on him.*"
(Acts 2:24, N.I.V.)

"*(Christ) was not left in hell (abandoned to the grave, N.I.V.), neither did his flesh see corruption. This Jesus hath God raised up.*"
(Acts 2:31 – 32)

"*Jesus our Lord . . . was delivered for our offences and raised again for our justification.*"
(Romans 4:24 – 25)

The crucifixion *and* the resurrection are involved in the process of redemption for sinful man. Unlike us, Jesus was in no way in need of redemption from sin; but, like us, he required salvation from death, and this was granted according as it is written:

"*Who in the days of his flesh, having offered up prayers and supplications with strong crying and tears unto him that was able to save him from death, and having been heard for his godly fear, though he was a Son, yet learned he obedience by the things which he suffered; and having been made perfect, he became unto all them that obey him the author of eternal salvation.*"
(Hebrews 5:7 – 9, R.V.)

The Lord Jesus Christ became the new starting point, the new head of the human race. The first man brought sin and death into the world; the new man brought righteousness and everlasting life. We belong to Adam by natural birth: we belong to Christ when we are re-born in true faith.

The death and resurrection of the Lord Jesus Christ are like precious jewels which shine with many splendours as they turn in

79

the light. The loving work of God in Christ lies at the heart of the Gospel; it is the means whereby everything else is secured.

Christ is the key to the fulfilment of the cherished promises made to Abraham, Isaac and Jacob, and again to David the king. The full blessings of the promises could not be released without the redemptive work of Jesus. How else could Abraham have everlasting life? How could there be an everlastingly righteous king on David's throne except the King himself be immortal? No one but Christ is sufficient for these things. He alone is the Royal Son of David, the Righteous Branch and King, and the Bearer of immortality. Christ is the seal to the everlasting covenant of promise.

Christ is everything for all God's children, whenever they have lived and whatever the stage reached in the revelation of God when their faith was kindled. As the Bible beautifully puts it:

"For no matter how many promises God has made, they are 'Yes' in Christ. And so through him the 'Amen' is spoken by us to the glory of God." (2 Corinthians 1:20, N.I.V.)

11

THE CHRIST: WHOSE SON IS HE?

T HE Bible reveals much more about the Lord Jesus than we
have considered thus far. It is well that we seek to know him
more, for *"in him are hid all the treasures of wisdom and
knowledge"* (Colossians 2:3).

Of all the aspects of Christ which devout men have looked upon
throughout the centuries, the Sonship of the Saviour has most
deeply engaged them. Strange as it may seem to others, there are
some who have been satisfied only when they have regarded Jesus
as the true son of Joseph, the husband of Mary. Such people do not
accept the record of the Virgin Birth, and generally believe that the
godly Sonship of Jesus stems only from his character and not also
from his exceptional paternity.

At the other end of the spectrum of beliefs is the idea that Jesus
was, and always had been, God the Son who took flesh in the
Virgin's womb. This teaching emerged only after some centuries
of theological discussion, and is now embodied in the accepted
creeds of the orthodox churches. To those who believe it, the
doctrine is exceptionally precious.

What then is the seeker for truth to do in these circumstances?
How should he endeavour to arrive at the right belief? Above all
else, he must approach this subject with the deepest humility and
reverence. We are on holy ground. We are not engaged in mere
speculation or in an academic exercise the results of which might
provide further stimulation to our intellect, or logical satisfaction
in having solved a spiritual equation. Let us remember that we
who are fleeting creatures of dust are seeking to understand the

81

Almighty God and the One who is described as His beloved Son. Let us approach our considerations with quiet respect (at least) and loving awe.

At the outset we can rest on one sure foundation. All that we know about the Lord Jesus Christ comes from the Bible. There is no other source on which to draw. All that men have written and churches believe would never have existed without this prime source of revelation and knowledge, the Word of God in our hands. Therefore any belief which goes beyond what is revealed or contradicts it must raise serious questions in our minds. It is evident that to contradict the Word of God is to introduce some other authority, some other arbiter in the matter of faith and practice. We are therefore entitled to ask for the source of such authority. Moreover, we place in jeopardy *all* of our beliefs and hopes, once we question the very foundation book of the Gospel of salvation.

The Virgin Birth

The belief that Jesus was the son of Joseph, though a very old belief in one form or other, cannot stand without denying the very clear narratives of the conception and birth of Christ as given in Matthew's and Luke's Gospel records. There are no grounds for such denial. It cannot be established that the text of those two Gospel accounts has been corrupted by the later addition to them of the sections on the Virgin Birth. The text is well-founded and is in any case supported by numerous allusions in other parts of Scripture. Therefore, any adherence to the Josephite teaching must stem from other considerations — an attitude to miracles for example — which can be summed up as a direct questioning of the authority of Scripture.

Firmly believing the Bible to be the wholly inspired and infallible record of God's revelation to man, Christadelphians cannot accept any view which casts doubt upon its clear teaching.

The Bible instruction about the Fatherhood of God in respect of Jesus stands clear in the whole of the Bible:

> "*I will be his father, and he shall be my son.*"
> (2 Samuel 7:14; 1 Chronicles 17:13)

> "*He shall cry unto me, Thou art my father, my God, and the rock of my salvation.*" (Psalm 89:26)

> "*The angel of the Lord appeared unto him in a dream, saying, Joseph,*

82

thou son of David, fear not to take unto thee Mary thy wife: for that which is conceived in her is of the Holy Spirit." (Matthew 1:20)

"And the angel said unto her, Fear not, Mary: for thou hast found favour with God. And, behold, thou shalt conceive in thy womb, and bring forth a son, and shalt call his name JESUS. He shall be great, and shall be called the son of the Highest . . . the Holy Spirit shall come upon thee, and the power of the Highest shall overshadow thee: therefore also that holy thing which shall be born of thee shall be called the Son of God." (Luke 1:30 – 35)

"And the Word was made flesh, and dwelt among us (and we beheld his glory, the glory as of the only begotten of the Father), full of grace and truth." (John 1:14)

"For God so loved the world, that he gave his only begotten Son, that whosoever believeth in him should not perish, but have everlasting life." (John 3:16)

"For unto which of the angels said he at any time, Thou art my Son, this day have I begotten thee? And again, I will be to him a Father, and he shall be to me a Son?" (Hebrews 1:5)

"Blessed be the God and Father of our Lord Jesus Christ." (1 Peter 1:3)

"When the fulness of the time was come, God sent forth his Son, made of a woman." (Galatians 4:4)

" Therefore the Lord himself shall give you a sign; Behold, a virgin shall conceive, and bear a son, and shall call his name Immanuel." (Isaiah 7:14; Matthew 1:23)

There can be no doubt from these Scriptures that God was the Father of the Lord Jesus Christ in a unique manner, a way quite different from the Fatherhood of God extended to believers. The expressions, "his only begotten Son", "the Son of the Highest", "the only begotten of the Father" and "the Son of God", are clear indications of the quite exceptional circumstances attending the conception and birth of the Lord Jesus.

To be Bible believers, we must therefore believe that Jesus was truly the Son of God, with no human father whatsoever.

It is when we consider the relationship between the begettal of Jesus and the birth of Jesus that we are brought to consider the declaration of these matters in church creeds. Here we find it declared that Jesus was begotten from eternity and was eternally the Son of God. He was so from all time and was truly, according to this teaching, "God the Son". Let us look at some of the words in which men have set forth this doctrine:

The Council of Nicaea in A.D. 325 declared:

> "I believe in one God the Father Almighty,
> Maker of heaven and earth,
> and of all things visible and invisible:
> And in one Lord Jesus Christ, the only begotten Son of God,
> Begotten of his Father before all worlds.
> God of God, Light of Light, Very God of Very God:
> Begotten not made.
> Being of one substance with the Father, by whom all things were made.
> Who for us men, and for our salvation came down from heaven
> And was incarnate by the Holy Ghost of the Virgin Mary,
> And was made man.

The Athanasian creed said:

> "We worship one God in Trinity, and Trinity in Unity: neither confounding the persons: nor dividing the substance. For there is one person of the Father, another of the Son, and another of the Holy Ghost. But the Godhead of the Father and of the Son and of the Holy Ghost is all one . . . the Son is God . . . the Son is of the Father alone: not made, nor created, but begotten."

The First of the 39 Articles of the Church of England says:

> "The Son which is the Word of the Father, begotten from everlasting of the Father. The Very and Eternal God, and of one substance with the Father, took man's nature in the womb of the blessed virgin of her substance so that two whole and perfect natures, that is to say the Godhead and Manhood were joined together in one person, never to be divided, whereof is one Christ, Very God and Very Man."

For many devout persons, these statements hold the sacred kernel of truth concerning the Son of God and provide a real comfort in an unstable and restless world. All of us have profound respect for the deepest feelings of other worshippers, as we would expect them to have for us. We would, therefore, courteously invite others to look into the feelings and beliefs of Christadelphians in this central area of faith, and examine how we have arrived at the position and belief which for us is fundamental truth and therefore precious.

The language of the creeds which we have quoted is exquisitely composed and memorable. It is a mixture of phrases from Scripture and phrases not to be found there. For example, the terms "eternally begotten", "two whole and perfect natures", and "Trinity in Unity" are not to be found in the Bible. They are human descriptions of what the writers believe to be truth. For this reason, we must compare them with Bible teaching. What do we then find?

The Son of God

In the first place, there is no hint in the Old Testament that the Son of God was already existent or in any way active at that time. There is no word from him and no word about him to suggest that an already existent Son of God would later appear on earth. Indeed, if the Old Testament had contained clear teaching of that kind, the Jews would not have had such difficulty in accepting him when he appeared. They were certainly waiting for the Messiah, but not for one already existent in heaven.

Bible teaching on the other hand is very clear in telling us that the Lord God Almighty had *promised* to provide the Christ:

> "*Christ . . . verily was* **fore-ordained** *before the foundation of the world, but was manifest in these last times for you . . .*"
>
> (1 Peter 1:20)

> "*We tell you the good news: What God promised our fathers he has fulfilled for us, their children, by raising up Jesus. As it is written in the second Psalm: You are my Son; today I have become your Father.*"
>
> (Acts 13:32 – 33, N.I.V.)

The Old Testament abounds with the promises made concerning the Christ who was to come. When these promises were fulfilled Christ was first begotten and then born. It is sometimes overlooked that the coming of Jesus is described as a birth. Birth would be a strange word to use if the Son of God had already existed. It is not simply that the words "Christ" and "Jesus" are used in connection with the word "birth". If this were so, it might be pressed that the Son of God had always existed, but was now appearing for the first time as Christ or Jesus. But this is not so.

The Bible is explicit in saying that it is the Son of God who is born of Mary:

> "*The Holy Spirit will come upon you, and the power of the Most High will overshadow you. So the holy one to be born will be called* **the Son of God.**" (Luke 1:35, N.I.V.)

> "*God sent forth* **his Son**, *made of a woman.*" (Galatians 4:4)

Whilst we may wonder at the nature of this birth and seek in our minds to explain how this could be, the facts are very clear: Jesus Christ, the Son of God, was first promised, and came into being only when he was born of the virgin Mary.

This leads us to our next consideration. It is an essential part of the doctrine set out in the creeds that it was an act of God the Son in heaven to become incarnate in Mary. We are well aware that the words expressing this belief are sung every year:

> "True God of True God,
> Light of light eternal,
> Lo! He abhors not the virgin's womb."

These words teach that it was God the Son who humbled himself to be "born" of Mary. There is one passage of Scripture particularly which is often relied on to establish this teaching:

> "*Let this mind be in you, which was also in Christ Jesus: who, being in the form of God, thought it not robbery to be equal with God: but made himself of no reputation, and took upon him the form of a servant, and was made in the likeness of men: and being found in fashion as a man, he humbled himself, and became obedient unto death, even the death of the cross. Wherefore God also hath highly exalted him, and given him a name which is above every name: that at the name of Jesus every knee should bow, of things in heaven, and things in earth, and things under the earth; and that every tongue should confess that Jesus Christ is Lord, to the glory of God the Father.*" (Philippians 2:5 – 11)

The nub of this magnificent passage lies in the words:

> "*Being in the form of God . . . made himself of no reputation.*"

To the man of the creeds this teaches that God the Son in heaven humbled Himself to be born of the virgin Mary. However, the words do not say anything about birth or about the virgin Mary; nevertheless it is felt by Trinitarians that they support the credal point of view.

We ask the question: When was Jesus "in the form of God"? Christadelphians believe that Jesus was in the form of God by his birth through begettal by the Father, by speaking the words of God and doing His works. They believe that "being in the form of God" is the way in which this passage of Scripture describes the Sonship of Jesus whilst he was here on earth. Otherwise there is no mention whatsoever of the Sonship of Jesus in these verses. It was his begettal and birth that made Jesus the Son of God, and made him "Immanuel . . . God with us", as in these actual words of Scripture:

> *"Behold, a virgin shall be with child, and shall bring forth **a son**, and they shall call his name Emmanuel, which being interpreted is, God with us."* (Matthew 1:23)

> *"The Holy Spirit shall come upon thee, and the power of the Highest shall overshadow thee: **therefore** also that holy thing which shall be born of thee **shall be called the Son of God.**"* (Luke 1:35)

When we accept that the Lord Jesus Christ was entitled to reverence and honour as Son of God by virtue of his birth we can understand what is meant by the succeeding words in Philippians, "made himself of no reputation". Those words are a clear description of the way in which the Lord Jesus Christ *made himself* servant of all. As other versions express it, "he emptied himself". This he did during his ministry, despite the privilege and status which were his as Son of God, when he girded himself with the towel of service as the humble menial, the living grace of God as the lowest servant.

We believe that the rightness of this interpretation of the words, "being in the form of God . . . made himself of no reputation", is confirmed by the words which lie between those two expressions. Here is the section in full:

> *"Who, being in the form of God, **thought it not robbery to be equal with God:** but **made himself of no reputation**, and took upon him the form of a servant."*

He who was "in the form of God" as God's Son took upon him the "form of a servant" by thinking it "not robbery to be equal with God." What could those words possibly mean? How could the word "robbery" be used about Jesus in heaven? He was already, according to the creed, co-equal with God; what else was there to be taken? This is how the phrase is translated in other versions:

87

"counted it not a prize to be on equality with God"   (R.V.)

"did not count equality with God a thing to be grasped"   (R.S.V.)

"did not consider equality with God something to be grasped"

                                                     (N.I.V.)

There is no doubt that these words are telling us that there was something which could be grasped, or snatched at, in an attempt to become truly equal with God, and that Jesus refused to do so. But, in heaven, those words could never have applied to Jesus. According to the creeds, he was already co-equal, co-glorious, co-eternal. There was nothing else to be sought. If, however, we believe that the words apply to Jesus whilst here on earth, the position is perfectly clear. The Lord Jesus Christ though born Son of God, had the choice of rebelling against God (the very basis of his temptation in the wilderness), or of humbly submitting in obedience and in service. The former would have been the way of Adam and Eve (the serpent having said: "Ye shall be as gods") when they stole from God's tree: the latter was the way of Christ when he finally yielded all on that other Tree.

God the Father

It is for this reason that he has been highly exalted by God. His ascension is not a simple resumption in heaven of what had been temporarily laid aside (according to the teaching of the creeds), but the gift of God. Most astounding of all is the teaching in this passage that Christ's present exaltation to heaven is for "the glory of God the Father" and not simply for the glory of the Son.

This understanding of a profound but highly informative passage of the Bible leads us to another very serious consideration, which lies at the heart of the relationship between God and His Son. It is this. Jesus *worships* God: God worships no one. Someone may be tempted to reply by saying that it is altogether reasonable to expect that Jesus, whilst here on earth, would render worship to God in heaven. Even if such an explanation sounds acceptable, it is wide of the mark. It was not only during his lifetime on earth that the Lord Jesus Christ worshipped God. God is *still* the God of Jesus and always will be. Here is the Bible evidence for this which includes words of Jesus before his death, after his resurrection *and* since his ascension to heaven:

> *"I thank thee, O Father,* **Lord of heaven and earth,** *because thou*

hast hid these things from the wise and prudent, and hast revealed them unto babes. Even so, Father: for so it seemed good in thy sight."
(Matthew 11:25 – 26)

"O my Father, if it be possible, let this cup pass from me: nevertheless **not as I will, but as thou wilt.** *"* (Matthew 26:39)

"My Father is greater than I." (John 14:28)

"But go to my brethren, and say unto them, I ascend unto my Father, and your Father; and to **my God, and your God.** *"* (John 20:17)

"Him that overcometh will I make a pillar in the temple of **my God**, *and he shall go no more out: and I will write upon him the name of* **my God**, *and the name of the city of* **my God**. *"* (Revelation 3:12)

"To him that overcometh will I grant to sit with me in my throne, even as I also overcame, and am set down with my Father **in his throne.** *"*
(Revelation 3:21)

"Unto you first **God**, *having* **raised up his Son** *Jesus,* **sent** *him to bless you."* (Acts 3:26)

*"***God** *hath made that same Jesus, whom ye have crucified, both Lord and Christ."* (Acts 2:36)

"But I would have you know, that the head of every man is Christ; and the head of the woman is the man; and **the head of Christ is God.** *"*
(1 Corinthians 11:3)

"Ye are Christ's; and Christ is God's." (1 Corinthians 3:23)

"Blessed be **the God and Father** *of our Lord Jesus Christ."*
(Ephesians 1:3; 1 Peter 1:3)

"The **God of our Lord Jesus Christ**, *the Father of glory."*
(Ephesians 1:17)

"Unto him that loveth us, and loosed us from our sins by his blood; and he made us to be a kingdom, to be priests unto **his God and Father.** *"*
(Revelation 1:5 – 6, R.V.)

These and many other testimonies in the Word of God provide us with a clear understanding of the relationship which existed and exists between the Lord God and His exalted Son. There is consistent Bible teaching, as demonstrated earlier in this book, that the Almighty God alone is from everlasting to everlasting; He is the Maker of heaven and earth, and is responsible for bringing

89

Christ into existence by his begettal through the Holy Spirit. Jesus was raised from the dead by God the Father, was glorified by the Father and shares the Father's royal throne.

At the end of his 1000 years' reign on earth, the Lord Jesus will render to his Father the perfected kingdom as an act of tribute and honour:

> "*When all things shall be subdued unto him (God), then shall the Son also himself be subject unto him . . .*"   (1 Corinthians 15:28)

But, it may be asked, if the Lord Jesus Christ is not *God the Son* from all eternity, is he not then "mere man" and thereby deprived of his rightful honour and glory? It is this question which we now proceed to examine. We shall find that the answer to it glorifies and honours the Lord Jesus Christ in a manner and to an extent made impossible by the doctrine in the creeds.

12

THE WORD WAS MADE FLESH

"*I*N *the beginning was the Word, and the Word was with God, and the Word was God. The same was in the beginning with God ... And the Word was made flesh, and dwelt among us (and we beheld his glory, the glory as of the only begotten of the Father), full of grace and truth.*"
(John 1:1 – 2,14)

These words from the Gospel of John are companions to the birth narratives in Matthew and Luke. John does not tell us of the virgin birth in terms such as Matthew and Luke were inspired to use; instead, he provides, under similar inspiration, a new insight into the same wondrous truth concerning the coming of the Son of God.

Matthew and Luke tell us that Jesus was the Son of God because he was conceived by the Holy Spirit, the power of the Highest. John tells us that Jesus was the Son of God because the Word was made, or became, flesh. In each case there is the clear teaching that God Himself is involved. Jesus is neither conceived nor born as "mere man". Here are three descriptions of him:

"*Immanuel — God with us*"	(Matthew 1:23)
"*The holy one*"	(Luke 1:35, N.I.V.)
"*The Word was made flesh*"	(John 1:14)

No other child has ever been truly "Immanuel"; no other, "the Word made flesh"; and none, "the holy one". Jesus is not mere man and Christadelphians have never believed that. *We believe that he is truly and uniquely the Son of God.*

91

Is it possible to go further in our understanding? And would it be profitable to do so? There is no value in seeking what God has not revealed, or in spinning words to make it look as though we were wise beyond what He has told us.

The way in which John tells us the great truth is itself a door to a larger understanding. "The Word was made flesh". In human terms a word is an expression of an idea or thought or a collection of thoughts. It is the formulation of what the mind has conceived. When made known to others our words convey our thoughts and, on occasion, our intentions. Man has limitations. His thoughts are not always coherent or consistent one with another and, however much he might wish it, he cannot always carry his intentions into fulfilment.

The Word of God

God's Word is different. God's Word is the mind of God, entirely self-consistent in content and quality. The Word of God has the quality of God Himself. It is God and does not exist without Him. When God expresses His mind, His will, there is no one who can say Him nay. Take, for example, these words of Scripture:

> "*Through faith we understand that the worlds were framed by the word of God, so that things which are seen were not made of things which do appear.*" (Hebrews 11:3)

> "*By the word of the Lord were the heavens made;*
> *and all the host of them by the breath of his mouth.*" (Psalm 33:6)

The universe around us came into being by the Word of God and it is an expression of His mind. This is why man, in his frequently godless probings to further his understanding of the things around him, discovers an underlying consistency and coherence which he sets down as the "laws" of science and nature and so on. The so-called laws are the consistent behaviour of God within His creation. We seek to read it like a book because, unknown to us, it is part of the book of the Word of God. Little wonder that man discovers that the more he knows the more there is to know. He is simply on the fringe of the fathomless mind of God.

Man struggles to find explanations for the origin of things, and will always fail in the end because he is working at the wrong level. It is little use looking at "things" in the hope of explaining their origin. "Things" did not come out of "things" (as man insists on declaring). The beginning was in God. With Him was the Word and when expressed it became what He had in mind:

> *"And God **said**, Let there be light: and there was light."*
>
> (Genesis 1:3)

All the light we see about us is expending itself. There is only one *Eternal Light* (in every sense of that word) and that is God. The Word which God spoke in the beginning, empowered by His Spirit, bore in itself the capacity to produce light and to sustain all the "laws" which govern light. And so with all creation. Creation is the Word of God made tangible or visible.

Before ever creation commenced, it existed in plan and potential in the mind of God. God had seen it all before ever it was made. He knew, He willed and it was. In all of this there is an interesting principle which extends beyond creation itself. The word which God spoke to men by His angels, or in revealed dreams or through His holy prophets, had the same consistency and potential as that which formed creation. It expressed God's purpose and intent, and sent forth by His Spirit, would accomplish what God had determined.

Within this revealed Word of God, indeed the very heartspring of it and the foundation of everything, was the purpose of God in Christ. Christ was the pre-eminent purpose in the mind of God, he was the promise within God's purpose, that which gave pattern to everything. That pattern was the first thing in the mind of God and preceded all others. When, for example, God said, *"Let there be light"*, the first step was taken towards that which God had first in mind, the coming of Christ the Light of the World. It was all one purpose. Christ was not the last resort, the final desperate attempt by God to cause His will to prevail; Christ was the Only Way in the mind of God from the beginning.

The Lord Jesus made plain this same teaching time and time again. On one occasion he was accused by his enemies of dishonouring Moses. But Jesus said, *"Moses wrote of me"* (John 5:46). Christ came to honour Moses, to complete what Moses had foretold, and to reveal and make full the real meaning of what Moses had said and ordained at God's hand:

> *"Think not that I am come to destroy the law, or the prophets: I am not come to destroy, but to fulfil."* (Matthew 5:17)

The law through Moses was a foreshadowing of Christ. Christ

93

himself was the substance which God had in mind before ever Moses climbed mount Sinai to receive the Law.

The Jews became aggrieved with Christ because they sensed, and rightly, that Christ, if his claims were true, was greater even than Abraham. But how could this young man born some 2000 years after Abraham be superior to the father of the Jewish race? Jesus puzzled them even more when he said:

> *"Before Abraham was, I am."* (John 8:58)

Jesus was not saying that he personally existed before the days of Abraham. We have shown from Scripture that this was not the case. What then, did the Lord mean? He was declaring a profound, yet simple, truth: he preceded everything in the purpose of God. Two thousand years before Abraham was born, Christ had already been promised as "the seed of the woman" (Genesis 3:15). This promise lived through the Old Testament, appearing in different forms and having different emphases according to the time and circumstances of the revelation. In the same chapter in which Christ said, "Before Abraham was, I am", we also read:

> *"Your father Abraham rejoiced to see my day: and he saw it, and was glad."* (John 8:56)

In other words, as Christ in the purpose of God had preceded all else, so Abraham was able by faith to see the day of his actual coming as the Seed. The Word reaches backwards and forwards. It is the same Word and the thread is unbreakable. The thread is God Himself in the Word of His purpose.

Christ in all the Scriptures

The truth of the promise of all the Scriptures became shiningly clear to the apostles when Christ explained the Scriptures to them after his resurrection from the dead:

> *"And beginning at Moses and all the prophets, he expounded unto them in all the scriptures the things concerning himself . . . And he said unto them, These are the words which I spake unto you, while I was yet with you, that all things must be fulfilled, which were written in the law of Moses, and in the prophets, and in the psalms, concerning me. Then opened he their understanding, that they might understand the scriptures, and he said unto them, Thus it is written, and thus it behoved Christ to suffer, and to rise from the dead the third day; and that repentance and*

remission of sins should be preached in his name among all nations.''
(Luke 24:27, 44 – 47)

Christ was the essence of the Old Testament. He it was who gave it its forward look and by its fulfilment was the seal to its truth. When Peter by the Holy Spirit wrote about the Old Testament writers he said that the prophets wondered what it was that:

"The Spirit of Christ which was in them did signify, when it testified beforehand the sufferings of Christ, and the glory that should follow.''
(1 Peter 1:11)

Peter knew as well as anyone else that the prophets spoke and wrote by the Spirit of God, and he wrote to that effect in his second letter when he declared:

"Holy men of God spake as they were moved by the Holy Spirit.''
(2 Peter 1:21)

When he writes that the *Spirit of Christ* was in them, he means that the Spirit of God by which they wrote was revealing through them the message concerning Christ. Christ was the message of the Spirit which filled the prophets. So it was that the prophets made known the glorious hope concerning Christ, and the Spirit in them bore the imprint of the coming Christ.

The Word of God is not a static thing, a word on a page or a dying word in the mouth of a prophet. Once the Word has been pronounced it is, as it were, a messenger of God gone out to fulfil His purpose. The Word will not return to source without having completed its mission. This is how God explains this truth through Isaiah the prophet:

"My counsel shall stand, and I will do all my pleasure.''
(Isaiah 46:10)

"For as the rain cometh down, and the snow from heaven, and returneth not thither, but watereth the earth, and maketh it bring forth and bud, that it may give seed to the sower, and bread to the eater: so shall my word be that goeth forth out of my mouth: it shall not return unto me void, but it shall accomplish that which I please, and it shall prosper in the thing whereto I sent it.''
(Isaiah 55:10 – 11)

The prophecies and promises which God had made known at different times were at work in one way and another during the

95

seemingly silent days of waiting for their fulfilment. For this reason, when Messiah finally appeared, everything was ready for him. The Jews had returned from captivity in Babylon in readiness for Christ's birth in Palestine. The time period of Daniel concerning the coming of Christ had run its course (Daniel 9:25). The Jewish maid of the House of David was grown to maturity in Nazareth, ready in mind and body for the great work which God had ordained for her. The Jews and Gentiles were in authority in the capital city, Jerusalem, for both had a work to do. Bethlehem was awaiting its promised child. Nothing had been left to chance. The Word of God under His blessing had done its work by the hands of angels and of men.

The angel Gabriel (who had given to Daniel the prophecy about Messiah) was sent to speak to Mary when everything was prepared. Elizabeth was already six months pregnant with John the Baptist, the appointed forerunner of Christ. Mary heard the message from Gabriel with humble wonder, and finally with joy and submissiveness. She knew the voices of the prophets, and she believed them. Her song, commonly known as the *Magnificat*, is composed almost entirely of lines from Old Testament Scripture woven into a beautiful tapestry of faith. Her faith.

She was to bear Messiah, the son of David. She was as yet unmarried, and in gentle but precise terms Gabriel made known to her the manner by which she would come to be with child. It was as though the Lord God waited for her consent before over-shadowing her by His Spirit. Her willingness is expressed in words which matched perfectly that which was to take place:

> "*Behold the handmaid of the Lord; be it unto me* **according to thy word.**" (Luke 1:38)

Thus it was that the Word became flesh. All of God's mighty purpose came to rest with active gentleness on the woman chosen as the meeting place, the place where all the many parts and diverse promises came together; the place where all the varied colours of the Old Testament were to blend together in the perfect whiteness of the Light of the World:

> "*In the past God spoke to our forefathers through the prophets at many times and in various ways, but in these last days he has* **spoken to us by his Son.**" (Hebrews 1:1 – 2, N.I.V.)

Could it have been expressed more simply? "The Word became

96

flesh" is presented to us as "God ... hath spoken to us by his Son". In *everything* about Jesus, the Word of God was speaking.

Born in Bethlehem

Mary carried Christ for the normal period of pregnancy. She waited in Nazareth. But Christ was to be born in Bethlehem. At the appointed time, seemingly of his own initiative, Caesar Augustus issued the decree that all the people of his empire should return to their ancestral home in order to be enrolled. So at census time Mary and Joseph travelled southwards from Galilee and came to Bethlehem, the city of David their forefather. All this was of God. Nothing was by chance. His declared Word of prophecy was at work and nothing could hold back its fulfilment in due time.

Even the fact that the many guests which crowded the inns of Bethlehem made it impossible for Joseph to find an adequate lodging for his wife and child to be was all of God. This was how it was and how it would be until the world would crowd out the Son of God and lead him to a shameful, lonely death — but still according to God's word.

Mary's eyes were as yet shielded from the sorrow to come, but she knew the present joy:

> *"But thou, Bethlehem Ephratah, though thou be little among the thousands of Judah, yet out of thee shall he come forth unto me that is to be ruler in Israel."* (Micah 5:2)

The child thus born according to the Word of God, the very embodiment of it in all its purposefulness, was one whole being. He was not part Word and part flesh. He was the Word made flesh. *His was one nature, not two.* There was not a God *and* a man separate and distinct within the one being. The Son of God was the Son of man, and the Son of man was the Son of God.

It may be asked, How then was Christ different from any other child? The answer is positive and simple: God was his Father. The marks of the Fatherhood of God were to be seen in Jesus. Jesus knew that God was his Father and by this means he had an affinity with God which no other person had ever known, even though he bore this affinity in the frailty of human flesh. His mind was wonderfully alert and active. At the age of twelve, when Mary and Joseph brought him to Jerusalem, the doctors of the law were astonished as Jesus sat in their midst, asking and answering questions with an extraordinary degree of understanding.

It will be recalled that Joseph and Mary commenced the homeward journey to Nazareth from Jerusalem believing that Jesus was somewhere in the company of pilgrims. They were mistaken. Jesus had remained behind in the city and it was three days before they found him there. They were distraught with anxiety and reproved Jesus when they found him. His reply was totally unexpected:

> "*How is it that ye sought me? wist ye not that I must be in my Father's house?*"
> (Luke 2:49, R.V.)

How could I be lost at home! His Father's house, as he termed the temple in whose precincts he had been found, was well known to all the worshippers who came to Jerusalem; but none of them would refer to it in that way. Jesus was wholly aware of his Father, even at the age of twelve.

From Boyhood to Manhood

It is possible for us to suppose that within the Lord Jesus from the day of his birth there lay a complete and perfect character. We should be wrong. Listen to the word of God:

> "*And Jesus **increased** in wisdom and stature, and in favour with God and man.*"
> (Luke 2:52)

Jesus grew, not only physically, but in wisdom and in favour with God. The character of Christ was developing. At each stage it was without sin, but nevertheless it experienced growth. One aspect of this growth is mentioned specifically elsewhere in Scripture:

> "*Though he were a Son, yet **learned** he obedience by the things which he suffered.*"
> (Hebrews 5:8)

> "*Being found in fashion as a man, he humbled himself, and **became** obedient unto death, even the death of the cross.*"   (Philippians 2:8)

The obedience of the Lord Jesus Christ grew and was tested under the stress of chastisement and the allurement of temptation. Each of these different tensions developed the mind of the Son of God and prepared him for the final trial of Gethsemane and Calvary. His Father, as a true father, cared for His Son on each step of that journey. Christ leaned on his Father and the Father blessed him day by day. The long nights on the mountain in prayer and meditation were times spent with God. His total acquaintance with the written Word of God afforded him insight and instruction beyond anything which Joseph and Mary could provide.

Man had never regarded his own relationship with God as the prime factor of his existence. He had always spent more time over his earthly relationships and his mortal ancestry than ever he had devoted to God. In Christ the true focus was to be found. In him man's true purpose and God's supremacy were perfected.

Christ had to resolve whether he would lean on his mortal ancestry leading back through the illustrious names of David and Abraham, but inevitably also back to sinful Adam; or seek to trust his heavenly Father and be His Son in truth. The problem had been hinted at in a famous Old Testament verse:

> *"I will be his father, **and** he shall be my son."*
>
> (1 Chronicles 17:13)

The first part of that verse — "I will be his Father" —·was entirely of God's initiative in which the Lord Jesus had no part. The second part — "and he shall be my son" — was Christ's response in loving, unfaltering and willing obedience to the will of God. His trust in God had long been foretold:

> *"He shall cry unto me, Thou art my father,*
> *My God, and the rock of my salvation."*   (Psalm 89:26)

Thus the likeness of the Father was made evident in the Son until, shortly before his death, the Lord could say to his disciples:

> *"He that hath seen me hath seen the Father."*   (John 14:9)

It was in this and in his common purpose with the Father that the saying was true:

> *"I and my Father are one."*   (John 10:30)

When the apostles were inspired to write their letters to believers, which are preserved for us in the New Testament, they set down how God saw His beloved Son:

> *"Who is the image of the invisible God."*   (Colossians 1:15)

> *"His Son . . . the brightness of his glory, and the express image of his person . . ."*   (Hebrews 1:2,3)

These verses hold distinct allusions to the very first verses of the Bible in which God had said, *"Let us make man in our image"* (Genesis 1:26). It was in Christ that the image was perfected.

God's greatest work had been performed and it was the beginning of a wonderful process. All who become Christ's will share the fruits of this work of redemption:

"And we know that to them that love God all things work together for good . . . to be conformed to the image of his Son . . ."
(Romans 8:28 – 29, R.V.)

"He (Christ) is the head of the body, the church: who is the beginning, the firstborn from the dead; that in all things he might have the pre-eminence. For it pleased the Father that in him should all fulness dwell."
(Colossians 1:18 – 19)

An image is not the original thing, however much like the original it might be. So Christ is the *image* of God. God is the first and the only underived One. Christ is of Him, born by His Spirit, and with His perfect *likeness*. Teaching could not be more clear and consistent.

The only begotten Son of God

It is sometimes insisted that because the Word was with God and the Word was God, then Jesus was the Word and Jesus was God. This is not so. The opening words of the Gospel of John teach us that when the Word *was made flesh, and not before*, there existed the only begotten of the Father. It is the Word made flesh who was begotten. There is nothing whatever in Scripture that tells us that the Word was begotten. Jesus was the Word made flesh. He was not the Word or the flesh alone. Jesus was the Word become flesh. This process began in begettal and conception, and resulted in the birth of the Son of God. It was then that he personally existed for the first time.

Only by this understanding can we believe that Jesus truly died. Christadelphians believe that Jesus truly died for our sins. They do not believe that he personally continued to exist at the instant of death. Such a view, however, has to be held by those who believe that he actually existed before he was born. Since, on that belief, Christ would be eternal, *he could not truly die*. Christ himself declares the truth:

"I am he that liveth, and was dead; and, behold, I am alive for evermore." (Revelation 1:18)

The "I" who lives is the "I" who was dead. Christadelphians truly believe that Jesus died, as he himself says he did. Thus, both in birth and in death, there is a simple fundamental truth concerning the nature of the Son of God.

We promised at the end of the previous chapter to show how the doctrine of the Son of God as believed by Christadelphians greatly exalts the Lord Jesus Christ without diminishing his glory as the Son of God. How great is his work! From the lowly beginnings when he shared our nature, he overcame the temptations of sin, entered and conquered death, and has ascended in immortality and abounding glory to the right hand of God in heaven. This is Bible teaching. We honour and praise the Son of God, believing that he was truly born, was truly tempted, truly died, truly rose and was truly exalted to the right hand of the Father. His honour and authority and power have been given to him by the Father:

"All authority **hath been given** *unto me in heaven and on earth."*
(Matthew 28:18, R.V.)

"(God) . . . raised him (Christ) from the dead, and made him to sit at his right hand . . . put all things in subjection under his feet, gave him to be head over all things . . ." (Ephesians 1:20 – 22, R.V.)

"God also hath highly exalted him, and given him a name which is above every name." (Philippians 2:9)

The power and glory and authority of Christ have been bestowed upon him by the Father. They are derived and none of them would be his if they had not been given to him by God the Father.

It is sometimes forgotten that the Lord Jesus constantly told his disciples that his words and his deeds were from his Father:

"For he whom God hath sent speaketh the words of God: for God giveth not the Spirit by measure unto him." (John 3:34)

"The word which ye hear is not mine, but the Father's which sent me."
(John 14:24)

"Believest thou not that I am in the Father, and the Father in me? the words that I speak unto you I speak not of myself . . ."
(John 14:10)

"My teaching is not mine, but his that sent me." (John 7:16)

"Many good works have I shewed you from my Father."
(John 10:32)

101

> *"God anointed Jesus of Nazareth with the Holy Spirit and with power: who went about doing good . . ."* (Acts 10:38)

> *"Jesus of Nazareth,* **a man approved of God** *among you by miracles and wonders and signs, which God did by him . . ."* (Acts 2:22)

The wondrous words of grace which he spoke, the deeds of healing and compassion which he performed and the power by which he stilled the storm on Galilee or fed the thousands, were all of God. Anointed by God with power at his baptism, he went forth in his Father's name. It is impossible to read the Bible without being told everywhere that what Christ was and is comes from God Himself.

Even the Holy Spirit which was poured forth at Pentecost was given to Christ by the Father (Acts 2:33). So it will be that when he bestows immortality on the faithful disciples, he will do so because God the Father has given him that power (John 5:26). Everything is of God the Father.

Wrongly to attribute to the Son as an inherent possession that which derives from God, is to dishonour the Father. An erroneous understanding of the Son inevitably leads to an erroneous understanding of the Father.

Comment is needed, however, on those verses of Scripture which have every appearance of attributing personal pre-existence to the Son of God. Here is a selection of them:

> *"Glorify thou me with thine own self (in thy presence, N.I.V.) with the glory which I had with thee before the world was."* (John 17:5)

> *"Before Abraham was, I am."* (John 8:58)

> *"He is before all things, and by him all things consist."* (Colossians 1:17)

The Bible passages already quoted in this chapter have shown that everything about Jesus was already planned in the mind of God long before his birth of Mary. This knowledge and purpose pre-existed: it had first to be in God's mind for it to have been prophesied in the Old Testament and for God to have brought it about. We believe that this is the basic explanation of the majority of verses which speak of Christ as though he personally was there before his birth. It is easier to understand this truth by examining a series of similar verses which we find much less difficult to comprehend:

> *"Thou (God) lovest me (Jesus) before the foundation of the world."* (John 17:24)

"(He) whose name hath not been written in the book of life of the Lamb that hath been slain from the foundation of the world."
(Revelation 13:8, R.V.)

"Every one whose name has not been written before the foundation of the world in the book of life of the Lamb that was slain."
(Revelation 13:8, R.S.V.)

"Blessed be the God and Father of our Lord Jesus Christ, who hath . . . chosen us in him before the foundation of the world."
(Ephesians 1:3 – 4)

"Come ye blessed of my Father, inherit the kingdom prepared for you from the foundation of the world." (Matthew 25:34)

"Christ . . . who verily was foreordained before the foundation of the world, but was manifest in these last times." (1 Peter 1:19 – 20)

"From the foundation of the world"

These passages provide an insight into the mind of God and the marvels of His foreknowledge. From the foundation of the world God knew the Lord Jesus Christ and those who would come to believe in him; He knew the names which will be found inscribed in the Lamb's book of life at the day of judgement; He had already prepared the kingdom which they would inherit; and had fully ordained all that Christ would do. All these were really there in the mind of God, though none of them actually existed at that time. It is as though the musical score was there from first note to last, but none of it had yet been played. In Bible words:

*"(God) calleth those things which be not as **though they were**."*
(Romans 4:17)

"Declaring the end from the beginning, and from ancient times the things that are not yet done." (Isaiah 46:10)

God Himself expresses it in the clearest words:

"Before I formed thee (Jeremiah) in the belly I knew thee; and before thou camest forth out of the womb I sanctified thee, and I ordained thee a prophet unto the nations." (Jeremiah 1:5)

We should have no difficulty in understanding the words, "The glory that I had with thee before the world was". Christ was not living at that time, but in the mind of God everything had been accomplished and Christ had died, had risen and had ascended to heaven in glory.

So the words which Christ would speak were known to God before Christ was born. They too were part of the Word of God. All who heard the teaching of Jesus were impressed by both the manner and content of the message. We read that:

> *"The people were astonished at his teaching: for he taught them as one having authority, and not as their scribes."*   (Matthew 7:28 – 29)

> *"And all bare him witness, and wondered at the gracious words which proceeded out of his mouth."*   (Luke 4:22)

The exquisite beauty of what he had to say was matched by the unfailing love, holiness and righteousness which he displayed. He fulfilled in an unforgettable way an Old Testament description:

> *"His mouth is sweetness itself;*
> *He is altogether lovely."*   (Song of Songs 5:16, N.I.V.)

No wonder that Peter, at a time when others were forsaking Christ, was constrained to exclaim:

> *"Lord, to whom shall we go? thou hast the words of eternal life."*
>   (John 6:68)

His message was such as to challenge the hearts of men and to offer them something they longed for but had never believed they could attain. He spoke of forgiveness, a new beginning, everlasting life and an inheritance in the Kingdom of God on earth. Humble listeners and believers were in contrast to the Jewish leaders who, though they were included in his compassionate call, would not respond, but instead sought to discomfit him with hard questions, sometimes deceitfully put, and went away marvelling at his answers.

But the word of Jesus in his preaching was accompanied by the word of equal power in his works of healing. He healed by his word:

> *"There came unto him a centurion, beseeching him, and saying, . . . Speak the word only, and my servant shall be healed . . . and Jesus said . . . Go thy way, as thou hast believed, so be it done unto thee. And his servant was healed in the self-same hour."*   (Matthew 8:5 – 13)

So it was that he who was the Word made flesh radiated that word in all he had to say and do. He was indeed the mind of God made known to man. Most wondrously, however, he translated all he said into his own life. If he spoke of the merciful, he was merciful: or the pure in heart, he was pure: or the peacemaker, such he was. He was indeed the Word made flesh in a double sense: first by birth and then by his life. And all of this was for the purpose of redeeming sinners:

> *"The word which God sent unto the children of Israel, preaching good tidings of peace by Jesus Christ . . . for God was with him."*
>
> (Acts 10:36,38, R.V.)

We can exclaim with those amazed men and women of his own time:

> *"What a word is this!"*   (Luke 4:36)

13

A PRIEST FOR EVER

MOST religious bodies have priests or people who hold special office above the ordinary members of their communities. Sometimes the authority vested in the priest is regarded as considerable, even to the extent of his being able to grant forgiveness of sins.

What was the position in the New Testament communities? What should the position be today? It is an important question. For some communities the priesthood is their anchor to Christ. The Roman Catholic church in particular has a priesthood which performs an important part in daily ministry, in officiating at the Mass, in relation to the confessional and, it is claimed, to absolution for the sins of the truly penitent.

Many people feel secure and greatly helped by the fact that a priest is available in time of need and is present to lead congregational worship. Others, however, look upon priestcraft as a hated and oppressive thing. What is the truth concerning this significant matter? Is it essential to have the services of a priest in order to gain access to the body of Christ and to share in communion?

God established a priesthood in the days of Moses for the benefit of the children of Israel. Their work was to have the custody of the written Word of God delivered to them by the prophets, to impart instruction to the people, and to minister in the Tabernacle worship under the guidance of Moses at God's command. This priesthood was chosen and established by God. The Chief Priest, known as the High Priest, is mentioned in the New Testament in the following terms:

"Every high priest . . . is ordained for men in things pertaining to God . . . And no man taketh this honour to himself, but he that is called of God." (Hebrews 5:1,4)

The heart of Israel's worship was the Tabernacle, and the heart of the Tabernacle was the solid gold mercy seat which rested on the gold-covered wooden chest, known as the Ark of the Testimony, in which, particularly, the tablets of stone bearing the Ten Commandments were placed. Once a year only, the mercy seat was sprinkled with blood, on a day known as the Day of Atonement. No member of the priesthood except the High Priest officiated in the Tent of Meeting on that special day.

The Tabernacle

We have learned from Scripture that the principal ordinances of the Old Testament were foreshadowings of Christ, either in the words used, the acts performed or the persons involved. This is particularly true of the Tabernacle, its ceremonies and the priesthood. Put simply, the position is:

"The law being a shadow of good things to come . . ." (Hebrews 10:1)

In fact, God had planned the worship under the law of Moses with Christ in mind, so that when he came men could recognise in him the reality of the things that were present only in shadow in former times.

The first tabernacle as erected by Moses pointed forward to the true — the real — tabernacle, the household of God of which the Lord Jesus Christ is the very heart. He is the true Ark: the Word of God was in him. He is the true mercy seat:

"For the law was given by Moses, but grace and truth came by Jesus Christ." (John 1:17)

"Christ Jesus: whom God hath set forth to be a propitiation (mercy seat) through faith in his blood, to declare his righteousness for the remission of sins that are past." (Romans 3:24 – 25)

Christ was the very essence of all the sacrifices and offerings, he was the way in which God's intentions of which those things spoke would be fulfilled once and for all. Jesus was in himself the Day of Atonement:

"This man . . . offered . . . one sacrifice for sins for ever . . . for by one

*offering he hath perfected for ever them that are sanctified. Therefore . . .
brethren . . . enter . . . the holy place by the blood of Jesus, by the way
he dedicated for us, a new and living way, through the veil, that is to say,
his flesh.''* (Hebrews 10:10,12,19 – 29, R.V.)

What then of the office of High Priest? How does Christ fulfil what
that office signified? What does the Bible say? The Bible tells us
something which is a great comfort and provides us with a mighty
source of blessing. In the first place we are told that Jesus is in
heaven and is a priest for ever. In other words, what the High
Priest performed for Israel in his limited way and despite his
physical limitations (he, too, was in need of help in respect of sins),
Christ fulfils in a greater and a much more effective way for the
believer. It is a work not of ritual but of reality. Christ is the
believer's access to God and the believer's source of help. Here are
the Scriptures on this matter:

*"We have such an high priest, who is set on the right hand of the throne
of the Majesty in the heavens . . ."* (Hebrews 8:1)

*"For such an high priest became us, who is holy, harmless, undefiled,
separate from sinners, and made higher than the heavens, who needeth not
daily, as those (Jewish) high priests, to offer up sacrifice, first for his
own sins, and then for the people's: for this he did once, when he offered
up himself.''* (Hebrews 7:26 – 27)

*"Wherefore in all things it behoved him to be made like unto his brethren,
that he might be a merciful and faithful high priest in things pertaining
to God, to make reconciliation for the sins of the people. For in that he
himself hath suffered being tempted, he is able to succour them that are
tempted.''* (Hebrews 2:17 – 18)

*"For we have not an high priest which cannot be touched with the feeling
of our infirmities; but was all in points tempted like as we are, yet
without sin. Let us therefore come boldly unto the throne of grace, that we
may obtain mercy, and find grace to help in time of need.''* (Hebrews 4:15 – 16)

*"Wherefore he is able also to save them to the uttermost that come unto
God by him, seeing he ever liveth to make intercession for them.''* (Hebrews 7:25)

*"Christ . . . entered . . . into heaven itself, now to appear in the presence
of God for us.''* (Hebrews 9:24)

"For there is one God, and one mediator between God and men, the man Christ Jesus." (1 Timothy 2:5)

"Christ . . . who is even at the right hand of God, who also maketh intercession for us." (Romans 8:34)

This is an impressive and comforting array of Scriptures for the believer. Christ, who offered himself for his sins, continues unceasingly to work on his behalf. Christ is the Mediator, the intercessor, the compassionate and understanding high priest, who is able to succour and save. Prayer is the link with God through the intercessor, who is Christ.

No longer is there any need for the old priesthood under the law of Moses. There is now something better and more enduring, the work of Christ who "ever liveth". Christ's priesthood abides unchanged and it abides continually.

Do we need Priests?

We can now return to consider our earlier questions about the need for a priesthood today. Do we need God-appointed ministers for the communities of true believers? What we are considering is what the Bible has to say on this subject about priests other than Christ himself.

The Bible knows nothing whatever about a special order of Christian priests in our everyday sense, nothing at all. Apart from those New Testament references which are commenting on the old Mosaic priesthood, the great preponderance of Scriptures about a priest make reference to Christ and to him alone. In addition there are five references to *all* true believers as a holy or royal priesthood, who will have a special work to do when Christ returns and the Kingdom of God is established:

"You also, like living stones, are being built into a spiritual house to be a holy priesthood, offering spiritual sacrifices acceptable to God through Jesus Christ.
But you are a chosen people, a royal priesthood, a holy nation, a people belonging to God, that you may declare the praises of him who called you out of darkness into his wonderful light." (1 Peter 2:5,9, N.I.V.)

"To him who loves us and has freed us from our sins by his blood, and has made us to be a kingdom and priests to serve his God and Father — to him be glory and power for ever and ever! Amen."
(Revelation 1:5 – 6, N.I.V.)

"With your blood you purchased men for God from every tribe and language and people and nation. You have made them to be a kingdom and priests to serve our God, and they will reign on the earth."

(Revelation 5:9 – 10, N.I.V.)

"Blessed and holy are those who have part in the first resurrection. The second death has no power over them, but they will be priests of God and of Christ and will reign with him for a thousand years."

(Revelation 20:6, N.I.V.)

Every true believer is called into this royal priesthood but he must remain faithful in order to inherit the blessing in its completeness. The nation of Israel were offered the same calling as can be read in Exodus 19:6 (from which the Apostle Peter is quoting in the first and second of the above citations). But Israel failed to respond acceptably and God has now made known that His purpose will be fulfilled when Christ returns. At that time all the faithful, whether living or dead, will be granted everlasting life and become the royal priesthood of the kingdom of God on earth.

But there are no Scriptures whatsoever to tell us that a priesthood should be established at the present time between the laity and God. A priesthood of this kind with particular authority in respect of the communion service or the absolution of sins is quite unknown in the New Testament.

The word "bishop" occurs in the New Testament, and this might lead us to think of the modern bishop and the nature of his authority. The Bible knows nothing of a bishop having authority over a diocese or a group of churches, nor of a priesthood subordinate to a bishop or archbishop. The word "bishop" simply means, "overseer", of whom there were several in each church or ecclesia (see Philippians 1:1 and Acts 20:28, R.V.). In no case do we read of one man having the rightful rule over a church. It is evident that the present hierarchical system is a development after Bible times and without Scriptural warrant.

There is another reason why a special human priesthood, in the modern sense, is wholly inappropriate. Scripture is quite specific in telling us that the new order in Christ is an unchangeable priesthood based on the fact that Christ lives for ever. Were there to be other priests of that same order, they too would have to be everliving in order to take their place in the unchangeable ministry. No-one today can meet those requirements. The immortalised saints will be embraced within that priesthood in the kingdom of God. Their great work will be instructing the world in the ways of God and overseeing some of the work in the great temple to be built in Jerusalem.

Having seen that there is no Scriptural basis for present-day priests (and certainly there are none to be found in the New Testament), we should also note that the forgiveness of sins is not mediated through men anywhere in the New Testament, with the exception of authority given by Christ to the apostles alone (John 20:21). There is nothing in Scripture permitting the extension of that authority to any kind of "successors" whatsoever.

The Only Mediator

Nor is there any Scriptural foundation for the practice of praying to dead saints in order to seek particular aid in special needs. In the first place, all who die are asleep in the grave and have neither part nor lot in any matters in heaven or in earth. Second, the Bible makes it plain that the true believer has direct access to God through Christ alone. There is no need to solicit the services of any other person, whether living or dead, in order to secure a more sympathetic ear or a more ready access to the Lord Jesus Christ. No-one has greater sympathy than Christ himself, and he is ever available as mediator for his beloved servants. This matter of prayer through saints and the Virgin Mary is one of the greatest departures from Scriptural teaching and practice.

The prevalent teaching about the Virgin Mary which makes her own conception immaculate, her bodily assumption to heaven a doctrine to be received and her personal title that of Queen of Heaven find no place whatsoever in the Bible. They are not part of the original Gospel as taught by the apostles of the Lord Jesus Christ. The Virgin Mary was a divinely chosen and deeply blessed maid of Israel for the mighty work of a wonderful and unique motherhood. Her own salvation from sin and death was bound up in the redemptive work of the Son of God. She will not receive everlasting life until the return of Christ from heaven.

The Lord Jesus Christ made no provision for successors to the twelve apostles. Their work and office were peculiar to them and were based on the fact that they had been with Christ throughout his earthly ministry and had seen him after his resurrection from the dead. They were empowered and authorised by Christ himself. They were not a priesthood and they did not ordain any believers

111

as priests with priestly duties in the local congregations of believers.

The manner in which the Lord provided for the time when the apostles would pass from the scene was already at work when the apostles were active. They were engaged in the ministry of the Word of God. Under the inspiration of the Holy Spirit, their teaching has been preserved in the New Testament. The apostles gave instruction of this kind:

> *"And the things that thou hast heard of me among many witnesses, the same commit thou to faithful men, who shall be able to teach others also."*
> (2 Timothy 2:2)

It is a tragedy of the centuries that the Word of God became less well known among believers and its authority was gradually eroded. At the same time the cleavage between the laity and the clergy became well established with the consequence that the Bible became even more remote from men and women. This resulted in men turning to the priest and his service rather than to the Word of God itself. The word of the priest and the authority of his church took the place of the authority of the Word of God with disastrous results.

As will be gathered from the foregoing, Christadelphians do not have an ordained priesthood. Services are conducted and the Word of God ministered entirely by laymen able to do the work. There is no superintending council over the congregations world-wide. Their coherence comes from the common acceptance of the same faith, and its application in the corporate and personal lives of members.

Nor are any special days or feasts to celebrate laid down or taught by Christ and the apostles, except for the breaking of bread on the first day of the week. First century Christians did not keep a holy day for the birth of Christ and did not celebrate Easter as a special time of year.

14

THE HOLY SPIRIT

WHAT or who is the Holy Spirit? What part does the Holy Spirit play in the work of God? These are questions to which answers should be found, if this is possible. It is possible, and once again the Bible is our ample guide.

At the outset let us clear whatever mystery or confusion may lie behind the word "Ghost" in the expression "Holy Ghost" in the King James (Authorised) version of the Bible. In Shakespeare's day "ghost" was a current word for "spirit" and a spiritual adviser was called a "ghostly confessor". Holy Ghost and Holy Spirit are translations of the same original words. The strange notions which now attach to our word "ghost" are not what the translators intended to convey. Later translations uniformly render the words, "Holy Spirit".

Several expressions are to be found in the Bible which are descriptive of the Holy Spirit and these include:

"*The Spirit of God*"	(Genesis 1:2; Matthew 3:16)
"*The spirit of the Lord*"	(Isaiah 11:2; Acts 8:39)
"*Thy good spirit*"	(Nehemiah 9:20)
"*The Spirit of the Lord God*"	(Isaiah 61:1)
"*His holy Spirit*"	(Isaiah 63:10 – 11)
"*The Spirit of your Father*"	(Matthew 10:20)
"*The Spirit*"	(John 1:32)

> *"The holy Spirit of God"*   (Ephesians 4:30)
>
> *"The power of the Lord"*   (Luke 5:17)

The words God the Holy Ghost, or God the Holy Spirit, are not to be found in the Bible. Nevertheless, there is clearly a very strong link between God and the Holy Spirit. Indeed, the Spirit is said to be "of God", "of the Lord", "of the Lord God", and "of your Father", in the list of expressions given above. If we make this the starting point of our journey through Scripture we shall find that progress is not difficult.

Look at the following descriptions of creation:

> *"In the beginning **God** created the heavens and the earth."*
>
> (Genesis 1:1)

> *"And the **Spirit of God** moved upon the face of the waters."*
>
> (Genesis 1:2)

> *"**The Lord God** formed man of the dust of the ground, and breathed into his nostrils the breath of life, and man became a living soul."*
>
> (Genesis 2:7)

> *"The **Spirit of God** hath made me, and **the breath of the Almighty** hath given me life."*   (Job 33:4)

> *"He hath made the earth by **his power**, he hath established the world by his wisdom, and hath stretched out the heavens by his discretion."*
>
> (Jeremiah 10:12 and 51:15)

These are but a few of the many evidences in the Bible about the work of God in creation. He alone by His wisdom conceived the wondrous plan, and it was executed by His Almighty power, His Spirit. God is Spirit (John 4:24, R.S.V.), and *whatever* He does is by His Spirit.

How is creation sustained in existence? Is it a huge clock, wound up by the Almighty and left gradually to run down? Or is the Lord God still involved and concerned with what He has made? The Bible in all its parts tells us that creation is upheld by God and He is everywhere present throughout and within all that He has made. Without Him nothing could exist or continue to exist:

> *"God that made the world and all things therein . . . giveth to all life, and breath, and all things . . . for in him we live, and move, and have our being."*   (Acts 17:24 – 28)

> *"If he set his heart upon man,*
> *If he gather unto himself his spirit and his breath;*
> *All flesh shall perish together,*
> *And man shall turn again unto dust."*   (Job 34:14 – 15)

> *"Can any hide himself in secret places that I shall not see him? saith the*
> *Lord. Do not I fill heaven and earth? saith the Lord."*
>   (Jeremiah 23:24)

> *"Seek him that maketh the seven stars and Orion, and turneth the shadow*
> *of death into the morning, and maketh the day dark with night: that*
> *calleth for the waters of the sea, and poureth them out upon the face of the*
> *earth: The Lord is his name."*   (Amos 5:8)

God fills His creation. All of its activity is because of His wise and sustaining Spirit, the divine energy working out His gracious purpose. The Spirit is not a "separate" or "other" person. It is God's own radiant power, ever outflowing from Him, by which His "everywhereness" is achieved. The Spirit is personal in that it is of God Himself: it is not personal in the sense of being some other person within the Godhead.

We have learned from the Scriptures that God has a redemptive purpose for man and for the earth on which he lives. It will come as no surprise to us to learn that the revelation of that will has come about by God Himself through His Spirit:

> *"We have the word of the prophets made more certain, and you will do*
> *well to pay attention to it . . . Above all, you must understand that no*
> *prophecy of Scripture came about by the prophet's own interpretation. For*
> *prophecy never had its origin in the will of man, but* **men spoke from**
> **God as they were carried along by the Holy Spirit.***"*
>   (2 Peter 1:19 – 21, N.I.V.)

The message is simple. God has revealed His will infallibly by the Holy Spirit upon chosen men called prophets. It was by this means that the contents of Scripture came into existence. Those who wrote were inspired by God's Spirit and what they set down upon the written page was inspired by God. Therefore, although all the prophets have long since died, we have a totally reliable and wholly inspired Word of God in our hands. God still speaks to us therein as surely as He spoke by the mouth of the prophets:

> *"The holy scriptures . . . are able to make thee wise unto salvation*
> *through faith which is in Christ Jesus.* **All scripture is given by**

115

> *inspiration of God* ... *that the man of God may be perfect,*
> *throughly furnished unto all good works.''* (2 Timothy 3:15 – 17)

The Word of God provided in this way carries to us the mind of God and all of the glorious attributes associated with His holy name. To resist the message and command of the Word of God is to resist God Himself. Indeed, it is to resist the Spirit of God in every sense of that word, including that broader meaning which we imply when we talk, for example, of the "spirit" of an agreement. This is how the Bible describes the resistance of the children of Israel to God's Word through the prophets:

> *"Yet many years didst thou forbear them, and testifiedst against them by thy spirit in thy prophets: yet would they not give ear ...''*
> (Nehemiah 9:30)

> *"In all their affliction he (God) was afflicted, and the angel of his presence saved them: in his love and in his pity he redeemed them; and he bare them, and carried them all the days of old. But they rebelled, and vexed his holy Spirit.''* (Isaiah 63:9 – 10)

> *" Ye stiffnecked and uncircumcised in heart and ears, ye do always resist the Holy Spirit: as your fathers did, so do ye.''* (Acts 7:51)

Clearly, it was not simply the naked power of God that the rebels resisted. They resisted the redeeming love and righteousness of God whether in His prophets or later in the Christ. They refused to humble themselves to serve God. This was the evil spirit of man contesting the Holy Spirit of God.

Miracles and Wonders

There were times, of course, when the powerful nature of the Spirit of God was made manifest. From time to time God intervened openly and worked wonders among men. This aspect of the Spirit whether in goodness or in severity is unmistakable:

> *"Our fathers understood not thy wonders in Egypt;*
> *They remembered not the multitude of thy mercies;*
> *But provoked him at the sea, even at the Red Sea.*
> *Nevertheless he saved them for his name's sake,*
> *That he might make* **his mighty power** *to be known.*
> *He rebuked the Red Sea also, and it was dried up ...''*
> (Psalm 106:7 – 9)

116

*"**He spake,** and the locusts came,
And caterpillars, and that without number,
And did eat up all the herbs in their land,
And devoured the fruit of their ground."*

(Psalm 105:34 – 35)

*"**The power of the Lord** was present to heal them. And, behold,
men brought in a bed a man which was taken with a palsy . . . and he
said to the sick of the palsy . . . Arise, and take up thy couch, and go into
thine house. And immediately he rose up . . . "* (Luke 5:17 – 25)

The miracles of the Lord Jesus Christ in stilling the storm on
Galilee, in causing miraculous draughts of fish, in feeding many
thousands at one time, and in healings of every kind, were strongly
reminiscent of the various works of God in the Old Testament. It
was as though the activity of the Spirit of God was focused, as
never before on earth, in the person of the Lord Jesus.

This was equally true of the words he spoke. His words and
miracles were wonderfully married together. It was as though the
Lord God had brought near to man in His Son everything He had
to say in a most compassionate and powerful form. The Spirit had
worked God's will in ages past, sometimes in signs and wonders,
fearful and gracious; sometimes in word or vision or dream; but
now, in Christ, the Lord God provided a wondrous and unforgettable manifestation, a Son filled with all the radiance of God's
Word and in himself a reflection of all that He spoke, and endued
with such power and authority as to extend the gracious Word in
saving acts of almost unbelievable kindness. In all of this the mind
and will of God were made known in such a way as to redeem the
destitute, to give hope to those who were bowed down with sin,
or oppressed by the man-made traditions and restrictions which
made life intolerable for the ordinary man in the days of Jesus.

Christ's words relieved the desolate and despairing. His deeds
brought spontaneous praise to their lips. His devoted death
provided the release from their sins. God had spoken through all of
these aspects of the life of Christ.

When at Calvary and in the tomb in the garden all seemed to
have been lost, the Lord moved again by His Spirit:

*"**By his power** God raised the Lord from the dead."*

(1 Corinthians 6:14, N.I.V.)

Thus the power of God, exercised in love and righteousness,

visited the silent sepulchre and brought forth the only begotten Son to receive glorious and unending life:

> *"God . . . raised him up from the dead, and gave him glory."*
> (1 Peter 1:21)

> *"His Son Jesus Christ our Lord . . . was made of the seed of David according to the flesh; and declared to be the Son of God with power, according to the spirit of holiness, by the resurrection from the dead."*
> (Romans 1:3 – 4)

> *"According to the working of his mighty power, which he wrought in Christ, when he raised him from the dead, and set him at his own right hand . . . and hath put all things under his feet."*
> (Ephesians 1:19 – 22)

> *"(Christ) is gone into heaven, and is on the right hand of God; angels and authorities and powers being made subject unto him."*
> (1 Peter 3:22)

The exaltation of Christ is a source of great joy and praise for believers. Christ is Saviour and Christ is Lord. Moreover, God who had raised His Son from the dead by the power of His Spirit continued His will and purpose in him after his resurrection:

> *"Of all that Jesus began both to do and teach, until the day in which he was taken up, after that he* **through the Holy Spirit** *had given commandments unto the apostles whom he had chosen."* (Acts 1:1,2)

> *"This Jesus hath God raised up, whereof we are witnesses. Therefore being by the right hand of God exalted, and having received* **of the Father the promise of the Holy Spirit** *. . ."* (Acts 2:32 – 33)

The exalted Christ is empowered and authorised by the Spirit of God.

The life which Jesus now lives is a life of the Spirit; he has been *"quickened by the Spirit"* (1 Peter 3:18) so that now, in the fullest sense, he lives by the Spirit. His mortality has been clothed upon with immortality. It has been swallowed up by life. Furthermore, the Lord Jesus is now *"a life-giving spirit"* (1 Corinthians 15:45, R.V.):

> *"For as the Father raiseth up the dead, and quickeneth them; even so the Son quickeneth whom he will."*
> (John 5:21)

The Lord Jesus Christ is now the source of life everlasting for all who truly believe in him. He is *"the firstborn among many brethren"* (Romans 8:29), the One who is to bring *"many sons to glory"*, and is *"the author of eternal salvation unto all them that obey him"* (Hebrews 2:10 and 5:9). It is impossible to over-estimate the significance of the present standing and office of the Lord Jesus Christ as Son of God. God has bestowed immortality upon him and given him the power to grant immortality to others. This is the glorious message of the New Testament. In Christ there is not only the promise of eternal salvation; he is the actual Forerunner, the one who has arrived, and has himself attained to immortality. This is the unshakable assurance for all who come to God by him. Christ is truly the Saviour granted to us by God. This is the pinnacle of the work of the Lord God by His Holy Spirit: prophesied in old time by the holy prophets and brought to perfection in the birth, life, death, resurrection and exaltation of Jesus Christ our Lord.

Therefore, the Gospel is now proclaimed "in his name", and the progress of the message of salvation on earth is now under his care. The apostles were sent to proclaim this good news. And they were directly empowered by the Spirit of God in Christ so that the words they were to speak and the wonders they were to perform would be integral parts of the one message of God made known in Jesus:

> *"Therefore being by the right hand of God exalted, and having received of the Father the promise of the Holy Spirit, he hath shed forth this, which ye now see and hear . . . And fear came upon every soul: and many wonders and signs were done by the apostles."* (Acts 2:33, 43)

> *"Be it known unto you all . . . by the name of Jesus Christ of Nazareth . . . which is become the head of the corner. Neither is there salvation in any other: for there is none other name under heaven given among men, whereby we must be saved."* (Acts 4:10 – 12)

To resist the mission of Christ by the apostles was to resist Christ: any who resisted were resisting the Holy Spirit as did their Old Testament counterparts (Isaiah 63:10 and Acts 7:51). The Jewish authorities who opposed the development of the Gospel were *"against the Lord, and against his Christ"* (Acts 4:26). Saul of Tarsus, who later became the beloved apostle Paul, bitterly persecuted the early believers but, when challenged by Jesus on the way to Damascus, was asked by Christ: *"Why persecutest thou me?"* (Acts 9:4).

Those, on the other hand, who believed were submissive to the Spirit's message and thereby to the Lord Jesus Christ and his

119

Father. The word of the Spirit convicted their hearts, bringing repentance and the hope of everlasting life. In the New Testament particularly, this message, the glad tidings of "*the things concerning the kingdom of God and the name of Jesus Christ*" (Acts 8:12), is plainly related to the Word and the Spirit:

> "*Hear ye therefore the parable of the sower . . . he that received seed into the good ground is he that heareth the word, and understandeth it; which also beareth fruit . . .*" (Matthew 13:18 – 23)

> " '*The word is near you; it is in your mouth and in your heart,*' *that is, the word of faith we are proclaiming . . . Consequently, faith comes from hearing the message, and the message is heard through the word of Christ.*" (Romans 10:8,17, N.I.V.)

> "*Except a man be born again, he cannot see the kingdom of God . . . Except a man be born of water and of the Spirit, he cannot enter into the kingdom of God.*" (John 3:3,5)

> "*Being born again, not of corruptible seed, but of incorruptible, by the word of God, which liveth and abideth for ever . . . And this is the word which by the gospel is preached unto you.*" (1 Peter 1:23 – 25)

> "*It is the spirit that quickeneth; the flesh profiteth nothing: the words that I (Jesus) speak unto you, they are spirit, and they are life.*" (John 6:63)

> "*Of his own will begat he us with the word of truth . . . Wherefore . . . receive with meekness the engrafted word, which is able to save your souls. But be ye doers of the word, and not hearers only, deceiving your own selves.*" (James 1:18 – 22)

> "*Put off your old self, which is being corrupted by its deceitful desires; to be made new in the attitude of your minds; and to put on the new self, created to be like God in true righteousness and holiness.*" (Ephesians 4:22 – 24, N.I.V.)

> "*Walk in the Spirit, and ye shall not fulfil the lust of the flesh. For the flesh lusteth against the Spirit, and the Spirit against the flesh . . . Be not deceived; God is not mocked: for whatsoever a man soweth, that shall he also reap. For he that soweth to his flesh shall of the flesh reap corruption; but he that soweth to the Spirit shall of the Spirit reap life everlasting.*" (Galatians 5:16 – 17 and 6:7 – 8)

> "*The fruit of the Spirit is love, joy, peace, longsuffering, gentleness, goodness, faith, meekness, temperance.*" (Galatians 5:22)

The Message of the Spirit

From these Scriptures it is evident that the way of salvation in Christ is the way of the Spirit. It is God's way. Salvation comes from God. The whole purpose and plan of salvation and its execution are of God. Man was altogether impotent and sterile. There was no goodness in him. God has made compassionate and gracious provision in Christ. God's will was brought into action by His Spirit. None of this is known other than by the Word of God which is the message of the Spirit:

> *"Who hath ears to hear, let him hear."*　　　　(Matthew 13:43)

> *"He that hath an ear, let him hear what the Spirit saith unto the churches."*　　　　(Revelation 2:7)

The message of salvation is the power of God (Romans 1:16) which brings man into contact with the mind of God, the Spirit of God. An entirely new force enters into his life when he hears or willingly receives the Word of God. Meekness in receiving the Word leads to faith. The Word illumines the mind and understanding, and commences a process of change which leads to repentance and conversion. We shall discuss these steps in greater detail later in the book.

God's Word written on the heart of man in this way by believing the written message in the Bible is said to be:

> *"written not with ink, but with the Spirit of the living God; not in tables of stone, but in fleshy tables of the heart."*　　(2 Corinthians 3:3)

This is a marvellous happening. It is truly the work of the Spirit of God engendered by a faithful acceptance of the glad tidings of the Gospel. At the beginning of human history Eve's mind had been polluted by the words of the serpent. They were words which spelt sin and death. The way of God is to teach man anew. The mind has to be redeemed from mere human, fleshly thinking. The thinking of God has to replace it.

> *"Be not conformed to this world: but be ye transformed by the renewing of your mind, that ye may prove what is that good, and acceptable, and perfect, will of God."*　　　　(Romans 12:2)

The Word of the Gospel is designed for this process. It is a seed which will bear spiritual fruit. The man who receives it into his heart will be caught up in the floodtide of God's saving love in the work of the Lord Jesus Christ.

A part of this on-sweeping work of God is to assure us of the care of God and of Christ for those who believe and seek to obey. This is what the Gospel is all about; it is designed to bring us to God through Christ:

"Come unto God by him (Jesus)." (Hebrews 7:19,25)

"Draw nigh to God, **and he will draw nigh to you.** *"*
(James 4:8)

We are assured of God's care and the shelter of Christ during our life of pilgrimage as we wait for the day of the Kingdom of God.

One of the ways in which God cares for His children is by means of the angels. This subject is dealt with more fully in Chapter 18 but the following verses are illustrative of the point which we are conveying at this juncture:

"Are not all angels ministering spirits sent to serve those who will inherit salvation?" (Hebrews 1:14, N.I.V.)

"The angel of the Lord encampeth round about them that fear him, and delivereth them." (Psalm 34:7)

We can therefore, when we become disciples of Christ, be assured that they that be with us are more and more effective than anything ranged against us in this life.

The Privilege of Prayer

Perhaps the greatest blessing afforded by the Gospel in this life is communion with God through the Lord Jesus by means of prayer. This is the lifeline. God hears prayer. Through the mediation of Christ in heaven our petitions and praises are taken to God and they are answered according to what is best for us in the will of God:

"It is Christ that died, yea rather, that is risen again, who is even at the right hand of God, who also maketh intercession for us. Who shall separate us from the love of Christ?" (Romans 8:34 – 35)

"We have an Advocate with the Father, Jesus Christ the righteous: and he is the propitiation for our sins." (1 John 2:1 – 2, R.V.)

"Wherefore he is able also to save them to the uttermost that come unto God by him, seeing he ever liveth to make intercession for them."
(Hebrews 7:25)

The unspeakable privilege of prayer is granted to us through the goodness of God by His Spirit. Our faintest whisper, or our unspoken petitions, reach Him through Jesus, when we truly belong; and He inclines His gracious ear to our cry. It is a means of unfailing access and help in our spiritual warfare.

Do we really obtain help by prayer? But, of course. God responds to our need. Prayer is not a substitute for the strength to be drawn from the Word of God. Prayer works with that Word of faith. Indeed, it is when we know the will and way of God from His Word that we discover the need for prayer in order that we might not enter into temptation. Prayer in its upward life counteracts the downward drag of our sinful natures. We need every source of help and sometimes we need it urgently. The reservoir of the Word of God in the mind, the mind of Christ dwelling in us richly, will always afford counsel and strength, because it is designed for that very purpose. Nothing could illustrate this more clearly than the manner in which Christ dispelled the temptations of the wilderness.

The records of the temptation of Christ are to be found in Matthew 4 and Luke 4 where the three-fold assault on his Sonship was made in the form of three questions, each of which appealed to self-will and would have denied the will of God had they been successful. The Lord Jesus found his replies, and the strength to make them, in his understanding of and reliance on the written Word of his Father in the Old Testament. Each temptation was rebutted with the words: "*It is written*", followed by the appropriate words of Scripture. "*The sword of the Spirit, which is the word of God*" (Ephesians 6:17) pierced the temptation at its heart and ensured the victory of Christ.

Even so, we must have the armour of prayer. Prayer was the Lord's refuge and comfort. It was a source of great blessing for him. If we faithfully ask God for help in our battle against sin, it will always be forthcoming:

> "*Let us therefore come boldly unto the throne of grace, that we may obtain mercy, and find grace to* **help in time of need**."
>
> (Hebrews 4:16)

> "*So that we may boldly say, The Lord is my helper, and I will not fear what man shall do unto me.*" (Hebrews 13:6)

The believer who passes into the family of God by faith and

baptism becomes a son to be cared for in every way: to be chastised from time to time, to be led in paths of righteousness for His name's sake, and to be blessed with strength from God in the life to be lived as he submits to the yoke of the Lord Jesus Christ. From morn to night, from day to day, a whole life long he hears the word of the Father:

"I will never leave thee, nor forsake thee."　　　　(Hebrews 13:5)

APPENDIX I

HOLY SPIRIT GIFTS AND HOLY SPIRIT GUIDANCE

SHORTLY before he ascended to heaven the Lord Jesus Christ made this promise to his apostles:

> "*Ye shall receive power, after that the Holy Spirit is come upon you: and ye shall be witnesses unto me.*" (Acts 1:8)

This promise was fulfilled in Jerusalem on the day of Pentecost. The Holy Spirit was poured down from heaven and forthwith the apostles stood forth openly in the city. A huge assembly of Jews from Palestine, Mediterranean lands and the Middle East flocked to hear, "*every man in his own language*" (Acts 2:6), the wonderful works of God proclaimed as never before. Everyone was amazed.

Peter explained that he and his fellow apostles were proclaiming the message given to them by the power of the Holy Spirit, and that their ability to do so in tongues intelligible to their hearers had also been bestowed by the same Spirit:

> "*Therefore being by the right hand of God exalted, and having received of the Father the promise of the Holy Spirit, he (Christ) hath shed forth this, which ye now see and hear.*" (Acts 2:33)

Peter repeated this same explanation when he later wrote a letter to believers concerning:

> "*the things, which are now reported unto you by them that have preached the gospel unto you with the Holy Spirit sent down from heaven.*"
> (1 Peter 1:12)

We are therefore assured that the message of the apostles (called the "*apostles' doctrine*", Acts 2:42) was precisely and only that which the Father and the Son wished to declare. Furthermore, their message was attested by speaking in a variety of languages, and by many signs and wonders such as miracles of healing and of raising the dead in the name of Christ (see Acts 2:43; 3:4 – 7).

The spoken word and the signs following provided a firm foundation for faith. Thousands believed and, because the visitors to Jerusalem carried the message away with them, the Gospel spread outwards to distant lands.

Groups of believers in widely separated places needed constant help in order to preserve the faith they had espoused, and to "*grow in grace, and in the knowledge of our Lord and Saviour Jesus Christ*" (2 Peter 3:18). It was physically impossible for the apostles to spend long periods in each place, although they clearly travelled ceaselessly in their labours for Christ. There was as yet no New Testament from which the whole of the apostles' message might be read and related to the Old Testament which was already in very wide circulation. The inspired written accounts of the Gospel writers and the special letters to individual congregations and individuals came into existence in the first century, for the most part before AD 70, and these — or copies of them — would quickly be known over a wide area. Moreover these writings were themselves a part of Scripture given by the Holy Spirit.

Special Powers

But how was the time-gap between the spoken message of the apostles and the divinely given account in writing to be bridged? The Holy Spirit was the means used by the Lord Jesus Christ. In addition to the apostles, certain other persons were given special powers which were designed to support the believers in the various congregations. These persons were prophets, evangelists, pastors and teachers (Ephesians 4:11), and the widespread gifts were those described as follows:

> "*For to one is given by the Spirit the word of wisdom; to another the word of knowledge by the same Spirit . . . to another the gifts of healing by the same Spirit; to another the working of miracles; to another prophecy; to another discerning of spirits; to another divers kinds of tongues; to another the interpretation of tongues . . .*"(1 Corinthians 12:8 – 10)

By this means members of each congregation or ecclesia were

equipped with gifts to help them exercise functions for the instruction, correction, exhortation and public witness of the group. No one had all of the gifts and the gifted members were therefore made dependent on one another for the total work.

None of the gifts provided for one member to pass on gifts to other members. Only the apostles were able to do this (*see* Acts 8:14 – 18).

We do not know precisely when the bestowal and operation of the gifts ceased to happen. That they would so cease is provided for in the words of the Spirit by Paul: "*Whether there be prophecies, they shall fail; whether there be tongues, they shall cease; whether there be knowledge, it shall vanish away*" (1 Corinthians 13:8). Moreover, the cessation of these gifts is coupled with the survival of three principal virtues: "*But now abideth faith, hope, love, these three*" (1 Corinthians 13:13, R.V.). Faith and hope will give place to reality and fulfilment at the return of the Lord Jesus Christ. Therefore the gifts were to cease before the return of Jesus because their cessation would leave faith and hope still unfulfilled.

By the end of the first century the New Testament had been completed and became available for all to read as the circulation and collation of the twenty-seven individual books gradually took place. In this way all of the ecclesias would have available to them the full accounts of the life of Christ together with the ministry and letters of the apostles. It is significant that God did not inspire any writings after the end of the first century. By this time, therefore, the gifts may have commenced to fade. From non-Biblical sources we learn that during the second century men arose who merely simulated possession of the gifts, evidence in itself that the true gifts were no longer widespread.

From time to time throughout the following centuries there have been groups claiming that once again the gifts were available to men. In modern times the Pentecostal and Charismatic movements have made such claims. Speaking with tongues, known as *glossolalia*, is the gift which exceeds all others in claims of this kind. Rarely is it claimed as an ability to speak foreign languages in the manner of the apostles (see Acts 2:4,6,11). Instead it is said that those concerned are given ecstatic utterance which they do not themselves understand but have to depend on others to provide the interpretation.

For the most part this manifestation is made known in meetings of committed members of the groups concerned. It is not used as a principal means for preaching the Gospel as they see it, and this is contrary to the direct instruction and practice laid down in Scripture (1 Corinthians 14:22 – 25). Indeed, there is no evidence whatsoever that the modern phenomenon is in any way related to the gift of tongues as described in the New Testament. Nor is it unique to "Christian" groups. The same occurrences are to be found amongst members of eastern religions and in the Mormon movement. We believe that the phenomenon arises from "religious excitation", an emotional state of mind, and not from any action by God through His Holy Spirit.

Similar considerations arise about the supposed "gift of healing". Healings wrought by the apostles were never carried out at "healing meetings". There was no religious service, no emotional fervour produced by hymn-singing and preaching, but instead direct and positive healing in the open, on the spot, for all to see; or in private by an apostle (see Acts 3:1 – 10 and 9:36 – 41). These miracles followed the pattern of the healings of the Lord Jesus Christ. For the most part, the Lord healed by a touch or by the spoken word and the results were evident.

Both the procedures and the results of modern healings are widely different from those of New Testament times. There are many failures and often a lack of permanence in the improvement achieved. Such was not the case with the apostles. In those days, a man who had never walked was healed in an instant and could run for joy (Acts 3:1 – 10). A dead woman was restored to life by the quiet prayer of one apostle and his spoken word to the corpse (Acts 9:36 – 41). Healers of today belong to non-Christian groups, Spiritualists, and others as well as Charismatics. The Holy Spirit cannot be the common factor. It is much more likely to be a result of the power of the mind of the healer upon the mind and will of the person who has come to be healed. Whatever may prove to be the explanation, there is a far more basic enquiry which must be conducted into the claims of those who profess to be moved by the Spirit.

The Test of Bible Teaching

The Bible provides us with a very positive test by which to determine the validity of the claims of those who say they are speaking or working by the direct influence of the Holy Spirit. The test does not question the conviction or sincerity of those concerned, and it does not question the subjective experiences which they are often said to have had. The test goes to the root of the matter: What is the doctrinal content of the message? Does it accord with Bible teaching? In other words, in our day, does the Gospel preached by, say, Charismatics, harmonize with the teachings of Christ and his apostles? It is for this reason that we are commanded to *"try the spirits whether they are of God: because many false prophets are gone out into the world"* (1 John 4:1).

Alongside this standard, the widespread evangelical movement is found to be woefully astray from Bible teaching. What they have to say about life after death, the devil, the Godhead and the Lord Jesus Christ, baptism and many other matters does not ring true. It is incredible that a community truly gifted by the Spirit could be basically at fault in this way, not in the beliefs of a few individuals amongst them, but in the message of the movement as a whole. When we examine carefully what is taking place, we discover that they place more stress on guidance by the Spirit than on the guidance in true teaching by the Word of God.

Guidance by the Holy Spirit

The foregoing considerations lead us to examine another feature of those who claim possession of the Holy Spirit, namely, claims to special guidance by the Spirit. Decision making is said to be determined by the Spirit. Answers are said to be provided by the Spirit in one way or another. It is not simply claimed that everything is put to the Lord in prayer (a practice with which we would have no cavil), but rather that explicit replies are given. All kinds of coincidences and "evidences" are adduced in support of this way of decision making.

We believe that this approach arises from a mistaken and confused understanding of Bible teaching. The root of the problem lies in an attitude to the authority of Scripture. The Bible is a book filled with guidance. Most of the questions of daily life are already fully answered within the pages of the Bible which is meant to be *"a lamp unto my feet, and a light unto my path"* (Psalm 119:105). The Book of Proverbs declares: *"For the commandment is a lamp; and the law is light; and reproofs of instruction are the way of life"* (6:23). Prayerful and regular Bible reading ensures that our feet are shown the path in which we should walk. The Bible is the Holy Spirit's book of guidance.

It is sometimes said by those who claim that the Spirit gives them guidance that such guidance is sought only where Scripture is silent. The writer's experience of several such claimants is that they seek guidance in areas where the Bible is quite clear in its teaching, and claim to be guided even when what they do is contrary to the direct teaching of the Word of God. In other words, "the Spirit" was made to over-ride the Word of God, and this conflict of authority lies at the base of the error in approach to spiritual decision making.

The disciple is assured that "*all things work together for good to them that love God*" (Romans 8:28). The lives of true believers are in the Lord's hands, and we are to seek Him constantly in prayer for His blessings on our journey through life. He has not promised to reveal to us openly what we should do. Provided that we are following the instruction of the Word of God and prayerfully seek the Lord's blessing and help in fulfilling His commands, we know that His oversight will ensure that life's path will lead us in the steps of the Master, and bring us safely, if we continue in faith, to everlasting life at the return of Christ.

Choice is one of the key functions of the life of a disciple. He must constantly decide between the alternatives which present themselves in everyday living. His decisions should be based on the word of the Bible. It is not a Scripturally acceptable method to shrink from making spiritual choices by handing everything over to the Lord or by asking God for answers. Revelation in this way is not promised in the Bible. We are expected to exercise our minds on the problems of life in the light of Bible teaching and in prayerful submission to God.

The Bible abounds in clear teaching which urges the believer to make the right choice based upon the principles set out in Scripture. For example:

"*I have set before you life and death, blessing and cursing: therefore choose life.*" (Deuteronomy 30:19)

"*Choose you this day whom ye will serve.*" (Joshua 24:15)

"*Good and upright is the Lord: therefore will he teach sinners in the way. The meek will he guide in judgment: and the meek will he teach his way. All the paths of the Lord are mercy and truth unto such as keep his covenant and his testimonies . . . What man is he that feareth the Lord? him shall he teach in the way that he shall choose.*"
(Psalm 25:8 – 10, 12)

"*All scripture is given by inspiration of God, and is profitable for*

130

doctrine, for reproof, for correction, for instruction in righteousness: that the man of God may be perfect, throughly furnished unto all good works."

(2 Timothy 3:16 – 17)

The Bible — Divine Instructor

The Word of God is the divine instructor of the mind and provides us with ample guidance on the everyday affairs of life. Therein is set forth clear teaching on the choices to be made in almost every aspect of Christian living. We neglect it at our peril. Moreover the Word of God is food for the mind and strengthens us in making the Christlike choice. If we humbly accept the teaching of the Word and resolve to follow it, we can rightly seek the blessing of God in prayer. He has promised never to leave us or to forsake us. When our choice is difficult to resolve even with the Bible in hand and on the heart, our course is to commit our way to the Lord in prayer and, without expecting direct revelation from Him, proceed to do in faith that which we believe to be wise before Him.

These simple guidelines are sufficient for the needs of life. Paul gave detailed tuition to disciples in his own time, many of whom had Spirit gifts, and concluded by saying:

"And now, brethren, I commend you to God, and to the word of his grace, which is able to build you up, and to give you an inheritance among all them which are sanctified."

(Acts 20:32)

15

A WORLD OF EVIL

THE problem of evil has greatly exercised the minds of the world's thinkers. All kinds of woes, sorrows, disasters, diseases and suffering afflict mankind, and it is not surprising that men have sought to find explanations for them, and to devise ways of alleviating or removing them. It would be unrealistic for us to ignore this important element of human experience. Faith must cope with these forms of evil, either by arriving at satisfying reasons for them, or, perhaps, simply by accepting them in trust without asking questions or exercising thought about them.

Evils can be broken down into two general classes: the first includes all of the natural occurrences such as storms, tempests, earthquakes, volcanic eruptions, accidents, disease and death; and the second covers man-made evils such as violence, war, political and industrial strife, exploitation of people and of their environment, the consequences of immorality, drug addiction and greed, and a host of other things which we have experienced, read about or feared.

Throughout the ages some men have attributed some or all of these things to forces, spirits and gods, outside the human sphere, and have taken what they have deemed to be appropriate action to avoid or minimise their occurrence. Codes of behaviour were said to be effective in warding off disasters or to reduce their effects. Rituals and sacrifices have been regarded from time immemorial as means of appeasing the gods.

On the other hand, it has been thought possible to call in aid against one's enemies the vast armoury of the spirit powers.

Vestigial traces of some of these practices can be found in some of the superstitious practices in almost every society. Charms, mascots, words and other things are thought by some to ward off possible dangers. Many people take steps of these kinds with explanations like, "You never know", "Just in case" or "It is better to be on the safe side". Conversely, many people seek means whereby they hope to procure luck or good fortune. Some of these devices are used by men and women who would also regard themselves as religious.

In addition many people in the 20th century believe that the Devil, or Satan, and demons are the cause of many of our worst troubles. We do not at this stage propose to examine the doctrine of the Devil and Satan, which we reserve for the next chapter, but we do intend examining whether God is in control of the evils which befall us.

Tragedy and Harm

All of us have a degree of fear about unseen evils. That fear is enhanced by the uncertainty which arises because we cannot see into the future or in any way truly determine what may happen in the days ahead. What follows is written from the standpoint of the common lot of mankind, and in the knowledge that some readers will have suffered considerably from one or more of the ills which befall us.

We should do well to bear in mind, however, that man's experiences are by no means uniformly evil. For every tragedy or harmful event it is possible to instance some completely opposite occurrence. There are bad harvests, but there are also good ones; there are imbeciles, and there are geniuses; and, there are infant deaths and cases of remarkable longevity.

Is God in control of the circumstances which produce evil for man? Or must we look elsewhere, to evil powers, for example, for an explanation? Let us look at those ills which come from the violence of nature — storm, flood, volcanic eruption, earthquake and the like. What does the Bible say about these things? The answer throughout Scripture is that all of these things are in God's hands. Otherwise how could God make statements like these?

"While the earth remaineth, seedtime and harvest, and cold and heat, and summer and winter, and day and night shall not cease."

(Genesis 8:22)

133

> *"Your Father in heaven . . . maketh his sun to rise on the evil and on the good, and sendeth rain on the just and on the unjust."*
>
> (Matthew 5:45)

> *"Ye should turn unto the living God which made heaven and earth, and the sea, and all things that are therein . . . he did good, and gave us rain from heaven, and fruitful seasons . . . ."* (Acts 14:15 – 17)

> *"He sendeth the springs into the valleys . . . they give drink to every beast of the field . . . the earth is satisfied with the fruit of thy works . . . He appointed the moon for seasons . . . the earth is full of thy riches. So is this great and wide sea."* (Psalm 104:10 – 13, 19, 24 – 25)

We must conclude, therefore, as we did earlier in this book, that nature is God at work. Moreover God's beneficence is, in these cases, bestowed irrespective of man's behaviour. We must therefore not seek to attribute bad events to bad deeds by the people who suffer or good events to the goodness of those who benefit from them. This is not necessarily so. It might be said that the Scriptures we have instanced concern only good things from God, but do not show that God is involved in serious evils from natural causes. We have no hesitation in saying that there is no evidence whatsoever in the Bible that natural evils come from any kind of evil powers. The very first evils following the sin of Adam and Eve were brought about by God – death and the curse on the ground. The adverse conditions in agriculture were of God:

> *"Cursed is the ground for thy sake; in sorrow shalt thou eat of it all the days of thy life; thorns also and thistles shall it bring forth to thee."*
>
> (Genesis 3:17 – 18)

When the plagues came upon Egypt in the time of Moses, we read:

> *"The Lord brought an east wind upon the land all that day, and all that night; and when it was morning, the east wind brought the locusts . . . over all the land of Egypt . . . (then Pharaoh said) I have sinned . . . and the Lord turned a mighty strong west wind, which took away the locusts . . . "* (Exodus 10:13 – 19)

When Jonah tried to run away from God to escape the task which God had given him, we read:

> *"But the Lord sent out a great wind into the sea, and there was a mighty tempest in the sea, so that the ship was like to be broken."*
>
> (Jonah 1:4)

We have established, therefore, that from time to time God has brought about evil circumstances in nature as punishment for particular sins. But what about seemingly indiscriminate evil such as arises from, say, a hurricane or an earthquake? We shall discuss this later on when we come to examine the problem of suffering. At this point we can say with confidence that the Bible never attributes indiscriminate sufferings to supernatural evil powers.

Suffering and Disease

There is one whole book in the Bible devoted to a consideration of the problems of tragedy and suffering. The book of Job describes what happened to a man of that name of whom God said at the outset that he was *"perfect, upright, and one that feared God"* (Job 1:1). Shortly afterwards he experienced a succession of sudden disasters which took away his earthly possessions, killed his children and left Job himself with a loathsome disease. This devastation of his life Job never attributed to an enemy or to evil powers, nor did the Lord God. Job said:

> *"Naked came I out of my mother's womb, and naked shall I return thither: the Lord gave, and the Lord hath taken away; blessed be the name of the Lord."* (1:21)

> *"What? shall we receive good at the hand of God, and shall we not receive evil?"* (2:10)

Job had three friends who came to see him in his distress. They were utterly confounded by what they saw. When their initial shock had passed they commenced a concerted and prolonged attack on Job's character by attributing his trials to deep-seated faults in Job's heart or grave shortcomings in his conduct, all of which were totally untrue. But they had no other way in which they could account for what had happened to their friend.

Whilst knowing that the accusations were false, Job in seeking to defend himself was driven to question the wisdom of God. Thus the friends and Job took the classic stance of seeking to find an immediate prior cause for the evil which had occurred.

In the closing chapters of the book, the Lord God speaks to Job. Unexpectedly the Lord's words provide no detailed exposition of the problem which the four men had grappled with. Instead the Lord opens up the wonders of creation with their evidences of the marvellous wisdom of God. Job acknowledges his error in thinking that God's wisdom might err and repents in dust and ashes. The

Lord accepts him, tells him to pray for his friends and rebukes them saying, "*Ye have not spoken of me the thing that is right, as my servant Job hath*" (42:7).

Man has wrestled with the problem of suffering and has often alleged that God is wrong. Job's experiences should cause us to think otherwise. It is ironical that man should make allegations about God in cases of unexplained suffering whilst failing to remember that man himself causes untold suffering to others when pursuing his own purposes or principles. The Book of Job has lessons for everyone.

Many questions are asked about the random way in which disease strikes us. It can afflict young or old, good or bad people, and sometimes passes by the people we might think were deserving of it, only to fall upon someone who is seemingly innocent or good. Is disease outside God's control or, if it is not wholly outside, is some of it caused by some evil power or influence?

There is nothing in the Bible to suggest that when disease occurs it is always attributable to particular sin by the sufferer. There are obvious cases to the contrary, some cases of venereal disease for example, but we have to remember that such diseases, too, are passed on to those who were not participants in the original immoral acts. The Bible does not invite us to assign each of our sicknesses to the sin or sins we have committed.

On one occasion Jesus was asked specifically about a man born blind, whether or not his condition was on account of sin. Jesus replied:

> "*Neither hath this man sinned, nor his parents.*"   (John 9:3)

On another occasion, a tragedy had occurred in Jerusalem and a tower had collapsed killing eighteen people. There were some who thought that the eighteen were guilty of sin and that their death was a direct punishment. However, Jesus said:

> "*Or those eighteen upon whom the tower in Siloam fell, and slew them, think ye that they were sinners above all men that dwelt in Jerusalem? I tell you, Nay . . .*"   (Luke 13:4 – 5)

Jesus accepted that there would be tragedies in a world where sinners live, without relating the accidents directly to particular sins of the victims involved.

There are, however, clear examples of divine judgement by disasters of which the Flood in the days of Noah and the

136

destruction of Sodom and Gomorrah are well known. Sometimes God has inflicted disease upon particular sinners:

> *"And after all this the Lord smote him . . . with an incurable disease."* (recorded in 2 Chronicles 21:18 about a king of Judah).

> *"Immediately, because Herod did not give praise to God, an angel of the Lord struck him down, and he was eaten by worms and died."*
>
> (Acts 12:23, N.I.V.)

The Lord Jesus Christ demonstrated his power over all kinds of disease when he carried out healings of every kind. These included those cases which are attributed to demons or unclean spirits, the nature of which we consider in chapter 17. The relationship of Satan to disease will be considered in chapter 16.

In addition to his supremacy over disease and death, the Lord Jesus exercised sway over the elements when he stilled the storm on Galilee. It is evident that the Scriptures are teaching us to look to Jesus the Son of God as the divine remedy for the world's ills. Evils occur within the containing power of the Lord God. They are not out of control or brought about by evil powers outside of the human sphere. Evil came as a consequence and punishment for sin. Evil will be removed when sin and death are banished as a result of Christ's return to the earth.

We must however take another look at the feelings of unfairness or injustice which arise in the minds of many people when disaster or disease remove young or innocent or "good" people. We may in fact feel outraged at such times.

The problem is particularly acute for anyone who believes in God. If we do not believe in God, we may have a philosophical problem, but we have no ultimate authority to appeal to. Indeed, if we believe in the randomness of circumstances which are said to have produced evolution, we must not be surprised if that randomness does things which displease us. In any case, if there is no God, who decides what is "right", "fair" and "proper"?

Consequences of Sin

In the following paragraphs, we attempt a line of thought which can prove helpful. Of course, no one can answer all the questions which arise, especially the ones about particular cases. What follows provides a basis for solving some of the problems. We have arrived at the conclusions purely by reading Scripture.

When God created man and placed him under a clear command,

137

He granted him freedom of choice. Thus Adam and Eve were told what would happen to them if they disobeyed. Nevertheless they were allowed to choose for themselves what they would do. It is implicit in this arrangement that a wrong choice, freely arrived at, would result in very serious consequences for the sinners and for their progeny in due course. These consequences included:

> Fear of death
> Death itself
> Sorrows together with hard toil because of the cursed ground, as long as life lasted.

All of these evils came from God. They were God's response to sin which is the greatest evil of all. Some people have found it difficult to accept that God creates evil. He does, and the following verses illustrate this fact:

> *"I (God) form the light, and create darkness:*
> *I make peace, and create evil:*
> *I the Lord do all these things."* (Isaiah 45:7)

> *"Shall there be evil in a city, and the Lord hath not done it?"*
> (Amos 3:6)

Evil came into the world because of sin. Whilst we may wonder at the extent of the evil, we can at least understand why it is there. What we are pursuing, however, is the feeling of outrage against our sense of "fairness" when evil falls on good people or on children.

Man's Freedom

We suggest that a great deal of man's suffering arises from his freedom of choice. When sinners have freedom of choice, they will from time to time produce evil for themselves or for others. The alternative is for God always to intervene when evil might result. Man would then be reduced to the role of a puppet.

Take man's violence against his fellow man as an example of evil springing from man's freedom of choice. When violence extends into war the evil is widespread and many innocent victims die, as when cities are bombed. We are often not entirely consistent in our attitudes. Perhaps we shrug our shoulders when the innocent die during wartime, saying, "That's war", yet at the same time feel a sense of outrage when a young mother is smitten by the scourge of cancer.

138

Man's freedom permits him to invent all kinds of things, some of which will bring random suffering or death. The invention of the aeroplane is an example of this. Hundreds die each year when aircraft crash. We accept this as one of the consequences of "progress", and many of us board aircraft knowing that accidents can take place.

Or more simply, man's freedom allows him to live in inhospitable places where he has to fight against the elements or take the risk of disaster should he reside in earthquake, hurricane or volcanic regions. Many disasters of this kind occur because men have chosen to live in such localities. None of us would wish to remove the freedom of choice any more than we seek to prevent our children learning to swim or climb or cycle or play games. Human life has its risks and some of them we choose to take when we could avoid them.

Man's freedom to enter into marriage and to choose his own partner is regarded as a "right". Most of us do not want arranged or forced marriages. But from our freedom of choice we may discover that there are such incompatibilities between partners as to result in deformities or deficiencies at the birth of children. It is a risk we take. Man's liberty to break up his marriage — and this, too, is increasingly regarded as one of man's freedoms — has brought misery to untold thousands of children and forsaken partners. Our sense of "outrage" seems to be diminished when man's freedom is at stake.

Let us now look further into the subject of disease and suffering. It is in this area that most of our problems of understanding or acceptance arise. We have indicated that a large part of the world's evils, even in the field of suffering, is brought about by man himself. Even so, there is a sizeable remainder which simply seems "to happen".

Why should we have a feeling of unfairness or harshness when disease strikes in a random fashion? What are the alternatives? Are we asking for no disease at all? If so, we are not accepting the plain teaching of Scripture that man is mortal. Moreover, we are then creating another evil, namely, that blatant sinners and everyone who is grossly evil should also escape from disease. Or, are we asking for the immediate punishment of individual sins, so that disease is directly related to sins? This would mean that men and women would be smitten with punishment at that instant — without regard to repentance — with a thousand and one other

139

immediate ills for other people as a result. Or are we asking for a deferred sentence, but nevertheless related to our individual sins? It will be seen that life under those conditions would be far more intolerable than it is alleged to be now. The only practical way seems to be to allow man freedom within his mortality and to allow disease to work with similar freedom.

Similarly we can consider the incidence of death. We may find it hard to bear that some die young or with exemplary characters, whilst others live seemingly too long or with less good reason for their continued existence. God has made it plain that all of us will die. It is the timing and manner of death which raise problems for us. Would we like everyone to live a stipulated length of time? The psychological problems under such a system would be disastrous. It is the uncertainty regarding death which creates optimism and hope, as well as room for tragedy. It is a merciful provision that we are not given a label at birth telling us the date when we must die. Even the cause and manner of death are left open, and that surely is how most of us would want it to be, if we have to die in the end. The comparatively few cases which offend our sense of justice are totally overwhelmed by the "benefits" which come from the system which God has instituted.

We need to remember that the Lord Jesus Christ did not question the ways in which disease and death came upon men, but he provided a consolation which makes them bearable. He offered eternal life and joy to those who, despite present circumstances, would seek God through him.

The flexibility which exists in the conditions which God has created allows for repentance and hope. Man does not live under the threat of immediate punishment nor does he find himself deprived of his freedom of choice.

The summary of all of the foregoing observations is that God is in control and there is no other power which is a source of potential blessing or cursing. God's grace and goodness provide the conditions and sustenance for life, and He does this generally without regard to man's behaviour. From time to time God has intervened and has said He will do so again.

Meanwhile the source of man's troubles is his mortal and sinful nature. Many of man's worst afflictions arise from man's own actions. Many evils arise from man's freedom of choice in things concerning everyday life. God does not punish man sin by sin as life goes along. Mortality demands that sooner or later we shall die, and God has so arranged in His mercy that for each individual the future remains unknown. Man can live in hope.

Taking the picture as a whole, we conclude that the way in which mortality works is the wisest and most merciful of all the alternatives, given the condition that God has seen fit to allow man freedom of choice.

Finally, there is a function of suffering which, though involving the same evils we have been considering, can be different in accomplishment. In the process of development of character which God desires for His children, there is an element of discipline and chastisement. Trials of one kind and another occur for those under God's care in order that faith, hope and patience might prove themselves.

> *"But God is faithful, who will not suffer you to be tempted above that ye are able; but will with the temptation also make a way to escape, that ye may be able to bear it."* (1 Corinthians 10:13)

What He desires is that, in response to this discipline, our characters will mature and we shall show forth attributes which are good and Godly.

> *"If ye endure chastening, God dealeth with you as with sons; for what son is he whom the father chasteneth not? . . . Now no chastening for the present seemeth to be joyous, but grievous: nevertheless afterward it yieldeth the peaceable fruit of righteousness unto them which are exercised thereby."* (Hebrews 12:7 – 11)

Evils will not continue for ever. God has promised to remove them completely when He fills the earth with His glory. The final picture which God gives us of the earth removes all our questions and dissolves all our fears:

> *"God shall wipe away all tears from their eyes; and there shall be no more death, neither sorrow, nor crying, neither shall there be any more pain."* (Revelation 21:4)

16

JESUS AND THE DEVIL

THE importance of this subject becomes clear to anyone who reads the New Testament. Even a superficial reading reveals that the Lord Jesus Christ is deeply involved in the problem of the Devil or Satan. Whatever or whoever the Devil is, its existence and influence are settled once and for all by Christ who is the victor. When the Bible story is complete, the Devil has been eradicated.

As we proceed with an examination of Scripture teaching, we shall need to take careful note of both what is and what is not said about the Devil and Satan.

If we were reading the Greek New Testament we would become aware that quite different words are used for "devil" and "Satan", and that these words are employed both with and without the definite article. It will be helpful to set down the words and their various translations in our English New Testament:

(1) *diabolos*   This is translated as "a devil" and "the devil" but *never* as "devils". Other translations are "false accuser" and "slanderer".

(2) *Satanas*   This is the Greek form of a Hebrew or Aramaic word and is always translated in the New Testament as "Satan", although as mentioned before it is often preceded in Greek by the definite article.

(3) *daimōn*   This is used only five times and is translated once as "the devil", twice as "the devils" and twice as "devils".

(4) *daimonizomai* this occurs more frequently and is translated as "possessed with a (or the) devil", "possessed with devils", "possessed of the devils", "vexed with a devil" and "hath a devil".

(5) *daimonion* Used frequently and always translated as "a devil", "the devil", "devil", "the devils", except once when the translation is "gods".

We shall consider items (3), (4) and (5) in the next chapter when we examine the subject of demons.

It will be seen that the word *diabolos* is not a unique name for a person or thing. It is a noun which describes certain kinds of people:

> "*Even so must their wives (the wives of deacons) be grave, not* **slanderers**, *sober, faithful in all things.*"   (1 Timothy 3:11)

> "*The aged women likewise, that they be in behaviour as becometh holiness, not* **false accusers**"   (Titus 2:3)

> "*In the last days . . . men shall be . . . unthankful, unholy, . . . truce-breakers,* **false accusers**.*"   (2 Timothy 3:1 – 3)

These verses tell us the *meaning* of the word *diabolos*. It is most useful to remember this when we consider the word "devil" which is not a translation but instead an anglicised form of the Greek word. For example, the first of the examples given above could have been rendered as: "Even their wives must be grave, not devils, sober, faithful in all things". In fact we have such an example in our English version: "*Have not I chosen you twelve, and one of you is a devil* (*diabolos*)" (John 6:70). Here we have a lead from the Lord Jesus Christ as to the meaning of the word. Judas Iscariot took his place among those who would falsely accuse the Lord Jesus Christ.

When we come to consider the special use which the New Testament makes of the *diabolos*, we shall find it useful to remember the root meanings of the word as given above. Here is a complete list excluding only those of the kind in the above examples:

Matthew 4:1,5,8,11; 13:39; 25:41. Luke 4:2,3,5,6,13; 8:12. John 8:44; 13:2. Acts 10:38; 13:10*. Ephesians 4:27; 6:11. 1 Timothy 3:6,7. 2 Timothy 2:26. Hebrews 2:14. James 4:7. 1 Peter 5:8*. 1 John 3:8,10. Jude 9. Revelation 2:10; 12:9*; 20:2*,10.

* indicates those verses where the definite article is shown in English but not in Greek.

Some readers may be surprised to learn that the words "the devil" do not occur in our English Old Testament. This significant fact must be given its due weight when arriving at the Bible's overall teaching on this subject. There are two Hebrew words which have given rise to the translation "devils". Their meanings are related to the topic of demons which we consider later.

We noted earlier that the Hebrew word Satan has been carried through into Greek and English. When the word first occurs it does not carry the sense of being a title or a proper name. Instead it is translated by our English word adversary. Here are some examples:

> *"And the angel of the Lord stood in the way for an adversary against him ... and the angel of the Lord said ... I went out to withstand thee (R.V. for an adversary)."* (Numbers 22:22,32)

> *"For my love they are my adversaries."* (Psalm 109:4)

The following are other occurrences:

1 Samuel 29:4; 2 Samuel 19:22; 1 Kings 5:4; 11:14,23,25. To these should be added a number of instances in which the almost identical Hebrew word is used in the sense of "being an adversary": Psalm 38:20; 71:13; 109:4,20,29.

Most frequently, however, the word comes through untranslated and appears as Satan. Sometimes in Hebrew the word Satan is preceded by the definite article and the same is true in Greek in the New Testament. Here are all the occurrences of the word Satan in both Hebrew and Greek which appear in our English Bible as Satan:

Old Testament
With the definite article: Job 1:6,7(twice),8,9,12(twice); 2:1,2(twice), 3,4,6(twice),7; Zechariah 3:1,2.
Without the definite article: 1 Chronicles 21:1; Psalm 109:6.

New Testament
With the definite article: Matthew 12:26; Luke 10:18; 11:18; 13:16; 22:31; John 13:27; Acts 5:3; 26:18; Romans 16:20; 1 Corinthians 5:5; 7:5; 2 Corinthians 2:11; 11:14; 1 Thessalonians 2:18; 2 Thessalonians 2:9; 1 Timothy 1:20; 5:15; Revelation 2:9,13,24; 3:9; 12:9; 20:2,7.
Without the definite article: Matthew 4:10; 16:23; Mark 3:23; 8:33; Luke 4:8; 22:3; 2 Corinthians 12:7.

144

Let us now proceed with our investigations. A reading of the Old Testament will reveal that

God never warned any one against the Devil;

God never warned any one against Satan.

It is very difficult to believe that this could be the case if, as many say, the Devil or Satan is the prime cause of the world's troubles and is the Chief Trouble Maker in person. Furthermore, if it were true, as many assert, that the serpent in the garden in Eden was Satan in disguise, why did not God warn Adam and Eve and, later, everyone else against the incursions of Satan into human affairs? It is no answer to point to the New Testament, since that Book was not in the hands of the servants of God of Old Testament times, and yet they proved to be faithful and many of them are listed in the catalogue of worthies in Hebrews 11.

But there is even more to come. The Old Testament never attributes temptation to do evil to anything other than man and his works. Even at the time of the Flood and of God's judgement upon that world, nothing is said about Satan or the Devil:

"And God saw that the wickedness of man was great in the earth, and that every imagination of the thoughts of his heart was only evil continually." (Genesis 6:5)

"The imagination of man's heart is evil from his youth." (Genesis 8:21)

No Old Testament character ever pleads with God that he has been tempted by a supernatural being. The Old Testament is silent on this subject. Man is held responsible for his sins and for the plight of mankind. His sources of temptation lie within himself and the world of man around him. Man is vulnerable to temptation.

Jesus' Temptations in the Wilderness

What then of the New Testament? In the first place, there is a considerable change of emphasis. The words Devil and Satan are given a prominence which is not found in the Old Testament. When Christ appears, the words are used with deliberate intent in the inspired Word of God. It is as though the two words have a special significance in relation to him. Here are some of the Scriptures:

> *"Then was Jesus led up of the Spirit into the wilderness to be tempted of the devil."* (Matthew 4:1)

> *"And he was there in the wilderness forty days, tempted of Satan; and was with the wild beasts; and the angels ministered unto him."* (Mark 1:13)

> *"Forasmuch then as the children (the people whom Jesus came to save) are partakers of flesh and blood, he also himself likewise took part of the same; that through death he might destroy him that had the power of death, that is, the devil; and deliver them who through fear of death were all their lifetime subject to bondage."* (Hebrews 2:14 – 15)

From these verses we gather that:

In the temptation of Christ, the words Devil and Satan are interchangeable. The meanings "accuser" or "adversary" would certainly describe the nature of the temptation.

Jesus is joining battle with the Devil or Satan. The battle is in respect of temptation. There is no sense of a display of power or any application of it by the Devil during the temptation.

In order to "destroy the devil", Jesus shared our nature, flesh and blood. It is impossible not to conclude that there must be a relationship between flesh and blood, temptation and the Devil; and, furthermore, the destruction of the devil is achieved *through death* which must indicate that death and the devil are related.

Our next step must be to examine the New Testament teaching about temptation. What is the main source of man's temptation? Here are the clear teachings of Scripture:

> *"It is no more I that do it, but sin that dwelleth in me. For I know that in me (that is, in my flesh) dwelleth no good thing: for to will is present with me; but how to perform that which is good I find not . . . When I would do good, evil is present with me . . . So then with the mind I myself serve the law of God; but with the flesh the law of sin."* (Romans 7:17 – 25)

> *"The flesh lusteth against the Spirit, and the Spirit against the flesh . . . now the works of the flesh are . . . these; adultery, fornication, uncleanness, lasciviousness, idolatry, witchcraft, hatred, variance, emulations, wrath, strife, seditions, heresies, envyings, murders, drunkenness, revellings, and such like . . . "* (Galatians 5:17 – 21)

"For all that is in the world, the lust of the flesh, and the lust of the eyes, and the pride of life, is not of the Father, but is of the world. And the world passeth away, and the lust thereof: but he that doeth the will of God abideth for ever."   (1 John 2:16 – 17)

"He that committeth sin is of the devil; for the devil sinneth from the beginning. For this purpose the Son of God was manifested that he might destroy the works of the devil."   (1 John 3:8)

"Let no man say when he is tempted, I am tempted of God: for God cannot be tempted with evil, neither tempteth he any man: but every man is tempted, when he is drawn away of his own lust, and enticed. Then when lust hath conceived, it bringeth forth sin: and sin, when it is finished, bringeth forth death."   (James 1:13 – 15)

If it is true that one of the major causes of sin is a personal Devil, why then does the passage from James, quoted above, make no mention of this overwhelming fact? The same is true of the comprehensive exposition of the origin of sin and death, and the redeeming work of Christ in the first eight chapters of Romans. No mention whatsoever is made of the Devil and Satan in these chapters. Hebrews 2:14 demands Christ's involvement with the Devil. Why does Paul omit any mention of the devil from his account in Romans?

The Scriptures quoted above, and there are many more, tell us plainly the facts about the seedbed of lust and sin. It is the flesh. The flesh has its own natural appetites which are flesh-centred, self-centred, and therefore opposed to God. All of the world's evils described in Galatians 5 above are *"works of the flesh"*, and these are described in 1 John 3 as, *"the works of the devil"*. This must mean that there is a strong connection between "the flesh" and "the devil". If the devil has its roots in the flesh, which is the only reasonable conclusion from these verses, it follows that the way to overcome it is to enter into conflict with it on its own ground, flesh and blood. This is exactly what the Lord Jesus Christ is described as doing when he *"partook of flesh and blood"* that he might *"destroy him that hath the power of death, that is, the devil"* (Hebrews 2:14).

The Conquering of Sin

We believe that the temptation of the Lord Jesus Christ in the wilderness was primarily his battle against "the lust of the eyes, the lust of the flesh, and the pride of life", and not against a supernatural being. If this was the case, why do the records of the

147

temptation present us with two opposing parties, the Lord himself and the devil or Satan? Only in this way could it be made clear that what was taking place was altogether different from anything that had happened before. "The devil" was the best way in which to emphasise the nature of Christ's conflict. All men who had gone before had repeatedly succumbed to sin, even the best of men. They were engaged in a battle with sin by which they had been wounded many times. Sin had left its mark on them.

Christ was not like other men. Although entirely of our nature and tempted as we are tempted, Christ was victorious. He never sinned. Actual sin never secured a foothold in him. He was the only sinless one in a world of sinners; his was the only life in all history free from personal transgression.

To have described his temptation in words used about everyone else would have placed him amongst sinners in an unacceptable way. He was with them but not of them. Despite temptation sin itself never took any part of his heart and mind. He kept it out. More than that: he kept the whole of the surrounding world in all its sinfulness outside his citadel of righteousness. More than that: he broke with history and every dictate of human precedent. History was to begin anew in him.

There is little wonder then to find his temptations described as a battle with the Devil or Satan. It was. He was engaged in mortal combat with the natural instincts of his nature and with the comprehensive sinfulness of a whole world of sinners. The world was ruled by Sin and Christ was come to bring deliverance, to break the power of sin and death, to "destroy him that hath the power of death, that is, the devil".

But how does *the devil* have the power of death? The Scripture tells us that God inflicted death on Adam and Eve. In what way does the devil have that power? Scripture is crystal clear:

> "... *him that hath the power of death, that is the devil.*"
> (Hebrews 2:14)

> "*Ye are of your father the devil, and the lust of your father ye will do.* **He was a murderer** *from the beginning, and abode not in the truth, because there is no truth in him.*" (John 8:44)

> "*Wherefore, as by one man sin entered into the world, and death by sin, (and) so death passed upon all men ...*" (Romans 5:12)

> "*For if by one man's offence death reigned ...*" (Romans 5:17)

"As sin hath reigned unto death . . ."	(Romans 5:21)
"For the wages of sin is death . . ."	(Romans 6:23)
"The sting of death is sin . . ."	(1 Corinthians 15:56)

We now have an unmistakable connection linking lust, the flesh, the devil, sin and death. It is impossible to escape this Scriptural conclusion. The devil is responsible for death. Sin is responsible for death. The flesh is responsible for death:

> *"Be not deceived; God is not mocked: for whatsoever a man soweth, that shall he also reap. For he that soweth to his flesh shall of the flesh reap corruption . . ."* (Galatians 6:7,8)

We must conclude from Scripture that flesh is fundamentally disposed to sin. Our natural urges or lusts (described in 1 John 1:16 as *"the lust of the eyes, the lust of the flesh and the pride of life"*) will, if allowed full expression, produce sin which ends in death. This explains why human nature is described as *"sinful flesh"* (Romans 8:3), and why the same part of Scripture says, *"If ye live after the flesh, ye shall die"* (v. 13). How, then, do we explain the words "the devil", and the comment we have read that *"he was a murderer from the beginning"* (John 8:44)?

There can be but one answer to meet all the known facts: the devil and sinfulness are so inter-related that we must conclude that in the context of the Scriptures we have quoted they are describing the same thing. Man's capacity for sinfulness is the devil; and *"by one man sin entered into the world, and **death by sin**"* (Romans 5:12).

When Adam and Eve sinned by surrendering to desires aroused by the words of the serpent they brought death into the world. Paul expressed it in this way: *"Sin . . . deceived me . . . and slew me"* (Romans 7:11). Death was not introduced by some outside evil power; it was the direct result of sin. The command given by God contained its own penalty clause which God brought into effect. No one else was involved. In the same way it is God who will finally remove sin from the face of the earth at the end of the millennium. In other words: when sin came, death came: when sin goes, death goes.

We conclude therefore that the basic sinfulness of man, his natural selfish disposition, is the true meaning of "the devil", in the passages we have been considering. In one sense that meaning is true for the word "Satan", as well. Sinfulness is the direct adversary of God. But we must proceed to look at the two words a little further, because they are not always interchangeable. We shall discover that while the devil is satisfactorily described, at least in a substantial part, by human sinfulness, it also has some clear extensions of meaning in a wider sense; and Satan has some particular significances also. Here is a broad selection of other verses which will help us in arriving at these wider meanings:

"And he (Jesus) called them unto him, and said unto them in parables, How can Satan cast out Satan? And if a kingdom be divided against itself, that kingdom cannot stand. And if a house be divided against itself, that house cannot stand. And if Satan rise up against himself, and be divided, he cannot stand, but hath an end. No man can enter into a strong man's house, and spoil his goods, except he first bind the strong man; and then he will spoil his house." (Mark 3:23 – 27)

"But Peter said, Ananias, why hath Satan filled thine heart to lie to the Holy Spirit?" (Acts 5:3)

"Then Peter said unto her (Ananias' wife), How is it that ye have agreed together to tempt the Spirit of the Lord?" (Acts 5:9)

"There was a woman which had a spirit of infirmity eighteen years, and was bowed together, and could in no wise lift up herself. (Jesus said), Woman, thou art loosed from thine infirmity. And he laid his hands on her: and immediately she was made straight, and glorified God. (The Lord said), Ought not this woman, being a daughter of Abraham, whom Satan hath bound, lo, these eighteen years, be loosed from his bond on the sabbath day?" (Luke 13:11 – 16)

"In the name of the Lord Jesus Christ, when ye are gathered together, and my spirit, with the power of our Lord Jesus Christ, to deliver such an one (a Christian who became deeply immoral) unto Satan for the destruction of the flesh, that the spirit may be saved, in the day of the Lord Jesus." (1 Corinthians 5:4,5)

"And lest I (Paul) should be exalted above measure . . . there was given to me a thorn in the flesh, the messenger of Satan . . . lest I should be exalted above measure. For this thing I besought the Lord thrice, that it might depart from me. And he said unto me, My grace is sufficient for thee: for my strength is made perfect in weakness." (2 Corinthians 12:7 – 9)

"Some . . . concerning the faith have made shipwreck . . . whom I have delivered unto Satan, that they may learn not to blaspheme." (1 Timothy 1:19,20)

"Give none occasion to the adversary to speak reproachfully. For some are already turned aside after Satan." (1 Timothy 5:14 – 15)

"And there was war in heaven: Michael and his angels fought against the dragon; and the dragon fought and his angels, and prevailed not; neither was their place found any more in heaven. And the great dragon was cast out, that old serpent, called the Devil, and Satan, which deceiveth the whole world: he was cast out into the earth, and his angels were cast out with him . . . And when the dragon saw that he was cast unto the earth, he persecuted the woman which brought forth the man child." (Revelation 12:7 – 13)

"An angel . . . laid hold on the dragon, that old serpent, which is the Devil, and Satan, and bound him a thousand years, and cast him into the bottomless pit, and shut him up . . . that he should deceive the nations no more, till the thousand years should be fulfilled: and after that he must be loosed a little season." (Revelation 20:1 – 3)

This selection of verses is a fair cross section of the kind to be found in the New Testament and, as will be seen, they are by no means uniform in what they have to say. What are we to make of all these elements of a total picture?

If we suppose that Satan is a supernatural person whose purpose it is to deceive others and to manipulate circumstances behind the scenes, we are faced with so many questions, some of which appear to reflect on the righteousness of God. Where did such a Satan come from? What rights does he have on earth? Does he have actual power to exert against believers? If he is like the popular idea of Satan who rebelled in heaven, why does God allow him to invade the earth? What possible connection could there be between such a Satan and human beings?

When we ask these questions we are sometimes told that God has not given us the answers for the most part, and that we should not be seeking what is not revealed. We find this unacceptable. Moreover, it is only because a supernatural Satan is assumed to exist that the questions arise. On the belief which we have been setting forward and now develop there *are* answers to questions of this kind.

But most pertinent of all is a question which *must* be answered because it lies at the heart of the Gospel: What real connection is there between an extra-terrestrial personal Satan and the atoning work of Christ? How could it be said that Jesus had to share human nature in order to break the power of the Devil, if the Devil is not

151

of that same nature? This question is crucial. The answers we have given in this book make the matter plain. Human sinfulness is the primary meaning of the expression "the devil", and Christ broke its power by living a sinless life *in human nature*. This wondrous triumph of righteousness by faith and obedience broke the power of sin and therefore the power of death.

Other views in this area rarely come anywhere near meeting this basic problem. In fact they leave us with more problems than we started with. If rebellion can take place in heaven because angels can sin, why should the saints be promised that they will be made like unto the angels to die no more? The Bible knows nothing of this teaching (but, see Appendix II). Angels always do the will of God (*"they are **all** ministering spirits"* — Hebrews 1:14), and they cannot die. The Satan of the Bible cannot be of that nature because in the end he is finally to be consumed as completely as death will be consumed at the end of the millennium. Here are some of the relevant passages of Scripture:

> *"They which shall be accounted worthy to obtain that world, and the resurrection from the dead, neither marry, nor are given in marriage: neither can they die any more: for they are equal unto the angels; and are the children of God, being the children of the resurrection."*
> (Luke 20: 35 – 36)

> *"Bless the Lord, ye his angels, that excel in strength, that do his commandments, hearkening unto the voice of his word. Bless ye the Lord, all ye his hosts; ye ministers of his, that do his pleasure."*
> (Psalm 103:20 – 21)

> *"The devil that deceived them was cast into the lake of fire . . . and death and hell were cast into the lake of fire."* (Revelation 20:10,14)

We believe that Satan is the sum total of everything in the world which has to do with mortality, including all the ills to which man is heir. Among men sin reigns as king and his empire is characterised by disease and mortality. The sum total of these things is Satan. It includes human sinfulness, and all the consequences of sin, and the total corporate and cumulative wickedness of man.

On this explanation it is easy to see how Satan had bound the infirm woman for eighteen years. She was a chronic sufferer from one of the consequences of Adam's sin, and Christ could heal her. All aspects of the mortal, sinful kingdom of man are to be removed ultimately because Christ has broken the source of them — sin and death. Meanwhile we continue to suffer. Paul was obviously suffering from some weakness of the flesh which he described as "a messenger of Satan". The Lord Jesus decided that it should not be removed, despite Paul's earnest prayers. One cannot believe that Christ would have left Paul in the hands of a malevolent, powerful and deceitful being, such as Satan is said to be. Surely, the one thing the Lord would wish is for his people to be removed from that influence.

On the other hand, Paul is said to have delivered certain people *to* Satan. One cannot imagine that he delivered them into the hands of the arch-enemy, especially when, in one case, he hoped to achieve good in the process. If one regards the "delivering to Satan" as excommunication from the congregation or possibly some physical punishment from God, the picture becomes plain. Paul excommunicated or punished them to teach a lesson, and in hope that they would return repentant.

As soon as we realise that Satan is everything adverse to the ultimate purpose of God, whether individual sinfulness, corporate wickedness or the present consequences of sin in the world, we have a key which unlocks many of the verses about the Devil and Satan. Some of the verses present more difficulty — they do so whether or not we believe in a personal devil — and we have to seek to work out the meaning by the sound principles we have learned. This we endeavour to do in the Appendix following this chapter.

Finally, we would like to examine two further passages of Scripture which are quoted in support of the popular orthodox view of the personal Devil and Satan, and demonstrate that they are better understood on the lines of what we have been setting forward thus far.

The first Scripture reads as follows:

> "*You hath he quickened, who were dead in trespasses and sins; wherein in time past ye walked according to the course of this world, according to the prince of the power of the air, the spirit that now worketh in the children of disobedience: among whom also we all had our conversation in times past (once lived, R.V.) in the lusts of our flesh, fulfilling the desires of the flesh and of the mind, and were by nature the children of wrath, even as others.*" (Ephesians 2:1 – 3)

Human sinfulness has generated so powerful a spirit of evil that it dominates all of the ways of the world. It is the "course of this world" or "the ways of this world" (N.I.V.). The citizens of Ephesus believed in all kinds of heathen ideas, but Paul was telling them that the real ruler of this world, both in its political manifestations and in its various religious systems, was the corporate wickedness of the desires and the minds of men of whom we have read that *"every imagination of the thoughts of his heart was only evil continually"* (Genesis 6:5).

A World of Wickedness

Corporate wickedness, the very spirit of the world, is extremely powerful, beyond that of individuals alone and sometimes beyond the sum total of all the individuals. What they have created by their wicked imaginations becomes the monster that destroys them. As John wrote, *"The whole world lieth in wickedness"* (1 John 5:19). Not only is it corporate, it is devastatingly singleminded in its sinfulness. Moreover, because sin deceives individuals (Romans 7:11), so the world is deceived, and sometimes discovers the enormity of its actions too late to be able to extricate itself from the toils of their consequences.

In the passage under consideration (Ephesians 2), alongside the highly descriptive language of verses 2 and 3, we have these descriptions of what had gone wrong:

"the spirit that now worketh in the children of disobedience"

"the lusts of our flesh"

"the desires of our flesh and of the mind"

"by nature the children of wrath"

The natural inclinations of men had taken possession of them so that they were totally ruled over by sin and its consequences. There is no need to suppose that some supernatural creature is involved in the process. Later in the same epistle the most influential people are called "world rulers" and "spiritual hosts of wickedness". They were ranged against godly men and women, not in physical combat of flesh and blood, but in the much more difficult encounter, the battle for the mind.

The spirit of sin is the ruler or prince of this world. Sin reigns (Romans 5:21). It exercises sway over the world in all its parts. Christ refused to be dominated and it cost him his life. The evil powers around him in the Jewish authorities and their Gentile political masters arraigned him before them. Christ had predicted everything and had said:

> "*The prince of this world cometh, and hath nothing in me.*"
> (John 14:30)

Christ was sinless, despite temptation. The temptations within and the evil forces without found no chink in his armour, no flaw in his perfect righteousness. They found no fault in him. Never before had sin gone away empty-handed. It was more than that:

> "*Now shall the prince of this world be cast out.*" (John 12:31)

Calvary would see the ultimate triumph:

> "*And having spoiled principalities and powers, he made a show of them openly, triumphing over them in it.*" (Colossians 2:15)

Truly, he had entered Satan's house, and had bound that which had been the binder, defeated that which had been the victor, spoiled that which had been the spoiler. Sin was finished for him and the victory would spread abroad in forgiveness for others. Death was vanquished for him, and immortality would come to light for all who would come to him.

And so the Gospel came to the Gentiles who lived in the land of the disobedient. Paul received the divine commission to preach to Gentiles:

> "*The Gentiles unto whom I now send thee, to open their eyes, and to turn them from darkness to light, and from the power of Satan unto God, that they may receive forgiveness of sins, and inheritance among them which are sanctified by faith that is in me (Christ).*" (Acts 26:17,18)

Under the blessing of God, Paul's preaching was mightily effective. We can compare what he achieved with what he was told to do:

"*Open their eyes.*"	=	"*The eyes of your understanding being enlightened.*" (Ephesians 1:18)
"*From darkness to light*"	=	"*For ye were once darkness, but are now light in the Lord.*" (Ephesians 5:8, R.V.)
"*The power of Satan unto God*"	=	"*Ye turned to God from idols to serve the living and true God.*" (1 Thessalonians 1:9)
"*Receive the forgiveness of sins*"	=	"*Through this man is preached unto you the forgiveness of sins.*" (Acts 13:38)

155

This is what Paul meant when he declared that "*the gospel is the power of God unto salvation*" (Romans 1:16). The Word of God was "*quick, and powerful, and sharper than any two-edged sword*" (Hebrews 4:12). The believers were sanctified and cleansed with the washing of water by the Word (Ephesians 5:26). Those who were appealed to were urged to turn from vanities "*unto the living God*" (Acts 14:15). Those who opposed this wonderful work were denounced:

> "*O full of all subtilty and all mischief, thou child of the devil, thou enemy of all righteousness, wilt thou not cease to pervert the right ways of the Lord.*" (Acts 13:10)

Neither the sinfulness of human nature nor its corporate manifestations nor the frailties of the flesh consequent upon Adam's sin, can in any way prove themselves stronger than faith in Christ Jesus by whom, said Paul, "*the world is crucified unto me, and I unto the world*" (Galatians 6:14).

APPENDIX II

"FALLEN ANGELS" AND SATAN

THERE are some problem passages of Scripture, cast in rather unusual language, which are sometimes said to lend credence to the view that angels can sin and rebel against God, and that Satan is the pre-eminent example of this rebellion. We propose to examine prominent representatives of this kind and provide an alternative explanation for them.

The following passage concerns "Lucifer, son of the morning":

> *"How art thou fallen from heaven, O Lucifer, son of the morning! how art thou cut down to the ground, which didst weaken the nations! For thou hast said in thine heart, I will ascend into heaven, I will exalt my throne above the stars of God: I will sit also upon the mount of the congregation, in the sides of north: I will ascend above the heights of the clouds: I will be like the most High. Yet thou shalt be brought down to hell, to the sides of the pit."* (Isaiah 14:12 – 15)

This passage was at one time used extensively by communities believing that the devil is a fallen angel. In recent years it has not featured so prominently. Perhaps this is due in part to the effectiveness of the exposition which Christadelphians have provided and used in discussion with those who hold the popular view.

A careful and unbiased reading of Isaiah 14:4 – 23 will cast considerable doubt on the view that it is describing the fall of an angel. Instead it will come to light that the passage is descriptive of God's judgements *on proud Babylon and its arrogant and ambitious king*. The language is graphic and presents a series of pictures portraying the overthrow of a mighty empire. It is like cutting down a tree greater than the cedars of Lebanon (verse 8); it is as though the worms in the earth were rousing themselves to receive the famous dead (verse 11); it is like a star cast down from heaven (verse 12); as though the dead in the grave were stirred in surprise to be joined by one so mighty (verses 16 – 17); and, yet, the king dies ignominiously with never a royal burial (verses 18 – 21).

All of this describes the end of *a man*, not an angel, as is clearly stated in verse 16:

> *"Is this* **the man** *that made the earth to tremble?"*

The place of the overthrow is not in heaven but an earthly kingdom whose capital city is swept away by the "besom of destruction" (verses 22 – 23).

There is certainly nothing in this chapter to support the orthodox doctrine of the Devil or Satan, neither of which is mentioned, and nothing to indicate a rebellion of angels, for neither are angels referred to in the record. One cannot avoid the conclusion that use of the passage to underpin orthodox views is based entirely on having brought the idea to the verses, and not on having arrived at it from the passage itself.

There are, however, two references in the New Testament which are of a different kind, and certainly require careful attention. Here they are:

> *"For if God spared not the angels that sinned, but cast them down to hell, and delivered them into chains of darkness, to be reserved unto judgment . . ."* (2 Peter 2:4)

> *"And the angels which kept not their first estate, but left their own habitation, he hath reserved in everlasting chains under darkness unto the judgment of the great day."* (Jude 6)

The interpretation of these verses presents a challenge to any Bible reader, not least because the information which they provide is very limited.

The word "angel" in our English Bible in Old and New Testament is the translation of a Hebrew or Greek word which means "messenger", and can be used to denote both human and divine messengers. The sense and context assist in deciding which of the two is intended. Generally, the translators have been sound in their judgement. They have used the word "angel" 289 times and "messenger" on 105 occasions. When the word "angel" has been used it usually denotes an angel of God, and "messenger" indicates a human messenger. On a few occasions the verse and its context do not provide positive indications as to which choice to make. The translators have done their best and have left the reader to judge for himself.

The verses from 2 Peter and Jude fall into this category. Although the translators have employed the word "angel(s)", there is some room for doubt. There is no mention of heaven and no leading phrase such as "angel of God". Moreover, we cannot determine with certainty what the events were which are being described or when they happened. This deprives us of the opportunity to take a cross bearing on the work of the translators.

For these reasons it would be unwise to seek to depend heavily on these verses for positive doctrinal teaching or to use them conclusively in support of such doctrine. It so happens that we believe it more probable that angels of God are not here intended and that the incidents relate to certain prominent men whose sins are recorded in the Old Testament; but we would not wish to force our view on others.

But there are some certainties which can be arrived at by a straightforward examination of the two verses. In the first place there is no reference to the Devil or Satan as the leader of a rebellion; indeed, there is no mention of a rebellion. There is no justification for saying that the incidents referred to took place in heaven. What is more, the "angels" concerned have had no part in any transactions on earth or anywhere else since the incidents took place; they are in everlasting chains of darkness awaiting the day of judgement (this is one of the reasons why we believe that men and not angels are involved). In other words, there is no support whatever in these verses for the orthodox doctrine of the Devil, and we need not fear that the angels can do us any harm since God has removed them altogether.

Last of all we must look at some verses in the last Book of the Bible:

> "*And there was war in heaven: Michael and his angels fought against the dragon; and the dragon fought and his angels, and prevailed not; neither was their place found any more in heaven. And the great dragon was cast out, that old serpent, called the Devil, and Satan, which deceiveth the whole world: he was cast out into the earth, and his angels were cast out with him . . . Therefore, rejoice, ye heavens, and ye that dwell in them.*

159

> *Woe to the inhabiters of the earth and of the sea: for the devil is come*
> *down unto you, having great wrath, because he knoweth that he hath but*
> *a short time."* (Revelation 12:7 – 12)

We now seem to have the full-blooded account of the rebellion in heaven whereby Satan was cast out and fell to earth. The language used is powerful and highly descriptive, and there is no way in which a facile or superficial exposition will satisfy the requirements of the chapter as a whole.

The Book of Revelation is God's last message to man which He gave to His Son, the Lord Jesus Christ (1:1). It is clearly a symbolic book as even a quick reading will show. The symbols and the events they portray are a prophetic outline of how human history under divine control would culminate in the return of the Lord Jesus Christ and the establishment of God's kingdom on earth (1:1; 4:1; 16:14,15; 11:15 – 18; 21:4). Consistent and sound exposition will not allow merely highly selective use of verses here and there; this would inevitably do violence to the fabric of the book as a whole.

Here are some facts which are evident from the chapter:

1. The incidents are intensely symbolic and there is no possibility of understanding the chapter unless the symbols are given meaning.

2. "Heaven" is used symbolically as representative of status and not as the dwelling place of God. A woman clothed in the sun, with twelve stars on her head and the moon under her feet is found in heaven and she is threatened by a great red dragon having seven heads bearing crowns and ten horns, and a tail drawing a third part of the stars of heaven which it casts down to the earth. This is picture language. We believe it describes actual events in world history involving nations and their rulers. This is not the place, however, to enter into detail. Suffice it to say that "heaven" in this passage is not the dwelling of God, but the arena of conflict of rival powers.

3. It follows that "earth" is used to represent more than the physical globe on which man lives. "Earth" is used to describe men and women as dominated by the ruling authorities, "the heaven". This usage is to be found throughout the Bible. For example, Christ is called "the star of Jacob" (Numbers 24:17) and the "sun of righteousness" (Malachi 4:3). The "earth" is used to denote its peoples as we read in Psalm 33:8: "*Let all the*

160

earth fear the Lord: let all the inhabitants of the world stand in awe of him".

4. The war in heaven described in Revelation 12 cannot relate to events prior to the Creation, as was at one time asserted and is still believed by some. The introduction (1:1) would lead us to expect that the things in the book of Revelation are forward looking. How could there have been a war in heaven where God dwells at any time subsequent to the ministry of the Lord Jesus Christ. He taught us to pray for "Thy kingdom (to) come" with the words "Thy will be done, on earth *as it is in heaven*". It is unthinkable that Christ would have used these words if heaven could become a place of rebellion and war. In that case the Lord's prayer would lose its meaning for us.

We have no hesitation in concluding that the events and symbols of this graphic chapter in the Book of Revelation are part of God's unfolding purpose here on earth which herald the coming of the kingdom. They are evidence that God is working amongst the nations as the people of God have always believed (*see* Daniel 2:20 – 21; 4:17).

If this is the case, why should the words "the Devil and Satan" be used to describe what is taking place? It should be noted that this passage of Scripture introduces us first of all to the great red dragon, and as we have seen this has reference to certain ruling authorities on earth. It is the dragon which is called "that old serpent, the Devil and Satan". It is not the Devil which is called "the dragon". The situation is very much as it was in the temptation of the Lord Jesus Christ. God's developing purpose in Revelation is opposed by a variety of powers in which human sinfulness is represented by corporate organisations such as empires or a powerful false church. The dragon is such a power and is ranged not only against other earthly powers but also against the true Gospel in the earth. It is appropriate to describe the dragon as the Devil and Satan because this pagan power would seek to eradicate the work of Christ in the earth.

17

DEMONS

WE live in an age when wickedness seems to be so powerful that more and more people regard the source of it as supernatural. We have already considered the question of the Devil and Satan, and have come to the conclusion that believing in some supernatural personal Devil is not the most satisfactory explanation: indeed, it is not Scriptural. But is there a possibility that there are evil spirits who are responsible for some of the world's wickedness?

Are there in fact beings, known as demons, who can cause evil to men, either because of their sins or out of sheer malevolence? These are serious questions and answers must again be brought from Scripture. Some people are tormented by the thought of demons waiting to attack them in some way. Others disregard the subject and let life take its course. Some people are genuinely puzzled by the references in the Bible to demons and do not quite know what to believe.

Let us approach the matter systematically and make full use of Scripture in arriving at our conclusions. Perhaps we should say at this stage that we would regard it as most odd were demons to be used to punish man for sins he has committed. Such a view would suggest that there is collaboration between the Lord God and the demons. Moreover, such punishment would have instructional value only if man knew it was taking place and why. The Bible would surely have told us to expect punishment in this way, if such were the case, but it remains absolutely silent in this regard.

In the King James' version of the Bible we come across the

words "devils" and "unclean spirits" which seem to be used interchangeably to describe the same phenomena. On page 142 we made reference to two Greek words, *daimon* and *daimonion* as the sources of the translation "devils", and to *daimonizomai* as the source of expressions like "possessed with a devil". It is unfortunate that the translators did not distinguish between the word for devil (*diabolos*) and that for devils in the sense of unclean spirits. Modern translations avoid this confusion by employing the word "demons". The distinction is essential because two entirely different subjects are involved. Here is a selection of passages about devils (demons) and unclean spirits:

> "*His fame spread throughout all Syria, and they brought him all the sick, those afflicted with various diseases and pains, **demoniacs**, epileptics, and paralytics, and he healed them.*"   (Matthew 4:24, R.S.V.)

> "*They sacrificed to **demons** which were no gods, to gods they had never known, to new gods that had come in of late, whom your fathers had never dreaded.*"   (Deuteronomy 32:17, R.S.V.)

> "*They served their **idols** . . . sacrificed their sons and their daughters unto devils . . . unto the idols of Canaan.*"   (Psalm 106:36 – 38)

> "*I say, that the things which the Gentiles sacrifice, they sacrifice to **devils**, and not to God*".   (1 Corinthians 10:20)

> "*We know that an **idol** is nothing in the world, and that there is none other God but one.*"   (1 Corinthians 8:4)

Heathen Gods

The first of these verses has to do with an affliction of a kind which is discussed later. The others refer to heathen gods. The Hebrew word for an idol means "a thing of nought". Paul expresses the same thought when he says, "an idol is nothing in the world". Even when the Jews in Greek countries used the words "demons" for "idols", they still believed that they did not actually exist, as witness this extract from the Greek translation of Isaiah 65:3:

> "*A people that provoketh me to anger continually to my face; that sacrificeth in gardens, and burneth incense upon altars of brick to **demons which exist not**.*"

Christadelphians do not believe that there are any such things as the personal demons worshipped by pagan nations. They practised idolatry, but there was no living spirit or any other kind of existence in the idol itself. God repeatedly contrasts His existence with the non-existence of heathen gods:

> "*From the beginning . . . I the Lord, the first and with the last; I am he . . . Shew the things that are to come hereafter, that we may know that ye are gods: yea, do good, or do evil, that we may be dismayed, and behold it together. Behold, ye are of nothing, and your work of nought . . . an abomination is he that chooseth you.*"
>
> (Isaiah 41:4 – 5, 23 – 24)

Despite the tenor of these words, some maintain that whilst they agree that an idol is nothing, that which lies behind it, the demon, is very much alive. This is pure assertion and renders meaningless the reasons which God advances against idols and those who worship them. It would be deception of the highest order were God to mock the wood or stone out of which the idol is made and at the same time not tell Israel that there is a powerful god behind it. This will not do. When the translators said that demons "exist not", they were asserting their total non-existence. They are a deception and a vanity, but the cults which men developed in this kind of worship were powerful enough, and it was these which Israel were to avoid. Such worship was often savage, always degrading and produced the most wicked practices:

> "*Thou shalt not let any of thy seed (children) pass through the fire to Molech, neither shalt thou profane the name of thy God . . . Thou shalt not lie with mankind, as with womankind . . . defile not ye yourselves in any of these things: for in all these the nations are defiled which I cast out before you.*"
>
> (Leviticus 18:21 – 25)

Man's need for worship was both exploited and abused by these systems of heathen worship. The Bible does not attribute their gross evils to anything other than the evil propensities which lie within us, and lays the blame squarely upon those who perpetrate or indulge in them.

In every age those who have developed and engaged in dark practices have reaped the harvest of their depravity. It was from these that the God of Israel sought to deliver the Jews, and seeks through the work of the Lord Jesus Christ to deliver us today.

But what about the "demons", "devils" and "unclean spirits" of the days of Jesus? The descriptions given of the healings performed by the Lord Jesus Christ are detailed and comprehensive. The supremacy of Christ over all kinds of afflictions and infirmities is clearly what the Gospels are seeking to convey. Thus, the blind, the dumb, the deaf, the palsied, the lunatic, the maimed, the lame, the leper, the continuously bleeding and all others, even the dead, were made alive and well. Men, women, children, rich, poor, Jews and Gentiles were among those who shared these glorious benefits.

And the blessings of Jesus' miracles extended even further. The hungry were fed, the stormy sea was stilled and, above all, sinners and the hopeless found compassion and restoration. Christ's power in all things was invincible.

His healing strength was linked with his spiritual mission, the bringing of the Gospel and forgiveness of sins to the people:

> "*But that ye may know that the Son of man hath power upon earth to forgive sins (he said unto the sick of the palsy), I say unto thee, Arise, and take up thy couch, and go into thine house. And immediately he rose up.*"
> (Luke 5:24)

The Lord's deepest purpose was the salvation of his hearers. His mighty powers and signs and acts of compassion were a demonstration of his power also to mend broken lives, to open the eyes of the mind and to give life to those who were dead in trespasses and sins.

The Demented and the Sick

Amongst his powers was his absolute control over demons. Let us assume, for purposes of discussion, that the demons were in fact spirit beings from an evil world who had invaded the human frame and mind. There are then questions to be asked. Does the Lord Jesus hold the sufferers from demons to be guilty and thus in some way to have deserved what has happened to them? Does he tell them, when he has cured them, that their suffering was because of their sins? Does he tell them how they came to be invaded in that way and, more particularly, how to avoid this same thing in the future? Does he warn people generally, those who have not suffered from demons, what to do in order to escape from the possibility of being similarly afflicted? The answer to all of these questions is, No. Jesus effects the cures, but gives no further instruction to the people about demons.

Is not this astonishing if there is a demon world ranged against mankind? The Gospel records are silent in this matter. Jesus does not tell potential sufferers or those around them what to do if ever they were to be invaded by such demons.

There is no evidence from the Gospels that any of the afflicted people whom Jesus healed were in any way associated with demon cults or that they had been indulging in gross sins. All that the demon appears to have produced were distressing blindness, dumbness, epilepsy or lunacy; or, it might be argued that the demons were associated with these afflictions. When these devils were removed, the people became normal.

Were we to believe in spirit beings called demons, there is still nothing in the teaching of Jesus telling us how to avoid being influenced by them. This total silence is baffling, and must raise serious doubt whether demons exist in the form which people today seem to believe. Certainly there is nothing in the teaching of Jesus telling us that we should be concerned. Again, there is nothing to suggest that any of those who were afflicted were in any way associated with the propagation of evil doctrine.

The more one reads the Gospel accounts and ponders them, the more one is drawn to the conclusion that demon distressed people are persons who are deprived in some way of normal senses or functions, either for a time or permanently. So the blind, the dumb and the deaf were unable to communicate normally with their fellows. The epileptic and the lunatic were altogether unable to have normal contact with their friends and family, either for a period or all the time. It is not as though two separate things were going on at the same time: we do not see the demon at work in the blind person other than in the blindness. The demon and the blindness are identified together. In one case, where the man is dumb, he is said to have a *dumb spirit* (Luke 11:14).

In other words, apart from the language used (which we discuss later), there seems to be little lost from the records of healing if we regard them as severe medical cases. If one so regards them, no teaching of Jesus is lost. Christadelphians do so regard them.

However, we have some additional areas of difficulty, as follows:

Jesus addresses the demons;
The demons respond;
The demons are cast out or depart.

Why should language of this kind be used if demons do not exist? Some people explain the language by saying that Jesus simply used the language of his day because that was how people thought and understood. Whilst this method of explanation has some value, it also has deficiencies. It looks as though the Lord Jesus Christ was contributing to the popular beliefs. A more understandable explanation is that Jesus had to use *for the sufferer* language which was helpful to him. The sufferer had been told by those around him that his trouble was demon possession. Jesus had to deal with that fact in the process of his healing work.

We must observe that Jesus never supports any of the current notions about demons (of which the Greeks and Jewish scholars had plenty), such as that demons were the spirits of dead people or were under the direction of Beelzebub. Nor does he associate them with the animal world, which is known to have been a belief of heathen people. Christ's language is most straightforward. He accomplishes his cures by his word. He makes no use of all the paraphernalia of the exorcists. It is the non-believers in Christ who from time to time are referred to as exorcists. Christ treats those who are said to be afflicted with evil spirits as sick people and he heals them. The language is the language of healing.

Why do the demons speak? Why does Jesus address them? The records are, in fact, a mixture of what is said to be the person speaking or the demon, but never of both at once. The records in which conversation takes place are those where the sufferer is mentally afflicted. It is important to take note of this fact. In his healing Jesus had need to communicate with the demented person, and he could do so only within the limitations of that person himself. It is interesting to note that whether the demon or the person answers, according to the record, the exchanges are all of a piece; there is no real evidence that there are two personalities in the conversation with Jesus.

The accounts can be understood well enough by regarding the conversations as being a demented person talking with the Lord in the only language he knew, and Christ sharing that language in order to deliver the sufferer from his plight. Talking as though there was a real demon is no different in essence from rebuking a fever as he did in the healing of Luke 4:39. It is very difficult to see what other kind of language the Lord could have used when speaking to a deluded person.

In another kind of healing, where an unclean spirit is not said to have been involved, Jesus mixed clay with his spittle to anoint the eyes of the blind man (John 9:6). His actions were very much like the so-called healers of his day, but he was not using, or contributing to the current beliefs in the magical qualities of the substance he used. He was using it as a means of communicating with the person to be healed, a means which the 'patient' would understand.

But what about words like this?

> *"He . . . cast out many devils; and suffered not the devils to speak, because they knew him . . ."*   (Mark 1:34)

We have indicated already that everything that is said by men and women who have an unclean spirit is said in the normal way of conversation. The voice and speech mechanism are those of the afflicted person. When such a person spoke he occasionally used words which indicated that he had some knowledge of the Lord Jesus Christ and made acknowledgement of him. How was the knowledge obtained?

It could, of course, have been entirely miraculous in that the nearness of Christ with intent to heal evoked a response from the demented person concerned, a response, as it were, beyond his normal capabilities. If this were the case, it is hard to see why Christ should wish to silence it. Similarly, if there were real demons and they were caused to confess Christ, it is again difficult to understand why the Lord would wish to silence their voices rather than encourage them.

A more profitable line of thought comes from realising that the fame of Jesus was widespread (Mark 1:28). In fact, it was this fame which caused some of the demented and afflicted to be brought to Jesus. It would not be surprising therefore for the afflicted person to have knowledge of Jesus. As a matter of fact, we have other examples of desperate but believing people making confession concerning Christ beyond what the average person was often prepared to do:

> *"Have mercy on me, O Lord, thou son of David; my daughter is grievously vexed with a devil."*   (Matthew 15:22)

> *"Behold, two blind men sitting by the way side . . . cried out, saying, Have mercy upon us, O Lord, thou son of David."*
>   (Matthew 20:30)

This leaves one other question to be answered. Why do the devils talk about being tormented before the time? Clearly, this is a reference to a belief that demons who caused afflictions would at some future time be tormented or punished. This view was held by some Jews and had been developed as a mixture of thoughts imported from non-Biblical sources. It was not, therefore, surprising to hear demented people talking in that way. Certainly, Christ gave no support whatsoever to that view and in no way endorsed what the voice said.

Before concluding this chapter, reference should be made to certain Scriptures written after the days of Christ's ministry which some people believe advance the doctrine of supernatural demons. Here are two of these Scriptures:

> *"Now the Spirit speaketh expressly, that in the latter times some shall depart from the faith, giving heed to seducing spirits, and doctrines of devils."* (1 Timothy 4:1)

> *"Put on the whole armour of God, that ye may be able to stand against the wiles of the devil. For we wrestle not against flesh and blood, but against principalities, against powers, against rulers of the darkness of this world, against spiritual wickedness in high places . . ."* (Ephesians 6:11 – 12)

False Christs and False Prophets

There are two possible ways of interpreting the passage from Timothy: either to believe that the doctrines emanate from demons, or that the doctrines have the effect of deranging the thinking of those who accept them, whatever the source from which they come. Christadelphians do not believe that there are demons who inject doctrines into the minds or systems of men. A parallel is being drawn by the apostle Paul between the afflictions of the people healed by Christ and the distortion and power of false doctrines of particular kinds generated by evil men. We have arrived at this conclusion from the words, "Now the Spirit speaketh expressly", at the opening of the passage under consideration. *When* did the Spirit speak expressly? Where in earlier Scriptures are there clear and express words about the introduction of powerful false doctrine? Here are two instances, one of them from the same Spirit-guided pen as the passage from the letter to Timothy:

> *"For there shall arise false Christs, and false prophets, and shall shew great signs and wonders; insomuch that, if it were possible, they shall deceive the very elect. Behold I (Jesus) have told you before."* (Matthew 24:24 – 25)

> *"For I know this, that after my departing shall grievous wolves enter in*

among you, not sparing the flock. Also of your own selves shall men arise, speaking perverse things, to draw away disciples after them."

(Acts 20:29 – 30)

These are good examples of the Spirit having spoken expressly. The believers had been warned. False Christs and false prophets would appear, seeking to attract followers and showing signs which the unstable would accept. It is this power to seduce and to deceive that makes these doctrines like the persuasive teachings about false gods in the Old Testament:

"Take heed to yourselves, that your heart be not deceived, and ye turn aside, and serve other gods, and worship them."

(Deuteronomy 11:16)

In the New Testament there is an example of a similar warning and of the response of those who heard it. When writing, probably to the congregation in Ephesus, the apostle John said:

"Beloved, believe not every spirit, but try the spirits whether they are of God: because many false prophets are gone out into the world . . . hereby know we the spirit of error." (1 John 4:1,6)

To that same congregation, the Lord Jesus sent a message recorded in the Book of Revelation:

"I know thy works, and thy labour, and thy patience, and how thou canst not bear them which are evil: and thou hast tried them which say they are apostles, and are not, and hast found them liars"

(Revelation 2:1 – 2)

The spirit of error was the message which the false apostles brought with them, which corresponds to "seducing spirits" and "doctrines of demons" about which Paul wrote to Timothy. Neither Christ nor Paul suggests that the real culprit is a spirit demon behind the false apostles. In each case it is false men who are examined and their teaching is rejected. The Bible tells us how to deal with actual problems when they arise. There is, however, no way detailed in Scripture by which to deal with evil spirits of the kind postulated.

But, someone may say, is not the language of Ephesians 6 quoted above sufficient to indicate that the believer is in fact fighting a spirit world? No! Paul is using a straightforward figure of speech to describe the Ephesian believers, who were surrounded by heathen beliefs in all kinds of evil powers, the kind of war we are waging. We are Christ's soldiers. But we are not fighting carnal warfare; we are engaged in spiritual conflict, the battle for the mind. On the one side there is the Word of God and on the other the religious systems of heathendom and heresy. These systems have their own hierarchies of authority which Paul describes as "principalities . . . powers . . . rulers of the darkness of this world . . . spiritual wickedness in high places". There are other Scriptures saying the same thing:

> *"The kings of the earth stood up, and the rulers were gathered together against the Lord, and against his Christ."* (Acts 4:26)

> *"We speak wisdom . . . yet not the wisdom of this world, but . . . the wisdom of God . . . which none of the princes of this world knew: for had they known it, they would not have crucified the Lord of glory."*
> (1 Corinthians 2:6 – 8)

Therefore, we can safely apply the same kind of speech to the words of Paul to the Ephesians. The battle of the believer was, and is, against all that would destroy his faith. He may have to suffer persecution from hostile civil authorities (as Paul did himself when in Ephesus), or stand up and be counted when false faiths arise, or when they infiltrate the congregation (as Paul did in Ephesus and in his defence of the Gospel against the Jewish authorities who opposed him and clung to the traditions of men). The concerted attacks of all that was evil would be broken upon the divine armour of the spiritual soldier and the weapons of the Word of God and prayer. There is nothing in the passage in Ephesians which requires the belief that a disciple's battle is really against extra-terrestrial spirit beings ranged against him. The Christian is seeking to preserve a true faith and a godly character against the onslaughts of the world in all its powers and influences. As the Lord Jesus said:

> *"Be of good cheer; I have overcome the world."* (John 16:33)

To which the apostle John adds this confident note:

> *"This is the victory that overcometh the world, even our faith."*
> (1 John 5:4)

18

ANGELS

ANGELS are mentioned very frequently in both Old and New Testaments, and we are clearly intended to have some understanding of them and their place among the affairs of men. For some people this subject is almost a closed book. Others associate angels very largely with cherubs, childlike but immortal creatures. For all of us, there may be an air of incompleteness in our understanding of the person and functions of angels simply because we have a limited amount of information on which to draw.

The Bible provides a great deal of background knowledge, but by no means answers all the questions we might care to ask. What we can know is what God wants us to know, because He has revealed it to us. We shall be unwise to add to it with conjectures of our own, or to diminish what is revealed. Here is a wide range of Scriptures in which angels are mentioned:

1. *"And the angel of the Lord found her (Hagar) by a fountain of water in the wilderness . . . and said . . . I will multiply thy seed exceedingly."*
(Genesis 16:7 – 10: the first occurrence of the word angel in Scripture.)

2. *"And the angel of God . . . went before the camp of Israel."*
(Exodus 14:19)

3. *"Behold, I send an Angel before thee, to keep thee in the way, and to bring thee into the place which I have prepared. Beware of him, and obey his voice, provoke him not; for he will not pardon your transgression: for my name is in him."* (Exodus 23:20 – 21)

172

4. *"As an angel of God, so is my lord the king to discern good and bad."* (2 Samuel 14:17)

5. *"The angel of the Lord encampeth round about them that fear him, and delivereth them."* (Psalm 34:7)

6. *"He (God) cast upon them the fierceness of his anger, wrath, and indignation, and trouble, by sending evil angels among them."* (Psalm 78:49)

7. *"My God hath sent his angel, and hath shut the lions' mouths, that they have not hurt me."* (Daniel 6:22)

8. *"The angel of the Lord appeared unto him in a dream, saying, Joseph, thou son of David, fear not to take unto thee Mary thy wife."* (Matthew 1:20)

9. *"The Son of man shall send forth his angels, and they shall gather out of his kingdom all things that offend."* (Matthew 13:41)

10. *"Depart from me, ye cursed, into everlasting fire, prepared for the devil and his angels."* (Matthew 25:41)

11. *They which shall be accounted worthy to obtain that world, and the resurrection from the dead, neither marry, nor are given in marriage: neither can they die any more: for they are equal unto the angels; and are the children of God, being the children of the resurrection."* (Luke 20:35,36)

12. *"And again, when he bringeth in the firstbegotten into the world, he saith, And let all the angels of God worship him. And of the angels he saith, Who maketh his angels spirits, and his ministers flames of fire."* (Hebrews 1:6 – 7)

13. *"Jesus Christ: who is gone into heaven, and is on the right hand of God; angels and authorities being made subject unto him."* (1 Peter 3:21,22)

From these verses we are able to draw a number of helpful and comforting conclusions, and to meet some difficulties regarding the work of angels.

God's Messengers

In the first five references, it is clear that angels do a good work for God. They are servants of God. As we learned earlier in both Old and New Testaments the word "angel" means "messenger", and is so translated on a number of occasions about human messengers.

173

The fifth reference says that those who fear God are under the care of angels. This comfort is reiterated in the New Testament where concerning the angels we read:

> *"Are they not **all** ministering spirits, sent forth to minister for them who shall be heirs of salvation?"* (Hebrews 1:14)

The angels are directly concerned, on behalf of God and the Lord Jesus Christ, in matters which have to do with the salvation of God's children. The extent of their work and care is not defined for us in Scripture, but it is there nevertheless. Some hint of their involvement is given in words such as:

> *"Likewise, I say unto you, there is joy in the presence of the angels of God over one sinner that repenteth."* (Luke 15:10)

Similarly we know that the angels will be there at the end, when the Lord returns, and will participate in those wonderful events which will accompany the resurrection of the dead and their gathering together unto the Lord, and the blessings that will follow for the faithful. In some of these matters the angels will have a personal role, as for example:

> *"The Lord Jesus shall be revealed from heaven with his mighty angels . . ."* (2 Thessalonians 1:7)

> *"And he shall send forth his angels with a great sound of a trumpet, and they shall gather together his elect from the four winds, from one end of heaven to the other."* (Matthew 24:31, R.V.)

This role of the angels as messengers, ambassadors and supervisors in respect of this world will yield in due course to the role which will be granted to the saints in the Kingdom of God on earth. The saints will be given *"the kingdom and dominion, and the greatness of the kingdom under the whole heaven"* (Daniel 7:27). It is for this reason that we read:

> *"For unto the angels hath he not put in subjection the world to come whereof we speak."* (Hebrews 2:5)

The angels' work on earth will be complete in major respects when the Kingdom of God is in the hands of Christ and of his saints. What other work the Lord God has in mind for these wonderful messengers who have been ceaselessly at work in affairs on earth ever since the creation we do not know.

In respect of their present work and knowledge, we have an insight granted to us in a number of places. Their knowledge does not extend to the omniscience enjoyed by God Himself. The angels know what God has revealed to them, but beyond that they may contemplate but not always arrive at further understanding. We know, for example, that they pondered the prophecies concerning the first coming of the Lord Jesus Christ but did not solve all of the mysteries which these contained! Peter says:

> "*Of which salvation the prophets have inquired . . . searching what, or what manner of time the Spirit of Christ which was in them did signify, when it testified beforehand the sufferings of Christ, and the glory that should follow . . . which things the angels desire to look into.*"
>
> (1 Peter 1:10 – 12)

If, as we have learned, *all* of the angels are God's unerring and faithful servants, what are we to understand by the evil angels of Psalm 78:49? Are they angels who work for God or against Him? Are they creatures who have an evil nature? A reading of the Psalm soon shows that the evil angels are engaged on work for God. He sends them to bring punishments on His disobedient people. They are called evil angels because of the work they do and not because they themselves are intrinsically evil. In other translations this is made clear. Thus the angels are known as "destroying angels" (R.S.V.) or "angels of evil" (R.V.). There are a number of examples of this kind in the Bible (see, for instance, 1 Chronicles 21:15). As God Himself brings evil upon mankind in its sinfulness, so the angels are used to perform such work for God.

Examples 7 – 9 in the list show us angels of God in a variety of roles — protector, messenger or destroyer — but all of them on behalf of God whose work they do.

"The devil and his angels"

In example 10 we have the intriguing words: "the devil and his angels." As will be seen the words are from a parable of the Lord concerning judgement day. Those acceptable to the Judge are invited to enter into everlasting life, but the condemned are told to depart into everlasting fire prepared for the devil and his angels.

Those who are rejected have themselves rejected the service of the Lord Jesus when they failed to live as true disciples and chose to follow the way of sin. That which Christ died to overcome, they preferred to follow. They went over to the enemy by perpetuating

175

their sinfulness. Instead of being messengers (angels) of Christlikeness like the faithful servants in the parable, they preferred to be messengers of Sin and the way of the world which Christ denotes as "the devil and his angels".

These are destined for the everlasting fire which describes the complete destruction of the unfaithful. The same words are used in Jude (v.7, R.V.) about the judgement of God on Sodom and Gomorrah which are said to have suffered the "punishment of eternal fire".

In the same way, fire is used to spell out the completeness of God's work in eliminating sin and sinfulness (corporately described as the devil), death and hell (the Bible word for grave) in the fulfilment of His purpose on earth:

> *"The devil that deceived them was cast into the lake of fire . . . and death and hell were cast into the lake of fire."*   (Revelation 20:10,14)

To return to the subject of angels, it is helpful to know that another Hebrew word as well as that for "messenger" is used to denote angels. It is the word "elohim" whose root lies in the words "power" and "might". Elohim is therefore appropriate to describe attributes of God Himself and is often made unique by attaching to it other words which then determine that the power and might are the underived almightiness of God.

The power which angels exercise is the derived power of God Himself which they are commissioned to use on His behalf. In this connection angels can bear the title "elohim", and an example of this is to be found in Exodus 3:2 – 4 where we are distinctly told that it was an angel that was like a flame of fire in the burning bush. Nevertheless when the angel speaks he is called "God" because the word used is "elohim". Angels are not God Himself, but are immortal, subservient beings used by Him as an extension of His power. He is the power and purpose in the angels. They were used at Creation (Job 38:7); in the destruction of Sodom and Gomorrah (Genesis 19:1,10,16); in leading the children of Israel through the wilderness (Exodus 23:20 – 23); in giving God's law to Moses at the mount Sinai (Acts 7:53); and in numerous other well-known incidents in the pages of Scripture.

It is therefore most apt to learn that those who are made immortal by the Lord Jesus Christ after their resurrection from the dead at his return will be called *"sons of God"* and be made *"like unto the angels"* (Luke 20:35 – 36) to die no more.

19

RESURRECTION AND JUDGEMENT

THE Bible makes it plain that the only way to everlasting life for faithful disciples who die before the return of Jesus Christ is by resurrection from the dead. All the righteous saints who have lived since the days of Abel, the righteous son of Adam, up to the last disciple to die before the Second Coming, share the sleep of death. They lie in dust awaiting the quickening voice of Jesus. The hope of the resurrection from the dead has been the comfort of the children of God since the earliest days. It is *the* hope. It is *the only* hope.

This is what the apostles preached:

> "*As they spake unto the people, the priests, and the captain of the temple, and the Sadducees, came upon them, being grieved that they taught the people, and proclaimed* **through Jesus the resurrection from the dead**." (Acts 4:1 – 2)

> "*For the Sadducees say there is no resurrection.*" (Acts 23:8)

> "*He preached unto them Jesus, and the resurrection.*" (Acts 17:18)

The resurrection of the Lord Jesus and the resurrection of the believer at the last day were indispensable parts of the first century Gospel. They were the keys to understanding the victory of the Lord Jesus Christ over sin and death. No one who heard the apostles preach could have failed to be impressed by their message that Jesus had been raised from the dead. They were witnesses to this glorious fact, and they made it the cornerstone of their belief in him:

"This Jesus hath God raised up, whereof we all are witnesses."
(Acts 2:32)

"The Prince of life, whom God hath raised from the dead."
(Acts 3:15)

"Jesus Christ of Nazareth, whom ye crucified, whom God raised from the dead ..." (Acts 4:10)

"The God of our fathers raised up Jesus, whom ye slew and hanged on a tree ..." (Acts 5:30)

"But God raised him from the dead." (Acts 10:40; 13:30)

"He (God) hath given assurance unto all men, in that he hath raised him from the dead ..." (Acts 17:31)

The apostolic message was clear: No resurrection of Jesus, no Gospel. Christ risen: repentance and remission of sins proclaimed. The resurrection of Jesus was the trumpet sound of his victory at Calvary:

"Our Saviour, Jesus Christ, who hath abolished death, and hath brought life and immortality to light through the gospel." (2 Timothy 1:10)

The whole edifice of the Christian faith would be in utter ruin were the foundation stone of the resurrection of Christ to be taken away. Without the empty tomb there would be no message to preach, and no hope to share:

*"If Christ be not raised, your faith is vain; ye are yet in your sins. Then they also which are fallen asleep in Christ **are perished** ... we are of all men most miserable."* (1 Corinthians 15:17 – 19)

The preaching of the cross without the preaching of Christ risen from the dead is impossible in New Testament terms. They are parts of one work of salvation. He who was lifted upon the tree of suffering, and lay in silence in the sepulchre, is he whose grave is everlastingly empty. It is the risen Christ who has ascended to heaven.

Readers will know from earlier parts of this book that Christadelphians believe the Bible teaching that when Jesus died on the cross he was truly dead. If that is not the true message, then Christ has not conquered death. We believe that he conquered death by "being obedient unto death". Any contrary Gospel which would have us believe that in reality the true Jesus was alive,

178

and that only his body slept, undermines both aspects of salvation, namely:

> *"He was delivered over to* **death** *for our sins and was raised to* **life** *for our justification."* (Romans 4:25, N.I.V.)

The Jesus who died is the Jesus who was raised and has ascended to heaven:

> *"Blessed be the God and Father of our Lord Jesus Christ, which according to his abundant mercy hath begotten us again unto a lively hope by the resurrection of Jesus Christ from the dead."* (1 Peter 1:3)

> *"The exceeding greatness of his (the Father's) power to us-ward who believe, according to the working of his mighty power, which he wrought in Christ, when he raised him from the dead."* (Ephesians 1:19 – 20)

> *"I am the Living One; I was dead, and behold I am alive for ever and ever! And I hold the keys of death and Hades."* (Revelation 1:18, N.I.V.)

The believers of the first century believed that the tomb was empty, and that the Lord Jesus Christ had risen bodily from the grave. No amount of explaining it away or of spiritualising of the message would do for them. The tomb was empty. Christ was risen. They knew this. They knew people who had gone into the tomb and had found it empty on the resurrection morning. They had spoken to those who themselves had heard angels say at the open tomb:

> *"He is not here: for he is risen, as he said. Come, see the place where the Lord lay."* (Matthew 28:6)

More that that, many of the first century believers had met people who had seen, spoken to and eaten with Jesus after his resurrection. They were sure. Moreover not even the enemies of Jesus ever denied that the tomb was empty, and neither they nor anyone else ever produced a body to confound the story of the resurrection which they hated. Above all, the same disciples who had trembled in confusion and fear behind locked doors when their Lord had been taken away, stood openly in Jerusalem and proclaimed boldly and clearly that Jesus was alive for evermore. Christ is risen!

Christ's resurrection from the dead became the basis for preaching the certainty of the resurrection of those who die believing in him. Here is how the Scriptures put it:

> "*They (Peter and John) taught the people, and preached through Jesus the resurrection from the dead.*" (Acts 4:2)

> "*The hope and resurrection of the dead. . .*" (Acts 23:6)

> "*There shall be a resurrection of the dead, both of the just and unjust.*" (Acts 24:15)

> "*Why should it be thought a thing incredible with you, that God should raise the dead.*" (Acts 26:8)

> "*That Christ would suffer and, as the **first** to rise from the dead, would proclaim light to his own people, and to the Gentiles.*"
> (Acts 26:23, N.I.V.)

Christ is Risen

Despite the certainty of the resurrection of Jesus, heresy crept into the company of believers in Corinth who at first heard the Gospel from the mouth of Apostle Paul. They were satisfied that Jesus had risen from the dead, but some of them began to cast doubt on the future resurrection of the believers. Paul's argument in rebuttal of this teaching contained the following phrase:

> "*If there be no resurrection of the dead, then is Christ not risen.*"
> (1 Corinthians 15:13)

What a strange argument! The heretics had been saying: We believe in the resurrection of Jesus, but we do not believe in the resurrection of the saints. Paul replied, much to their surprise: If you do not believe in the resurrection of the saints, you cannot believe in the resurrection of Christ. To deny one, said Paul, is to deny the other. But why was such an argument valid? What was the telling point which Paul had in mind? After all, at first sight, it does not make sense to say that because someone does not believe in the resurrection of the dead in the future he is, in fact, denying the resurrection of Christ two thousand years ago.

The answer is simple and intriguing. The future resurrection and the resurrection of Jesus are parts of *one* resurrection. It is as though some early ripe grain had been taken from a field and the main harvest is still to come. That is exactly what the apostles believed:

*"That Christ should suffer and that he should be **the first** that should rise from the dead ..."* (Acts 26:23)

*"For since by man came death, by man came also the resurrection of the dead. For as in Adam all die, even so in Christ shall all be made alive. But every man in his own order: Christ the **first fruits, afterward** they that are Christ's **at his coming**."*

(1 Corinthians 15:21 – 23)

In other words, on the basis of the Gospel message, it is impossible to believe the resurrection of Christ without also believing in the resurrection of the saints. To deny the one, therefore, is to deny both. And that would put an end to any hope of salvation:

"For if the dead rise not, then is not Christ raised: and if Christ be not raised, your faith is vain; ye are yet in your sins. Then they also which are fallen asleep in Christ are perished."

(1 Corinthians 15:16 – 18)

Wholehearted affirmation in the belief of the resurrection of Jesus is also to declare one's belief that dead saints will attain unto immortality by resurrection from the dead at Christ's Second Coming. All parts of the Gospel message are solidly parts of the whole. To destroy any one part, is to place in jeopardy all saving truth.

It will come as no surprise to the reader to learn that Old Testament worthies shared the same hope of resurrection from the dead:

"As for me, I will behold thy face in righteousness:
*I shall be satisfied, **when I awake**, with thy likeness."*

(Psalm 17:15)

"This is the fate of those who trust in themselves ...
death will feed on them. The upright will rule over
them in the morning; their forms will decay in the grave
*far from their princely mansions. But God **will redeem my soul** from the grave; he will surely take me to himself."*

(Psalm 49:13 – 15, N.I.V.)

"But your dead will live; their bodies will rise. You who dwell in the dust, wake up and shout for joy. Your dew is like the dew of the morning; the earth will give birth to her dead."

(Isaiah 26:19, N.I.V.)

181

> *"I will ransom them from the power of the grave; I will redeem them from death: O death, I will be thy plagues; O grave, I will be thy destruction."* (Hosea 13:14)

> *"There shall be a time of trouble, such as never was since there was a nation even to that same time: and at that time thy people shall be delivered, every one that shall be found written in the book. And many of them that sleep in the dust of the earth shall awake, some to everlasting life, and some to shame and everlasting contempt."*
> (Daniel 12:1 – 2)

The Sleep of Death

The language throughout these verses is consistent. The dead are to awaken and come forth from the grave in which they presently sleep in dust. This will be a joyful morning for the upright because the outcome of their awakening will be everlasting life; death will have no further dominion over them. This was a simple truth, the simple truth. They believed that the dead are truly dead, and that everlasting life will come by resurrection. Compare these two Scriptures which illustrate exactly what the ancient believers held as their faith and hope:

> *"Put not your trust in princes, nor in the son of man, in whom there is no help. His breath goeth forth, he returneth to his earth; in that very day his thoughts perish. Happy is he that hath the God of Jacob for his help, whose hope is in the Lord his God."* (Psalm 146:3 – 5)

> *"But your dead will live; their dead bodies will rise. You who dwell in the dust, wake up . . ."* (Isaiah 26:19, N.I.V.)

Resurrection is a reversal of the process of death. The word used by the New Testament writers means "a standing again". God who in the beginning created man from the dust can recreate those who sleep in dust.

The human body bears all the marks of its imperfection. It is born with death already at work within its members, and it labours under the influence of its sinfulness. Its final descent into the grave is the appropriate end to it all.

> *"All flesh is as grass, and all the glory of man as the flower of grass. The grass withereth, and the flower thereof falleth away."*
> (1 Peter 1:24)

For the redeemed, the burdensomeness of flesh is to be removed.

It is not to be shed like some great weight, leaving us light as air, like a colourful butterfly emerging from the winter of its chrysalis. Such a dream is not the Bible way to happiness. In any case it smacks of defeat despite the imaginativeness of the figures of speech. It is as though God had failed in respect of our bodies, the fearful and wonderful things which He has made, and is forced to produce redemption by some other method.

Hope of Immortality

This will not do. Bible teaching is clear and altogether different. True salvation includes the salvation of the body. As the body is essential to this present existence, so will it be to the eternal existence. However, this human frame, burdened and frail as it is, will be redeemed and transformed into a thing of glory and beauty. Resurrection from the dead is the prelude to this remarkable and permanent change which the faithful, and only the faithful, will enjoy. Here are the New Testament declarations:

> *"The creation itself will be liberated from its bondage to decay and brought into the glorious freedom of the children of God . . . we wait eagerly for our adoption as sons, **the redemption of our bodies**."*
> (Romans 8:21 – 23, N.I.V.)

> *"We eagerly await a Saviour . . . who, by the power that enables him to bring everything under his control, **will tranform our lowly bodies so that they will be like his glorious body**."*
> (Philippians 3:20 – 21, N.I.V.)

> *"We groan, earnestly desiring to be clothed upon with our house which is from heaven . . . for we that are in this tabernacle do groan, being burdened: not for that we would be unclothed, but **clothed upon**, that mortality might be swallowed up of life."* (2 Corinthians 5:2 – 4)

> *"For this corruptible must **must put on** incorruption and this mortal must **put on** immortality. So when this corruptible shall have **put on** incorruption . . . then shall be brought to pass the saying that is written, Death is swallowed up in victory . . ."* (1 Corinthians 15:53 – 54)

The victory over death comes not by surviving its initial impact in the moment of decease, but by resurrection from the dead, and by the supreme happiness of the faithful when, by Jesus Christ, immortality is bestowed upon them. It was belief in this which Paul offered as comfort to those in Thessalonica who had been bereaved and whose loved ones had fallen asleep believing in

183

Christ. He did not offer a different hope in those circumstances. There is only one hope. Here it is:

> "*I would not have you to be ignorant, brethren, concerning them which are asleep, that ye sorrow not, even as others which have no hope. For if we believe that Jesus died and rose again, even so them also which sleep in Jesus will God bring with him . . . For the Lord himself shall descend from heaven with a shout, with the voice of the archangel, and with the trump of God: and the dead in Christ shall rise first . . . and so shall we ever be with the Lord. Wherefore comfort one another with these words.*"
>
> (1 Thessalonians 4:13 – 18)

> "*When he (Jesus) shall come to be glorified in his saints, and to be admired in all them that believe.*"   (2 Thessalonians 1:10)

> "*Henceforth there is laid up for me a crown of righteousness, which the Lord, the righteous judge, shall give me* **at that day:** *and not to me only, but unto all them also that love* **his appearing.**"
>
> (2 Timothy 4:8)

> "*Beloved, now are we the sons of God, and it doth not yet appear what we shall be: but we know that,* **when he shall appear**, *we shall be like him; for we shall see him as he is.*"   (1 John 3:2)

> "*For* **the Son of man shall come** *in the glory of his Father with his angels; and* **then** *shall he reward every man according to his works.*"
>
> (Matthew 16:27)

> "*And as it is appointed unto men once to die, but after this the judgement: so Christ was once offered to bear the sins of many; and unto them that look for him* **shall he appear** *the second time without sin unto salvation.*"   (Hebrews 9:27 – 28)

The weight and consistency of these Scriptures is truly remarkable. The day of the Second Coming is the time of reward, of glory and of salvation. It is for these all-powerful reasons that the doctrine of the Second Coming has such prominence in the New Testament. Without the Second Coming, all is lost.

The Judgement

The observant reader will have noticed that a number of the verses which have been quoted speak of "the judgement", "the righteous Judge", and "rewarding every man according to his works".

When is Judgement Day? What is determined or made apparent at the Judgement? Who will be judged? What will happen to the rejected at the Judgement?

Bible teaching is clear. The day of judgement is the time of Christ's return to earth:

> *"I charge thee therefore before God, and the Lord Jesus Christ, who shall* **judge** *the quick (the living) and the dead* **at his appearing** *and his kingdom."* (2 Timothy 4:1)

> *"It is he (Jesus) which was ordained of God to be the Judge of quick and dead."* (Acts 10:42)

> *"The righteous* **judge** *... at ...* **his appearing.***"*
> (2 Timothy 4:8)

> *"In the day when God shall judge the secrets of men by Jesus Christ."*
> (Romans 2:16)

> *"We shall all* **stand before the judgement seat of Christ** *... every one of us shall give account of himself to God."*
> (Romans 14:10,12)

> *"We must all* **appear before the judgement seat of Christ***; that every one may receive the things done in his body, according to that he hath done, whether it be good or bad."* (2 Corinthians 5:10)

> *"Therefore judge nothing before the appointed time; wait* **till the Lord comes***. He will bring to light what is hidden in darkness and will expose the motives of men's hearts.* **At that time** *each will receive his praise from God."* (1 Corinthians 4:5, N.I.V.)

> *"Behold,* **I come quickly***; and my reward is with me, to give to every man according as his work shall be."* (Revelation 22:12)

> *"The day of wrath and revelation of the righteous judgment of God; who will render to every man according to his deeds ...* **in the day** *when God shall judge the secrets of men by Jesus Christ."*
> (Romans 2:5,16)

God has committed this work of judgement into the hands of His Son. Judgement day will be when the Lord Jesus returns to earth. Those to be judged will consist of two classes of people: those who will be approved, and those who will not. In other words the purpose of the judgement will be to make manifest the righteous

185

assessment of God. The Judge's decision will be critical and final. The issue is life everlasting or rejection. Nothing could be more serious. Some of the observations of Scripture on this aspect should be considered by all of us:

> *"Therefore the ungodly shall not stand in the judgement, nor sinners in the congregation of the righteous. For the Lord knoweth the way of the righteous: but the way of the ungodly shall perish."* (Psalm 1:5 – 6)

> *"Many that sleep in the dust of the earth shall awake, some to everlasting life, and some to shame and everlasting contempt."* (Daniel 12:2)

> *"For the hour is coming, in the which all that are in the graves shall hear his voice, and shall come forth; they that have done good, unto the resurrection of life; and they that have done evil, unto the resurrection of damnation (will rise to be condemned, N.I.V.)."* (John 5:28 – 29)

> *"A good man out of the good treasure of the heart bringeth forth good things: and an evil man out of the evil treasure bringeth forth evil things . . . they shall give account thereof in the day of judgement. For by thy words thou shalt be justified, and by thy words thou shalt be condemned."* (Matthew 12:35 – 37)

Clearly the nature of the judgement pronounced by the Lord Jesus Christ will be determined by the character, the Christlikeness, of the persons concerned. There is no doubt that the Lord Jesus is both merciful and compassionate, and, like the Lord God himself, does not desire that any should perish. Even so, some will perish. They will be eternally dismissed from the presence of Christ who had been willing to save them. Such people will have frustrated his grace by the deliberate inconsistency of their lives. For example, those who have treated their fellows harshly and unforgivingly, will reap what they have sown:

> *"For in the same way you judge others, you will be judged, and with the measure you use, it will be measured to you."*
>
> (Matthew 7:2, N.I.V.)

Those who have been avaricious or covetous in the pursuit of material gain and have forgotten the precious treasure of eternal things, will discover, all too late, the folly of their ways:

> *"For the love of money is a root of all kinds of evil: which some reaching after have been led astray from the faith, and have pierced themselves through with many sorrows."* (1 Timothy 6:10, R.V.)

186

"Be not deceived, God is not mocked: for whatsoever a man soweth that shall he also reap. For he that soweth to his flesh shall of the flesh reap corruption." (Galatians 6:7 – 8)

Similarly, those who depart from the basic truths of the doctrine of Christ will not enter the Kingdom of God:

"But shun profane and vain babblings: for they will increase unto more ungodliness. And their word will eat as doth a canker . . . (men) who concerning the truth have erred, saying that the resurrection is past already." (2 Timothy 2:16 – 18)

Such persons at the judgement seat of Christ will be cast into outer darkness. That is where they will truly belong, since they have chosen the way of darkness rather than the way of light. Despite all their opportunities, and their knowledge of the way of salvation, they will be miserable failures on account of their self-will. Instead of Christ, they will have chosen self; instead of seeking first the Kingdom of God and His righteousness, they will have pursued worldly ends of whatever kind.

What happens to those who are rejected by Christ? In the first place they will suffer irreversible and irremediable remorse: *"There shall be weeping and gnashing of teeth"* (Matthew 8:12). This is the remorse which spells out their desolating realisation that the path they have chosen has led them to destruction, even though they have stood before the Lord of life. Their bitter regrets will be to no avail, the time for repentance is past. It will be the moment of truth.

Will there be an end to this lamentable condition? Yes. It cannot last for ever since the rejected are not themselves everlasting. Like all who rise from the dead they will be mortal and, unlike the faithful who will be clothed upon with immortality, will finally reap corruption. Will this corruption be imposed upon them? Or will they have to await death in the normal way? Scripture is not precise and it would not be wise to dogmatise beyond what is written. There are some hints, however:

"Fear not them which kill the body, but are not able to kill the soul: but rather fear him which is able to destroy both soul and body in hell."

(Matthew 10:28)

"Be thou faithful unto death, and I will give thee a crown of life . . . he that overcometh shall not be hurt of the second death."

(Revelation 2:10 – 11)

187

The destiny of the rejected is to be "hurt of the second death", to suffer destruction of soul and body. There is perhaps in these words a hint of an inflicted end, rather than of waiting for death in the normal way. It will be the second death and there will be no possibility of being raised again. The destruction of soul and body speaks of complete annihilation, the body to corruption and the life we have had on lease from God being taken away eternally.

Hell

Some have wondered about the meaning of the word "hell", in Matthew 10:28, and whether this portends a conscious and everlasting suffering for the rejected. Eternal punishments or torments in a burning hell is a belief which came in the first place from the doctrine of the immortality of the soul. On such a doctrine it was essential to determine at the instant of death what the destiny of the good and of the bad would be. It was customary to assign the good to heaven and the bad to the burning hell (though very little was said about this in funeral services). Such a belief makes a travesty of Scripture. It assigns judgement day to the day of one's death, and this is altogether without warrant in Scripture. Judgement day is the day of Christ, the day of the Second Coming.

It so happens, however, that the word "hell" in Matthew 10:28 *is* associated with fire, but not the hell-fire of popular superstition. It is the hell which Jesus uses to denote the destiny of the rejected at the judgement seat, and has nothing to do with the false doctrine of hell-fire for departed souls. This word is Gehenna whose meaning we discussed earlier. To every Jew Gehenna had a special meaning. They had used the word or its Hebrew original for centuries. The word meant "Valley of (the son of) Hinnom" (see Joshua 15:8), and was the place of infamous memory south west of Jerusalem. Cruel idolatry had been practised there and little children had been burned to the god Molech (see 2 Chronicles 28:3 and Jeremiah 32:35). These detestable and wicked rites were eradicated by one of Judah's better kings and the place itself was defiled by him (2 Kings 23:10). Gehenna appears to have become a burning refuse heap, and even the bodies of criminals are said to have been cast there. How apt then for Christ to use this word to denote the final extinction of the wicked. They will be obliterated as though they had never been:

"... *like the chaff which the wind driveth away.*"   (Psalm 1:4)

"All that do wickedly shall be stubble: and the day that cometh shall burn them up, saith the Lord of hosts, that it shall leave them neither root nor branch." (Malachi 4:1)

". . . the chaff he will burn up with unquenchable fire." (Matthew 3:12, R.V.)

The distinction between the righteous and the unrighteous at the day of judgement will be the difference between everlasting joy and everlasting death.

Finally, what kind of people will stand before Christ for judgement? Will all men who have ever lived come forth? If not, what will determine the selection of those who will be there? Obviously, as in any judgement, there is a relationship between the persons to be judged and the law by which they are judged. In this case it is the law of God and the judge appointed by God is the Lord Jesus Christ:

"The Father judgeth no man, but hath committed all judgement unto the Son: that all men should honour the Son, even as they honour the Father. He that honoureth not the Son honoureth not the Father which hath sent him." (John 5:22 – 23)

The beginning of the relationship with Christ, and thus with the Father, is through the message of the Gospel and the degree of our willingness to receive it:

"He that heareth my word, and believeth on him that sent me, hath everlasting life, and shall not come into condemnation." (John 5:24)

"I am come a light into the world, that whosoever believeth on me should not abide in darkness. And if any man hear my words, and believe not, I judge him not: for I came not to judge the world, but to save the world. He that rejecteth me, and receiveth not my words, hath one that judgeth him: the word that I have spoken, the same shall judge him in the last day." (John 12:46 – 48)

The word of Christ is the word of salvation, and it is also the word of judgement. The man who hears and receives it in humble faith and obedience can be saved; the man who knowingly rejects the Lord and his word will be judged by that same Lord according to that same word:

189

> *"The day . . . of the righteous judgement of God . . . when God shall judge the secrets of men by Jesus Christ according to my gospel."*
>
> (Romans 2:5, 16)
>
> *"As many as have sinned under law shall be judged by law."*
>
> (Romans 2:12, R.V.)
>
> *"So speak ye, and so do, as they that shall be judged by the law of liberty."* (James 2:12)

But who will be raised to be judged by the word of God in Christ? We know that the faithful and unfaithful servants will be present, because that is what the New Testament teaches. So the Roman congregation was told:

> *"We shall all stand before the judgement seat of Christ . . . so then every one of us shall give account of himself to God."*
>
> (Romans 14:10 – 12)

Paul made it clear, therefore, that all who had responded to the call in belief and baptism would appear before Christ to give an account of their stewardship. This they would do whether their stewardship had been good or bad.

But what of men who knowingly rejected the service of Christ and never entered into it? What judgement are they exposed to? The Bible tells us that they are exposed to the judgement of Christ, and that Christ will exercise his judgement when he returns to this earth. What are the principles upon which this judgement will be exercised? First and foremost, those to be judged are fully aware of what they have done. There is nothing casual about their involvement in the day of judgement. Such persons have taken a deliberate decision in respect of Christ and his word. Here are phrases from John 12:

> *"I am come a light into the world . . . "*
> *"If any man rejecteth me and my word . . . "*
> *"The word that I have spoken shall judge him at the last day"*.

The rejector is a man who is aware of Christ as the light and has decided to reject him: he is aware of the demands of the Word of God and will not accept them as his own. God knows who are answerable to Christ on this basis. Doubtless the persons themselves are aware.

There are obvious examples of this kind of person among the

rulers in the day of Christ, and they were told that they would be present at the judgement seat:

> "*Ye shall see Abraham, and Isaac, and Jacob, and all the prophets, in the kingdom of God, and you yourselves thrust out.*"   (Luke 13:28)

There are further examples later in the New Testament. Peter writing to believers who were being oppressed in his day because they belonged to Christ, said:

> "*The Gentiles . . . are surprised that you do not now join them in the same wild profligacy, and they abuse you; but they will give account to him who is ready to judge the living and the dead.*"

> (1 Peter 4:3 – 5, R.S.V.)

Responsibility before God

The Gentiles concerned in these remarks were knowingly passing judgement on the lives of the believers who had lived and preached among them. Reading earlier parts of the epistle, we gather that those who were being abused had had to defend themselves before their accusers who, perforce, would learn something further of the faith which they held (1 Peter 3:13 – 16).

We have a specific example of someone who had considerable knowledge of the Gospel, but had no intention of obeying it. He was Felix, a Roman governor, of whom we read:

> That he heard Paul defend himself and talk about resurrection of the dead, both just and unjust (Acts 24:10,15);
> That, in any case, he had more exact knowledge concerning the Way (v.22, R.V.);
> That he heard Paul in private telling him about "the faith in Christ" (v.24);
> That he heard Paul privately on more than one occasion. Paul reasoned with him about righteousness, temperance and the judgement to come (v.25, R.V.).

There can be no doubt at all that Felix had a considerable knowledge of the way of Christ from various sources, not least from Paul himself on several occasions. When Paul spoke of "the judgement to come", Felix trembled. He knew of his responsibility before God and was afraid.

In our day men do not meet Christ or Paul, nor do they see the miracles which were performed in those days. Nevertheless it is still possible to know that Christ is the light of the world, and to know about his words; it is still possible to learn about righteousness, temperance and the judgement to come. Certainly it is still possible to respond and to be saved; and it is possible to reject, and to be accountable before Christ.

In the end, the Judge of all the earth will be just.

From the Scriptures it is clear that "*many* who sleep in the dust of the earth" will be raised, but evidently there will be those whose sleep will not be disturbed. It would seem from various references in different parts of the Bible that those who remain asleep will be those who have not been in contact with the Word of God, and therefore cannot be said to be accountable to it at the coming of Jesus.

To every reader of these words there comes the hope of everlasting life by greater acquaintance with the light of the world and with the Word of God. We would earnestly commend you to God, and to the Word of His grace, which is able to provide the means whereby you might have an inheritance among all them that are sanctified by faith which is in Jesus Christ. This gracious invitation is made by the Lord God Almighty and has been vouchsafed to us by the death of His beloved Son. We should therefore take heed and the more so because we are told that "*God commandeth all men everywhere to repent*" (Acts 17:30).

20

REPENTANCE AND CONVERSION

TO some people these are old-fashioned words; they are good Bible words nevertheless. The idea of repentance and conversion has, however, been rendered suspect by various cult religions, sometimes with a "Christian" label attached to them. These cults apply such pressure to the minds of their converts as to render them almost incapable of thinking for themselves — even to the point where, in extreme cases, the converts are unable to respond to normal communication from their parents and former friends. For reasons of this kind it is understandable that people would shy away from considering repentance and conversion for fear of being swept along by irresistible emotion or by pressured thinking with no time to apply a critical examination to the process taking place.

Bible repentance and conversion are of an altogether different kind. But are they matters of the mind or of the heart or of both? Are they free responses or are the processes entirely involuntary? In any case, what do repentance and conversion consist of? What do the words mean?

Repentance is an essential part of the Gospel message, and it is impossible to be a disciple of the Lord Jesus Christ without it. Jesus said:

"Except ye repent, ye shall all likewise perish." (Luke 13:3)

"I am not come to call the righteous, but sinners to repentance."

(Luke 5:32, R.V.)

193

The same message was repeated by the apostles over and over again:

> "*Repent, and be baptized every one of you in the name of Jesus Christ for the remission of sins.*" (Acts 2:38)

> "*Then hath God granted to the Gentiles repentance unto life.*"
> (Acts 11:18)

> "*Repent ye therefore, and be converted, that your sins may be blotted out.*" (Acts 3:19)

> "*Now (God) commandeth all men everywhere to repent.*"
> (Acts 17:30)

> "*Testifying both to the Jews, and also to the Greeks, repentance toward God, and faith toward our Lord Jesus Christ.*" (Acts 20:21)

> "*Shewed ... to the Gentiles, that they should repent and turn to God, and do works meet for repentance.*" (Acts 26:20)

There is no doubt, therefore, that repentance is commanded by God and that without it there is no forgiveness of sins or hope of life everlasting. In other words it is impossible to be a Christian or have the Christian hope without manifesting repentance. What, then, is repentance, and how do we achieve it?

Let us start with the more fundamental question: Why do we need to repent? The answer is plain. Man is naturally sinful and God is righteous. Man has to acknowledge his plight by believing wholeheartedly in the Gospel of the Kingdom of God and the name of Jesus Christ and seeking to forsake his old way of life. Scriptures teach these basic truths:

> "*The heart (of man) is deceitful above all things, and it is desperately sick.*" (Jeremiah 17:9, R.V.)

> "*From within, out of the heart of men, proceed evil thoughts, adulteries, fornications, murders, thefts, covetousness, wickedness, deceit, lasciviousness, an evil eye, blasphemy, pride, foolishness: all these evil things come from within and defile the man.*" (Mark 7:21 – 23)

> "*Remember that Gentiles in the flesh ... are ... without Christ, being aliens from the commonwealth of Israel, and strangers from the covenants of promise, having no hope, and without God in the world.*"
> (Ephesians 2:11 – 12)

194

"Seek ye the Lord while he may be found, call ye upon him while he is near: let the wicked forsake his way, and the unrighteous man his thoughts: and let him return unto the Lord, and he will have mercy upon him; and to our God, for he will abundantly pardon. For my thoughts are not your thoughts, neither are your ways my ways, saith the Lord. For as the heavens are higher than the earth, so are my ways higher than your ways, and my thoughts than your thoughts." (Isaiah 55:6 – 9)

"This I say therefore, and testify in the Lord, that ye henceforth walk not as other Gentiles walk, in the vanity of their mind, having the understanding darkened, being alienated from the life of God through the ignorance that is in them, because of the blindness of their heart."

(Ephesians 4:17 – 18)

"Ye should turn from these vanities unto the living God, which made heaven and earth, and the sea, and all things therein." (Acts 14:15)

"Be it known therefore unto you, that the salvation of God is sent unto the Gentiles, and that they will hear it." (Acts 28:28)

"Paul . . . preaching the kingdom of God, and teaching those things which concern the Lord Jesus Christ . . ." (Acts 28:31)

"He expounded and testified the kingdom of God, persuading them concerning Jesus, both out of the law of Moses, and out of the prophets . . . and some believed . . . and some believed not."

(Acts 28:23 – 24)

"These . . . received the word with all readiness of mind, and searched the scriptures daily . . ." (Acts 17:11)

"Believe on the Lord Jesus Christ, and thou shalt be saved . . . and they spake unto him the word of the Lord . . . and (he) was baptized . . . and rejoiced, believing in God." (Acts 16:31 – 34)

"Assuming that you have heard about him and were taught in him, as truth is in Jesus, put off your old nature which belongs to your former manner of life, and is corrupt through deceitful lusts, and be renewed in the spirit of your minds, and put on the new nature, created after the likeness of God in true righteousness and holiness."

(Ephesians 4:21 – 23, R.S.V.)

The essence of repentance, conversion and the commencement of discipleship in Christ is to be found in these verses. We would recommend that they be read several times.

195

Repentance means "to have another mind". Repentance takes place in the mind, although the emotions are also caught up in the process. It is, however, important to observe that the process does not take place the other way round. Repentance is not an emotional experience which leaves the mind behind struggling, as it were, to keep up. *Any* willing person can come to repentance. It is a development which can be fostered or frustrated by the individual. Individual responsibility is not removed or abandoned by Biblical repentance; rather is such responsibility a vital part of the process of repentance.

How then do we come to repentance? How can we have "another mind"? The answer is to allow the Word of God to have free and welcome access to the mind we already have. The Word of God is divinely adapted to achieving a change of mind in the one who hears, understands and keeps the message. Those three steps are vital. "Hearing" the Word of God is more than merely reading it. Bible hearing is listening humbly with the intention of being instructed. In the Old Testament it is often described as "inclining the ear", as though one were listening to someone who has a message for him personally. Anyone who reads the Bible in this way will soon discover that the whole book is designed for the personal reader, the one who wants to know.

> "*Ho, everyone that thirsteth, come ye to the waters, and he that hath no money; come ye, buy, and eat; yea, come, buy wine and milk without money and without price.*" (Isaiah 55:1)

But how can a man buy without money? Buying is an exchange of one thing for another. It is not taking without giving. In reading the Word of God, a man must give himself. He must open the door of his mind and let the refreshing Word of God enter in. He must provide room in his mind for the message to have a place. This is the secret behind repentance and conversion. The Word of God, given root in the mind, will do its work without fail. Divine thoughts are imparted by the Word of God and the humble reader will soon begin to think the thoughts of God. He will begin to have "another mind":

> "*The law of the Lord is perfect,* **converting the soul***:*
> *The testimony of the Lord is sure, making wise the simple.*
> *The statutes of the Lord are right, rejoicing the heart:*
> *The commandment of the Lord is pure, enlightening the eyes* . . .

Moreover by them is thy servant warned:
And in keeping of them there is great reward."   (Psalm 19:7 – 11)

"Thy word is a lamp unto my feet, and a light unto my path."
(Psalm 119:105)

The first of the parables of the Lord Jesus, the Parable of the Sower, teaches us the principle of the working of the Word of God, and warns us of the consequences of neglecting it:

> *"He that received the seed into the good ground is he that heareth the word, and understandeth it; which also beareth fruit, and bringeth forth, some an hundredfold, some sixty, some thirty . . . . He also that received the seed among the thorns is he that heareth the word; and the care of this world, and the deceitfulness of riches, choke the word, and he becometh unfruitful."*   (Matthew 13:23, 22)

A Receptive Mind

The Word of God will grow in a receptive mind (*"the good ground", "an honest and good heart"*: Luke 8:15). It will bear fruit in daily living and carry within the heart the hope of everlasting life. On the other hand, the preoccupied mind, the mind filled with caring for the things of this world, will choke the growing seed and make it fruitless. The Word of God requires our willing co-operation in order to do its work. Unless there be first a willing mind, there is no progress. God holds out great blessings in His words, but these can be lost by the resistance of self-will:

> *"By hearing ye shall hear, and shall not understand; and seeing ye shall see, and shall not perceive: for this people's heart is waxed gross, and their ears are dull of hearing, and their eyes they have closed; lest at any time they should see with their eyes, and hear with their ears, and should understand with their heart, and should be converted, and I should heal them."*   (Matthew 13:14 – 15; quoted from Isaiah)

If men refuse to hear, to see and to understand, for whatever reasons, repentance and conversion will not take place, and God's healing process of forgiveness and restoration will not be accomplished. God knocks at the door, but He does not break it down; He invites, but He does not compel; He offers, but He does not force anyone to receive. As we have seen repeatedly through this book, God is active and redemptive and willing to save, but man is allowed his free choice.

197

There is no danger then of brain-washing. The Word of God does not obliterate the mind of the man who receives it; it instructs, edifies and converts him, but always with his knowing agreement, so that in the end he will be able to say:

*"So then with the mind, **I myself** serve the law of God."*

(Romans 7:25)

The new mind is formed by faith. *"Faith cometh by hearing, and hearing by the word of God"* (Romans 10:17). What commences as willingness to hear and be instructed, develops into understanding and belief in the Word and its message. We become sure about Bible teaching. We discover the beauty of the life of the Lord Jesus Christ and his teaching, and we begin to know our need of forgiveness. We become convinced that there is forgiveness with God, and a promise of everlasting life through repentance, baptism and conversion.

The Word of God is the revelation of the mind of God presented in the best way for teaching man who already has so many ideas, experiences, hopes and fears active within him. It takes time to produce order out of chaos, and enlightenment for the proper ordering of a relationship with God by faith through the Lord Jesus Christ.

Repentance is a change of mind for the better; in fact, for the best: not by violence or pressure, but by the gentle power of the seed of the Word of God taking root and growing. Salvation is not possible without repentance, and repentance is not possible without the Word of God. Once we realise how deeply offensive to God is a sinful and godless life, we are filled with a deep sorrow for the past. This is described as:

"Godly sorrow worketh repentance to salvation not to be repented of."

(2 Corinthians 7:10)

The sorrow seems to be all the more poignant because we know that God has prepared forgiveness, before ever we are brought to ask for it. We were lost, and God sent His only begotten Son to look for us. Repentance confesses the fruitless past and wants to leave it behind. Repentance develops the forward look of hope. Repentance wants to shape its life in readiness for the coming Kingdom of God.

What part, then, does conversion play?

Here are two Scriptures already quoted in this chapter:

198

"Repent, and be baptized every one of you in the name of Jesus Christ for the remission of sins." (Acts 2:38)

"Repent ye therefore, and be converted, that your sins may be blotted out . . ." (Acts 3:19)

There are three parts to the process of acceptance with God: repentance, baptism and conversion. We consider baptism in greater detail in a subsequent chapter, but at this point we should note that baptism is as necessary as repentance and conversion. It is the means whereby a faithful person is washed clean and is reborn to a new life in Christ Jesus. Bible baptism, without any doubt whatsoever, is full immersion in water of an adult who repents, believing the things concerning the Kingdom of God and the name of Jesus Christ.

The word "conversion" means to come again, to be restored, to return, to turn again or to turn about. Obviously conversion is closely related to repentance. It is the new thrust of life in a Godward direction. Conversion is the restoration of man to the care of God in a life which is seeking to please God in faith and righteousness. The Lord Jesus Christ expressed what is involved in a most comforting way:

"Come unto me, all ye that labour and are heavy laden, and I will give you rest. Take my yoke upon you, and learn of me; for I am meek and lowly in heart: and ye shall find rest unto your souls. For my yoke is easy, and my burden is light." (Matthew 11:28 – 30)

Conversion is a change of direction to take on the yoke of discipleship. Hitherto we have laboured under the burden of life without God and without any permanent and effective answers to life's true problems. The short-lived fruits of a Christless life may seem sweet at the time, but they leave a bitter taste when life's course has been run or life's tragedies and trials beset us. Jesus tells us that there is no need to labour and toil or to carry so great a burden of sin and anxiety. He is telling us that it is useless merely to pursue happiness by human effort. In the end, we discover that life of that kind is *"vanity and vexation of spirit (a striving after wind, R.V.)"* (Ecclesiastes 1:14).

There is an emptiness in human gain of almost every kind; it is the pursuit of a mirage. At best it does not truly solve the human dilemma, and at worst it is self-destructive and vain. The yoke of Christ makes an almost unbelievable difference to everything.

199

To any reader who knows himself and the world he lives in, we would say: You will find no message as true as the Gospel and no friend as true as Christ. He has never failed any one who has come to him humbly, believing what the Gospel teaches.

In the Parable of the Prodigal Son (Luke 15) we find the essence of repentance and conversion. The prodigal gets "another mind" or, as the parable puts it, "he came to himself". He took the first repentant steps towards home rehearsing carefully what he would say to his father when he arrived at his father's home. He would tell him that he had sinned against God and home by his way of life since he left his father. When he came within sight of home, sorry and ready to do the most menial tasks if his father would accept him, he received an unexpected and moving welcome. Although he was still a long way off, he discovered that his father was looking his way and, recognising his son, ran to meet him. He had wondered, perhaps, how stern and angry his father would be — he deserved everything his father could say — but was surprised by joy when he found himself overwhelmed by his father's embrace and was hastened homewards with unrestrained gladness. Instead of menial tasks there was a marvellous celebration of his homecoming, and he was restored to sonship without stint and with no further questions. The son was home, and his father was glad.

This fine parable is for us. There is only transient joy away from home. At home there is joy for evermore. Joy of forgiveness, joy of acceptance, joy of hope and joy of being with God through Jesus Christ our Lord.

These same truths are expressed throughout the Bible:

"The Lord hath done great things for us;
Whereof we are glad." (Psalm 126:3)

"Incline your ear, and come unto me: hear, and your soul shall live; and I will make an everlasting covenant with you, even the sure mercies of David." (Isaiah 55:3)

"Blessed is he whose transgression is forgiven, whose sin is covered . . .
I acknowledged my sin unto thee, and mine iniquity have I not hid.
I said, I will confess my transgressions unto the Lord;
And thou forgavest the iniquity of my sin.
For this shall every one that is godly pray unto thee in a time when thou mayest be found." (Psalm 32:1,5 – 6)

"I (Jesus) say unto you, there is joy in the presence of the angels of God over one sinner that repenteth." (Luke 15:10)

There can be no true peace and no true stability of life, nor can there be the fullest use of our human powers, until we enter into the service of God. He made us, and there is deep and abiding satisfaction in using ourselves as God intended. The human mind, renewed by divine instruction from the Word of God and thus brought to repentance, discovers undreamed of dimensions for itself when engaged in worship and godliness. Repentance and conversion bring a fulfilment which remains unattained and unknown until we enter upon it.

Repentance and conversion are not milestones which we pass on the way of life and never see again. This would be to misconceive their true meaning. It is true that life is like a journey (we shall consider the journey later on when we think about Walking with God), but there are abiding principles which are essential for the whole journey and not simply for its commencement. Certainly, repentance has a beginning and comes to a special maturity when we see our need for forgiveness and for union with Christ and the Lord God. But, the fruits of repentance appear at all seasons of life, and keep us in a humble attachment to God. Moreover, when sin appears in our discipleship — and there is no disciple who does not sin — the wells of repentance spring up again as we make confession to God and seek His face. It is for this reason that "Forgive us our trespasses" appears in the Lord's pattern prayer.

Similarly conversion is not a once and for all decision. It is a turning and returning to God throughout our lives. We take up our cross at the beginning, and we have to take it up every day. Constantly we have to take our bearings afresh, like mariners at sea, and correct our course towards God:

"I thought on my ways,
And turned my feet unto thy testimonies." (Psalm 119:59)

The threads of repentance and conversion are continuous in the wondrous pattern of life.

21

WHY SHOULD I NOT BE BAPTIZED?

THIS is the crucial question for every one who comes to an understanding of the Gospel. The mighty promises of God about the coming Kingdom of God on earth will have made their impact upon him. In his mind's eye, he will have come to Palestine and seen Christ walking its hills, teaching in its towns and villages, healing everywhere, and will have followed him on his final journey to Jerusalem. He will have stood in the halls of judgement and seen the Lord arraigned before Jews and Gentiles, mocked by soldiers, scourged and derided, crucified between two thieves, buried in a borrowed tomb and raised to glory. He will have seen the ever-empty tomb.

No man can reflect on these things without feeling himself moved and challenged. Whatever he decides to do about what he now knows, life will never be the same again. He has heard and learned, and felt the call of Christ: "Come unto me". He has reached a moment of responsibility – to himself and to God. He has been granted the most precious knowledge on earth, the knowledge of how to attain unto everlasting life at the cost of the death of the Son of God. To turn on his heel and spurn Christ's life and death, is to place himself with the men who rejected him so long ago. If we now judge Christ unworthy of our commitment, we cannot rid ourselves of the consequences of knowing him thus far.

It was the infamous and vacillating Pontius Pilate who asked the question of the Jewish authorities which we now ask of ourselves: "What shall I do then with Jesus who is called Christ?" Pilate did not know how every word of that question was itself a question.

What shall I do with Jesus? What *shall* I do with Jesus? What shall *I* do with Jesus? What shall I *do* with Jesus? What shall I do with *Jesus*? I am given the choice. I am not compelled. Unless it be that like Paul I exclaim, "The love of Christ constraineth me!"

This is the dilemma. Everything I know about the wonderful purpose of God shines with His love made undying in Christ. To leave this love unrequited is unthinkable, yet my inner selfishness, my deluding desire to please myself, pulls hard and would seek to turn my eyes away from his gaze. The alluring glitter of the world and my independence in it are like a light which calls me to it as a moth to the fatal candle. What doth hinder me to be baptized? Nothing, but myself.

If I truly know the things concerning the Kingdom of God and the name of Jesus Christ, there is nothing standing between me and baptism, except myself. I can turn away, unrepentant and still in my sins, or I can take the narrow way, the living way to God and life for evermore:

> "*If any man would come after me, let him deny himself, and take up his cross, and follow me. For whosoever would save his life shall lose it: and whosoever shall lose his life for my sake shall find it. For what shall a man be profited, if he shall gain the whole world, and forfeit his life? or what shall a man give in exchange for his life?*"
>
> (Matthew 16:24–26, R.V.)

What did Jesus mean when he talked about saving life and losing it, and losing and saving it? What we are to do with our life is the most important question we have to decide. Saving our life is keeping it for ourselves, living for ourselves regardless of God. Jesus says this will end in loss; life is slipping away and at its end it will have gone, even though we imagined we were saving it. To lose our life willingly, in the sense Jesus had in mind, is to surrender it to the service of Christ, to exchange our so-called freedom for discipleship. Why should I die to my old life in order to live henceforward as a yokefellow of Christ? The answer is plain: it is the way to everlasting life with Christ when he returns to earth.

Is it not folly to run counter to the Word of God? God cannot be wrong. Christ's words must be true. The man who pursues his own selfish way must certainly lose everything in the end. The man who chooses the way of repentance and conversion will have blessings beyond compare, both in this present life and in that which is to come.

203

Where does baptism fit into this choice? Is baptism necessary for salvation? Does the method of baptism matter at all? These are important questions and we proceed to answer them.

Among the last things said by Jesus is this command which he passed on to his apostles:

> *"All authority hath been given unto me in heaven and on earth. Go ye therefore, and make disciples of all the nations, baptizing them into the name of the Father and of the Son and of the Holy Spirit: teaching them to observe all things whatsoever I have commanded you: and lo, I am with you alway, even unto the end of the world."*

(Matthew 28:18 – 20, R.V.)

> *"And he said unto them, Go ye into all the world, and preach the gospel to every creature. He that believeth and is baptized shall be saved; but he that believeth not shall be damned."* (Mark 16:15 – 16)

Clearly the apostles were instructed to include baptism in their preaching of the Gospel message. But as Jesus said, baptism was to be preceded by belief. Baptism was to be "in the name". The Gospel gives us understanding and therefrom springs our faith which should lead us to baptism. Baptism is the means whereby we enter into Christ and are covered by the gracious effectiveness of his blood. It will be realised that these things are for mature decision. Baptism is for adults.

There is no record anywhere in Scripture of the baptism of babies. The practice of christening was introduced gradually from the second century A.D., and became the accepted practice much later on; but it has no place in the Gospel as Christ and the apostles preached it. There is a good reason for this.

There is no guilt attaching to newborn babies from which they can or need to be freed. Truly, they are born of Adam and share our common mortality and proneness to sin, but there is no guilt attaching to babies simply on account of their birth. None of us is guilty because we are human: we had no choice in the matter. We are responsible for the sins we ourselves commit. There is no "original sin" which christening can remove, or adult baptism for that matter. The original sin was Adam's: we share the consequences but do not bear the blame for that sin.

What does faithful baptism achieve for us? Consider the following passages:

> *"Repent, and be baptized every one of you in the name of Jesus Christ for*

the remission of sins, and ye shall receive the gift of the Holy Spirit."
                                                    (Acts 2:38)

"Then they that gladly received his word were baptized: and the same day there were added unto them about 3000 souls."   (Acts 2:41)

"But when they believed Philip preaching the things concerning the kingdom of God, and the name of Jesus Christ, they were baptized, both men and women."   (Acts 8:12)

"Then Philip opened his mouth, and . . . told him the good news of Jesus. And as they went along the road they came to some water, and the eunuch said, 'See, here is water! What is to prevent my being baptized?' . . . and they both went down into the water, Philip and the eunuch, and he baptized him. And when they came up out of the water . . . the eunuch . . . went on his way rejoicing."   (Acts 8:35 – 39, R.S.V.)

"Then answered Peter, Can any man forbid the water that these should not be baptized . . . and he commanded them to be baptized in the name of Jesus Christ."   (Acts 10:47, 48, R.V.)

"Believe on the Lord Jesus Christ, and thou shalt be saved, and thy house. And they spake unto him the word of the Lord, and to all that were in his house. And (he) was baptized, he and all his straightway."
                                                    (Acts 16:31 – 33)

"And now why tarriest thou? arise, and be baptized, and wash away thy sins, calling on the name of the Lord."   (Acts 22:16)

"Know ye not, that so many of us as were baptized into Jesus Christ were baptized into his death? Therefore we are buried with him by baptism into death: that like as Christ was raised up from the dead by the glory of the Father, even so we also should walk in newness of life."

                                                    (Romans 6:3 – 5)

"For ye are all the children of God by faith in Christ Jesus. For as many of you as have been baptized into Christ have put on Christ . . . and if ye be Christ's, then are ye Abraham's seed, and heirs according to the promise."   (Galatians 3:26 – 29)

"There is one body, and one Spirit, even as ye are called in one hope of your calling; one Lord, one faith, one baptism, one God and Father of all, who is above all, and through all, and in you all."

                                                    (Ephesians 4:4 – 6)

> *"Buried with him in baptism, wherein also ye are risen with him through the faith of the operation of God, who hath raised him from the dead."* (Colossians 2:12)

> *"The longsuffering of God waited in the days of Noah, while the ark was a preparing, wherein few, that is, eight souls were saved by water. The like figure whereunto even baptism doth also now save us (not the putting away of the filth of the flesh, but the answer of a good conscience toward God), by the resurrection of Jesus Christ."* (1 Peter 3:20 – 21)

These Scriptures make clear the importance of baptism. To neglect this teaching is to neglect an essential part of the Gospel. To get the principles of baptism clear in one's mind is to grasp hold of a truth which links together numerous other parts of the Gospel.

Immersion in Water

The word "baptize" has been carried through from Greek almost unchanged. It was an everyday word, not one with solely a religious meaning. Dipping one's hands in water was to baptize them. To immerse a garment in a bath of dye was to baptize it. Anything baptized was completely covered in water. It was therefore a most appropriate word to use for baptism by which the believer was totally immersed in water. Immersion was the first century method of administering baptism.

When the Lord himself was baptized by John the Baptist, we read that "he went from Galilee to Jordan unto John to be baptized of him". The baptism took place in the river and the record in Matthew 3 continues, "and Jesus, when he was baptized, went up straightway out of the water".

Similarly, when Philip baptized the government official of the queen of the Ethiopians, we read that *"they went down both into the water, both Philip and the eunuch; and he baptized him. And when they were come up out of the water ..."* (Acts 8:38 – 39). The practice, therefore, of the earliest Christians was to baptize adults and to do it by immersion in water. The candidates for baptism were believers in the Gospel. There is no reason whatever to depart in the twentieth century from this practice and command. The arguments sometimes advanced would have been as applicable in the first century as in the twentieth, had they been true. We would earnestly entreat readers to look again at all the verses of Scripture quoted in this chapter. *Baptism is not optional: it is a command of Christ and of his apostles.*

The Bible description of baptism in Romans 6 and Colossians 2 is "Burial in water". Why is burial an apt figure for the act of baptism? Clearly it teaches that baptism is related to death. Whose death? In the first place, the death of the Lord Jesus Christ:

> "*So many of us as were baptized into Jesus Christ were baptized into his death.*" (Romans 6:3)

Baptism in faith is our meeting point with the saving death of Jesus without which there is no forgiveness of sins and therefore no hope. Calvary is at the heart of Christianity. Baptism is our open confession of our need for and acceptance of Calvary's redeeming grace. In baptism we meet Jesus in his death in the way appointed by Christ himself.

Baptism's burial is also a confession of our mortality, a recognition that by nature and without Christ we shall end our days in death. Moreover, baptism is an act of burying our old life that we might come forth to a "newness of life" in Christ. The old man dies, that the new man might live. Baptism is the token that we are crucified with Christ. We share his dying in putting away our old way of life.

It is important to reflect on forgiveness. How do we obtain this gracious blessing from God? There is only one way: baptism. Baptism is the divinely appointed means whereby a true believer in the Gospel may be cleansed from all of his past sins. Some readers may feel that forgiveness comes to the repentant sinner as soon as he makes confession of his need. That is not the case. We know that an old hymn contains the words:

> "The vilest offender who truly believes,
> That moment from Jesus a pardon receives."

Well-intentioned as these words may be, they are not Scriptural in their content. The cross of Jesus is made effective in baptism, and not simply by confession of need. Notice again how clearly forgiveness is related to the believer's repentance and baptism:

> "*Repent, and be baptized every one of you in the name of Jesus Christ for the remission of sins.*" (Acts 2:38)

> "*Arise, and be baptized, and wash away thy sins, calling on the name of the Lord.*" (Acts 22:16)

A believing, repentant person receives forgiveness of sins by being baptized. That is Bible teaching. Perhaps the best illustration of the truth of this teaching is the apostle Paul. When as Saul of Tarsus he was apprehended by Christ on the journey to Damascus, he knew and confessed that Jesus was the Lord. The pricks of conscience, the blinding light and the challenging voice left him no option: he knew that Christ was risen and victorious, and he cast away all his former hardness and opposition and unbelief in the words:

> *"What shall I do, Lord?"* (Acts 22:10)

This dramatic change in the life of a former enemy of Christ and a persecutor of his followers has been hailed through the centuries as an example of repentance and conversion. And so it is. The inner struggle which had been taking place in the mind of Saul was brought to a crisis and resolved. But when were Saul's sins forgiven? On the way to Damascus? The Bible answer is that Saul's sins were washed away three days later when he was baptized. It was at that time that Ananias, Christ's faithful messenger to the blinded Saul, said:

> *"And now why tarriest thou? arise, and be baptized, and **wash away thy sins**, calling on the name of the Lord."* (Acts 22:16)

Baptism is that act of belief and repentance by which the believer submits himself to Christ and has his personal sins forgiven. Baptism is not simply a ritual washing, but a matter of conscience, as it is expressed by Peter:

> *"Not as a removal of dirt from the body but as an appeal to God for a clear conscience, through the resurrection of Jesus Christ."*
>
> (1 Peter 3:21, R.S.V.)

True baptism removes past sins. But baptism is not confined to looking back. It brings rebirth to a new life, a life in Christ, about which Jesus said:

> *"Except a man be born again, he cannot see the kingdom of God. . . . Except a man be born of water and of the Spirit, he cannot enter into the kingdom of God: . . . Marvel not that I said unto thee, Ye must be born again."* (John 3:3,5,7)

The incorruptible seed of the Word of God (1 Peter 1:23) working in the faithful heart, blessed by God, brings forth the new man through baptism by bringing the believer into Christ. *"If any man be in Christ, he is a new creature: old things are passed away; behold, all things are become new"* (2 Corinthians 5:17). Our former fleshly birth, which was ours by nature, is superseded by this new spiritual birth by which we become sons of God:

> *"For ye are all the children of God by faith in Christ Jesus. For as many of you as have been baptized into Christ have put on Christ."*
>
> (Galatians 3:26 – 27)

Baptism is also the token of a larger process by which finally the faithful disciple will enter into everlasting life. At that time his flesh and blood will be swallowed up of life by being clothed upon with immortality (1 Corinthians 15:50 – 54 and 2 Corinthians 5:4). This process too is compared to a birth:

> *"For . . . the whole creation groaneth and travaileth in pain together until now. And . . . even we ourselves groan within ourselves, waiting for the adoption, to wit, the redemption of our body."*
>
> (Romans 8:22 – 23)

Baptism makes us heirs of the promises of God made to the fathers of old. This aspect of the work of baptism is both important and comforting. The great and precious promises which God made to Abraham and his seed are also available to us. When we are baptized into Christ we become heirs with Christ:

> *"If ye be Christ's, then are ye Abraham's seed, and heirs according to the promise."* (Galatians 3:29)

Thus we become part of the spiritual family of Abraham, the man of faith, and share the hopes and the blessings which God bestowed upon him:

> *"That he might be the father of all them that believe . . . who also walk in the steps of that faith of our father Abraham . . . For the promise, that he should be heir of the world, was not to Abraham, or to his seed, through the law, but through the righteousness of faith . . . that . . . the promise might be sure to all the seed . . . of the faith of Abraham; who is the father of us all."* (Romans 4:11 – 13,16)

The covenant which God made with Abraham thus embraces the true believer who is baptized and becomes a member of the family of the everlasting covenant, in which alone there is hope of everlasting life:

> *"This is my blood of the covenant, which is poured out for many for the forgiveness of sins."* (Matthew 26:28, R.S.V.)

> *"This cup is the new covenant in my blood. Do this, as often as you drink it, in remembrance of me."* (1 Corinthians 11:25, R.S.V.)

> *"Jesus, the mediator of the new covenant . . ."* (Hebrews 12:24)

> *"Now the God of peace, that brought again from the dead our Lord Jesus, that great shepherd of the sheep, through the blood of the everlasting covenant, make you perfect in every good work to do his will."*
>
> (Hebrews 13:20 – 21)

Children of the covenant are born by faithful baptism. Cleansed from sin by the blood of Christ they are brought within the family of Abraham and have hope of the inheritance of the Kingdom and of life everlasting.

Baptism translates us into an entirely new set of relationships. We become members of the household of God, and are enrolled as citizens of the kingdom of God (Ephesians 2:19). Our names are inscribed in the book of life, in which they will remain unless we prove to be unfaithful to our calling (Philippians 4:3). We have entered into the race for life eternal in which we compete, not to displace or vanquish others, but to complete the course in patient endurance (1 Corinthians 9:24 – 25). Though still in Adam as regards our earthly natures, we become God's own children and enjoy all the privileges and share the responsibilities of the new family of which God is Father. All of these things come by forgiveness of sins in true baptism from whose waters we rise to a new life, as by resurrection, to be lived in love, faithfulness and fruitfulness (Romans 6:4,18,22).

Therefore the wonderful work of baptism is essential to salvation. Surely it is impossible to resist the conclusion that baptism is a command of Christ which it would be disaster to disobey. New Testament disciples were baptized disciples. If we wish to tread the same path, we should pass through the same cleansing waters. Peter the faithful apostle once wrote:

> *"Baptism . . . saves you."* (1 Peter 3:21, R.S.V.)

No one who wants everlasting life and understands these teachings should ever seek to avoid the call of Christ to believe and be baptized. We must cry out with the eunuch:

"What is to prevent my being baptized?"   (Acts 8:36, R.S.V.)

A good and honest heart will eagerly desire baptism and the abundant blessing of God which accompanies it. Gladly will such a person come, as it were, to the waters of Jordan that its flowing stream may pass over him and bear all his sins away, as though by the blood of Christ:

> *"Though your sins be as scarlet, they shall be white as snow; though they be red like crimson, they shall be as wool. If ye be willing and obedient."*

(Isaiah 1:18 – 19)

211

22

WALKING WITH GOD

DISCIPLESHIP is a journey to the Kingdom of God. Not until the journey is over is the process of salvation completed. Salvation is not a once-for-all, irreversible happening. To claim otherwise is to misunderstand both the nature of salvation and the way in which it is accomplished. The Bible tells us:

> "*To those who by persistence in doing good **seek** glory, honour and immortality, he (God) **will give** eternal life ... This will take place **on the day** when God will judge men's secrets through Jesus Christ, as my gospel declares.*" (Romans 2:7,16, N.I.V.)

> "*For the word of the cross is folly to those who are perishing, but to us who **are being saved** it is the power of God.*"
> (1 Corinthians 1:18, R.S.V.)

> "*The gospel which I preached unto you ... by which also ye are saved, **if ye keep in memory** what I preached unto you.*"
> (1 Corinthians 15:1 – 2)

This work of salvation continues throughout the life of the disciple. He is saved finally because he has held fast to the lifeline secured in Christ. Salvation commences in the initial change by which, from being servants to sin, we enter the family of God; it is demonstrated in faith by living godly lives, and it is completed when, at the hands of Christ when he returns, the disciple is granted the glorious gift of immortality. Thereby the true believer becomes for ever a son of God.

212

Meanwhile the disciple must reflect in this present life the hope of the life to come. He must make known that he belongs to the Lord Jesus Christ by being Christlike. His character has to develop those likenesses to Jesus which are made known in the Sermon on the Mount and throughout the pages of the New Testament. His new life must not look as though it is rooted in this life. Rather must he be a pilgrim, a sojourner, a traveller making a journey.

The Bible uses many descriptive phrases to tell us about the pilgrim aspect of the disciple's life. One of these is "walking with God". The easiest and best way to understand those words is to read a number of verses of the Bible in which the subject is mentioned:

"Enoch walked with God . . . " (Genesis 5:22,24)

"Noah was a just man and perfect in his generations, and . . . walked with God." (Genesis 6:9)

"I am the Almighty God; walk before me, and be thou perfect." (Genesis 17:1)

"He hath shewed thee, O man, what is good; and what doth the Lord require of thee, but to do justly, and to love mercy, and to walk humbly with thy God?" (Micah 6:8)

"Who is wise, and he shall understand these things? prudent, and he shall know them? for the ways of the Lord are right, and the just shall walk in them: but the transgressors shall fall therein." (Hosea 14:9)

"All them that believe . . . who also walk in the steps of that faith of our father Abraham . . . " (Romans 4:11,12)

"Walk worthy of God, who hath called you unto his kingdom and glory . . . " (1 Thessalonians 2:12)

"Be ye therefore . . . as dear children; and walk in love, as Christ also hath loved us, and hath given himself for us . . . walk as children of light . . . have no fellowship with the unfruitful works of darkness . . . see then that ye walk circumspectly, not as fools, but as wise, redeeming the time, because the days are evil." (Ephesians 5:1 – 15)

"As ye have therefore received Christ Jesus the Lord, so walk ye in him: rooted and built up in him, and stablished in the faith, as ye have been taught, abounding therein with thanksgiving." (Colossians 2:6 – 7)

213

"Yea, though I walk through the valley of the shadow of death, I will fear no evil: for thou art with me." (Psalm 23:4)

"For he hath said, I will never leave thee, nor forsake thee. So that we may boldly say, The Lord is my helper, and I will not fear . . ."
(Hebrews 13:5 – 6)

It is evident from these words of God that the life of the disciple is not that of someone who is already at the end of a journey, resting and well satisfied that travelling is over, his mission accomplished. Discipleship is the response to the initiation into the family of God, and a ready acceptance of the responsibility to seek to live a life of faithful waiting for the return of the King.

Discipleship

The disciple has entered the narrow way to everlasting life, and he must journey in faith until death closes his eyes in sleep in his Lord, or, should it be so, the Lord himself comes back in the midst of his travelling. The narrow way is well marked with good signposts. The path itself is imprinted with the footsteps of those who also have walked the pilgrim way, including the Lord Jesus Christ, who commanded us to follow him.

The Bible is full of guidance. It tells us about the path, about the snares and pitfalls, about the places of refreshment and about the true companions on the way:

"Thy word is a lamp unto my feet,
and a light unto my path . . ." (Psalm 119:105)

"The commandment is a lamp; and the law is a light."
(Proverbs 6:23)

"Trust in the Lord with all thine heart; and lean not to thine own understanding. In all thy ways acknowledge him, and he shall direct thy paths." (Proverbs 3:5 – 6)

"Then shalt thou walk in thy way safely, and thy foot shall not stumble. When thou liest down, thou shalt not be afraid: yea, thou shalt lie down, and thy sleep shall be sweet." (Proverbs 3:23 – 24)

"For the Lord shall be thy confidence, and shall keep thy foot from being taken." (Proverbs 3:26)

"Enter not into the path of the wicked, and walk not in the way of evil

men. Avoid it, pass not by it, turn from it, and pass on."

(Proverbs 4:14, R.V.)

"*There is a way that seemeth right unto a man, but the end thereof are the ways of death.*" (Proverbs 16:25)

"*The path of the righteous is like the first gleam of dawn, shining ever brighter till the full light of day.*" (Proverbs 4:18, N.I.V.)

Such counsel is practical and sound. There are things which have to be done, and those which must be altogether avoided. Discipleship is a way of life. We must follow the footsteps of the men of Scripture, particularly those of the Lord himself. The Bible is the inspired handbook, the traveller's compass and road map; it provides unfailing, positive and clear advice for everyday living. No man can keep a true course without using the Bible. It is to be read every day.

Daily Bible Reading

Faithful Bible reading is the true source of the revealed wisdom of God. The disciple must not be merely selective in his reading. Naturally, every Bible reader has his favourite verses from which he draws sustenance and solace. However, the "pick and choose" method of reading has very serious shortcomings. Anyone who reads, say, the New Testament soon becomes aware that Christ and his apostles ranged widely over the Old Testament for purposes of instruction and consolation. A more careful reading of the New Testament will reveal that there are very few books of the Old Testament which are not quoted or alluded to in some way. Many of the well-known texts of the New Testament and much of the parables are to be found in the Old Testament. The Word of God is the whole of the Bible.

Furthermore this dependence of the New Testament on the Old is the key to the unity of Scripture and provides evidence of the common origin in God of the whole Bible. The Old Testament is equally dependent on the New. The many hundreds of verses in the Old containing promises and prophecy about the coming Saviour and King are given their fulness in the New Testament revelation concerning the Lord Jesus Christ.

We urge once more therefore that every Bible reader should be a reader of the whole Bible. It is not left to man to decide what is good for him. If the Lord Jesus Christ referred his disciples to the

215

law, the prophets and the Psalms, then we, too, must read them. If they were good enough for Jesus, they must be good enough for us.

The apostle Paul, when talking to the elders of one of the congregations he had visited, told them that he had not shunned to declare unto them *"the whole counsel of God"* (Acts 20:27, R.V.). His writings and speeches are ample proof of his extensive use of a very wide range of Scripture which formed part of the essential armoury of his life and preaching.

"The whole counsel of God"

Therefore disciples cannot do better than to follow the footsteps of these good men as they walk through the palace of the Bible. This is one of the ways in which we walk with God. As we traverse His word, He speaks His counsel to us — everywhere, and often in the most unexpected of places within the holy pages. We must remember that there is no knowledge of salvation from any other source than the Bible. It would be the deepest folly to neglect the Book. God asks: *"Can two walk together, except they be agreed?"* (Amos 3:3). How can we agree with God except by learning of His mind and purpose? Thereby we shall get mutual understanding. The Bible makes known the mind of the Lord for the benefit of man:

> *"The holy scriptures . . . are able to make thee wise unto salvation through faith which is in Christ Jesus. All scripture is given by inspiration of God, and is profitable for doctrine, for reproof, for correction, for instruction in righteousness: that the man of God may be perfect, throughly furnished unto all good works."*
>
> (2 Timothy 3:15 – 17)

The central place of the Word of God in the life of the true disciple is therefore beyond all doubt. To place it elsewhere will be seriously to err.

It is the Bible which points us and leads us to another relationship which, while resting on the Word of God, is additional to it. The relationship is with God Himself. The man who becomes a disciple in the way we have outlined elsewhere passes into God's personal care. He is no longer a spiritual waif and stray. He is a living member of the living family of God. He is, too, within the flock of the Good Shepherd. There is no more secure or more reassuring haven of safety: no other source of unfailing love and constant welfare. Listen to the comforting voice of God:

"As God hath said, I will dwell in them, and walk in them; and I will be their God, and they shall be my people. Wherefore, come out from among them, and be ye separate, saith the Lord, and touch not the unclean thing; and I will receive you, and will be a Father unto you, and ye shall be my sons and daughters, saith the Lord Almighty."

(2 Corinthians 6:16 – 18)

"My sheep hear my voice, and I know them, and they follow me: and I give unto them eternal life; and they shall never perish, neither shall any man pluck them out of my hand. My Father, which gave them me, is greater than all; and no man is able to pluck them out of my Father's hand."

(John 10:27 – 29)

"He that hath my commandments, and keepeth them, he it is that loveth me: and he that loveth me shall be loved of my Father, and I will love him, and will manifest myself to him . . . if a man love me, he will keep my words: and my Father will love him, and we will come unto him, and make our abode with him."

(John 14:21,23)

"Humble yourselves therefore under the mighty hand of God, that he may exalt you in due time: casting all your care upon him; for he careth for you."

(1 Peter 5:6 – 7)

"Draw nigh to God, and he will draw nigh to you . . . humble yourselves in the sight of the Lord, and he shall lift you up."

(James 4:8,10)

"Now unto him that is able to keep you from falling, and to present you faultless before the presence of his glory with exceeding joy, to the only wise God our Saviour, be glory and majesty, dominion and power, both now and ever. Amen."

(Jude 24 – 25)

What more could the disciple need than to know that he is in the supreme care of God and His Son? These are blessings beyond compare, and they are revealed and made available for our eternal salvation. They are both individual and collective, for each sheep and for the flock.

But the benefits are not indiscriminately given. A re-reading of the above list of passages will reveal that the blessings flow in defined and free channels. A man must be humble and submissive to the Word of God. God can find no way into a proud heart: it is too fully occupied with self-importance. It is not that the blessings have to be earned. We have to make ourselves acceptable to receive them:

"Come out . . . and be ye separate"
"Hear my voice . . . follow me"
"Hath my commandments, and keepeth them"
"Humble yourselves . . . cast all your care upon him"
"Draw nigh to God . . . humble yourselves . . ."

The above lines are extracts from verses we have previously examined, and they tell us of the ways in which the channels of blessings can be opened for the disciple. It is useless to live a life which is not taking the Word of God as its guide. To be materialistic or pleasure seeking or untruthful or unscrupulous, is to leave the path of Christ and to block all the channels through which blessings would flow. Love for God is not simply "a good and warm feeling"; it is defined by Jesus in the following straightforward terms:

> *"He that hath my commandments, and keepeth them, he it is that loveth me."* (John 14:21)

Love keeps close to the Word of God.

Peace of Mind

If we do these things, shall we have a serene and happy existence without storms or snares? The disciple on reading his Bible will become aware of two totally different but, in the end, complementary strands of teaching concerning the experiences of the life of a disciple. Here are verses of the first kind:

> *"Peace I leave with you, my peace I give unto you"* (John 14:27)

> *"These things have I spoken unto you, that my joy might remain in you, and that your joy might be full."* (John 15:11)

> *"These things I have spoken unto you, that in me ye might have peace."* (John 16:33)

> *"Therefore being justified by faith, we have peace with God through our Lord Jesus Christ."* (Romans 5:1)

> *"And the peace of God, which passeth all understanding, shall keep your hearts and minds through Christ Jesus."* (Philippians 4:7)

Peace and joy are the privilege of the believer when he is justified by faith. The origin of these blessings is in God and in His Son; they are not a simple personal ecstasy nor what is commonly held

218

by everyday people to be joy or happiness. They run deeper, much deeper, than that. The secret lies in their abiding nature and their sure links with things which are eternal and truly blessed. For example, examine the following verse of Scripture and see whether or not it conveys to you a sense of marvellous assurance on the part of the inspired writer (Paul), despite the difficult circumstances of his life which might otherwise have been thought to be destructive of joy, peace and certainty:

> *"Our light affliction, which is but for a moment, worketh for us a far more exceeding and eternal weight of glory; while we look not at the things which are seen, but at the things which are not seen: for the things which are seen are temporal, but the things which are not seen are eternal."*
>
> (2 Corinthians 4:17 – 18)

The secret of this peace does not lie in a trouble-free existence, as though one sailed under cloudless skies on calm waters. The peace of mind comes first from the forgiveness of sins in Christ, and then from the certainty that the journey on which we have embarked in him leads to everlasting life. Our part is to remain faithful to him.

Life's experiences in the hands of the Father and the Good Shepherd are designed, if the disciple will receive them as such, to fashion him for eternity. They are character-building. The rough rock of humanity will be shaped thereby and polished for use in God's eternal building. The silver is being purified in the fire. In another figure, man is in the hands of the Divine Potter who seeks to make an honourable vessel for His house. Starting with our human frame, and a heart and mind already well-used in the ways of sin, the Lord works His wonders of change and transformation. This cannot be achieved without pain and tribulation from time to time. These thoughts introduce us to the second strand of Scripture thought which tells of trial and testing, but always for our good:

> *"These things have I spoken unto you, that my joy may be in you, and that your joy may be fulfilled."* (John 15:11, R.V.)

> *"These things I have spoken unto you, that in me ye might have peace. In the world ye shall have tribulation: but be of good cheer; I have overcome the world."* (John 16:33)

> *"Confirming the souls of the disciples, and exhorting them to continue in the faith, and that we must through much tribulation enter into the kingdom of God."* (Acts 14:22)

"If children, then heirs; heirs of God, and joint-heirs with Christ; if so be that we suffer with him, that we may be also glorified with him."
(Romans 8:17, R.V.)

"That I may know him (Christ), and the power of his resurrection, and the fellowship of his sufferings, being made conformable unto his death . . . forgetting those things which are behind, and reaching forth unto those things which are before, I press toward the mark for the prize of the high calling of God in Christ Jesus." (Philippians 3:10 – 14)

"Ye have forgotten the exhortation which speaketh unto you as unto children, My son, despise not thou the chastening of the Lord, nor faint when thou art rebuked of him: for whom the Lord loveth he chasteneth, and scourgeth every son whom he receiveth . . . Now no chastening for the present seemeth to be joyous, but grievous: nevertheless afterward it yieldeth the peaceable fruit of righteousness unto them which are exercised thereby." (Hebrews 12:5 – 11)

"Count it all joy, my brethren, when ye fall into manifold temptations; knowing that the proof of your faith worketh patience. And let patience have its perfect work, that ye may be perfect and entire, lacking in nothing." (James 1:2 – 4, R.V.)

"Blessed is the man that endureth temptation: for when he hath been approved, he shall receive the crown of life, which the Lord promised to them that love him." (James 1:12, R.V.)

"As many as I (Jesus) love, I rebuke and chasten: be zealous therefore, and repent." (Revelation 3:19)

Peace with God in Christ; proof of our faith whilst on probation; eternal peace in the Kingdom of God: that is the divinely prescribed order of progression. We deceive ourselves if we think otherwise. The surest way of discovering the truth of these things is to read the lives of faithful men throughout the Bible. Some of them had trials beyond our imaginings:

"Others had trials of cruel mockings and scourgings, yea, moreover of bonds and imprisonment: they were stoned, they were sawn asunder, were tempted, were slain with the sword: they wandered about in sheepskins and goatskins; being destitute, afflicted, tormented; (of whom the world was not worthy:) they wandered in deserts, and in mountains, and in dens and caves of the earth." (Hebrews 11:36 – 38)

The Fire of Affliction

These were not forsaken men and women: they were the precious and chosen of God who, passing through the fire of affliction, were prepared for the final inheritance. *"They shall walk with me in white"*, says the Lord, *"for they are worthy"* (Revelation 3:4). Persecution has occurred not infrequently, but it is not the lot of believers generally. Nor should the disciple seek it or provoke it. Christ told his disciples not to linger in those places where the Gospel was spurned and the preacher ill-used. The preacher is not to persist simply to bear pain. On the other hand, when converts had been made, Paul would suffer for them, and endure hardness. Foolhardiness and deliberately seeking ill-treatment to prove our strength is contrary to the basic principles of the Lord's prayer:

"Lead me not into temptation, but deliver me from evil."

Chastisement and challenge will come in the ordinary things of life. Living righteously in an evil world is sure to produce trials enough. Learning to control the runaway or bitter tongue, doing an honest day's work for our employers, treasuring our marriage, instructing our children in the ways of truth, mastering evil thoughts, enduring ill-treatment for wrongs we have not committed and a thousand and one other things in the normal life of man and woman, will be sources of continual testing of our spiritual defences.

But the disciple need not fear that things outside his control will become so powerful as to overcome him completely. God has promised that the believer will be cared for and kept from trials which he cannot withstand:

"There hath no temptation taken you but such as man can bear: but God is faithful, who will not suffer you to be tempted above that ye are able; but will with the temptation make also the way of escape, that ye may be able to endure it." (1 Corinthians 10:13, R.V.)

"The Lord knoweth how to deliver the godly out of temptations." (2 Peter 2:9)

"The angel of the Lord encampeth round about them that fear him, and delivereth them." (Psalm 34:7)

God's care is actual and constant. Whether by angels, or by working in the circumstances of daily life and in response to our cries in prayer, the Lord works for His disciples:

221

"He that dwelleth in the secret place of the Most High
Shall abide under the shadow of the Almighty.
I will say of the Lord, He is my refuge and my fortress:
My God; in him will I trust.
Surely he shall deliver thee . . ."

(Psalm 91:1 – 3)

But how does the disciple find his strength in which to endure and to overcome? Each disciple knows his own weaknesses and the unreliability of human nature, however good-intentioned he might appear to be. There is no magical way by which a man overcomes. There is no wand to wave, no effortless access of power. The disciple must slip his hand into the outstretched hand of God, surrendering his own will and all his self-trust, and, equipped with the counsel of the Word of God, ask God in prayer for blessing and help. Prayer is the disciple's line of communication. It is ever open, and God is never absent:

"The righteous cry, and the Lord heareth,
And delivereth them out of all their troubles.
The eyes of the Lord are upon the righteous,
And his ears are open to their cry."   (Psalm 34:17,15)

"The steps of a good man are ordered by the Lord:
And he delighteth in his way.
Though he fall, he shall not be utterly cast down:
For the Lord upholdeth him with his hand."   (Psalm 37:23 – 24)

"When I said, My foot slippeth;
thy mercy, O Lord, held me up."   (Psalm 94:18)

"And we know that all things work together for good to them that love God, to them who are the called according to his purpose . . . What shall we say then to these things? If God be for us, who can be against us? . . . Who shall separate us from the love of Christ? shall tribulation, or distress, or persecution, or famine, or nakedness, or peril, or sword? . . . Nay, in all these things we are more than conquerors through him that loved us."   (Romans 8:28,31,35 – 37)

"That he (Jesus) might be a merciful and faithful high priest in things pertaining to God, to make reconciliation for the sins of the people. For in that he himself hath suffered being tempted, he is able to succour them that are tempted."   (Hebrews 2:17 – 18)

"We have not an high priest which cannot be touched with the feeling of

222

our infirmities; but was in all points tempted like as we are, yet without sin. Let us therefore come boldly unto the throne of grace, that we may obtain mercy, and find grace to help in time of need."

(Hebrews 4:15 – 16)

The disciple has limitless comfort, help and strength. The power of prayer is effective and unfailing. With Christ as mediator in heaven for us, who could want more? Everything is secure in him, and he has anchored us to himself — if we are truly his disciples:

"That . . . we might have a strong consolation, who have fled for refuge to lay hold upon the hope set before us: which hope we have as an anchor of the soul, both sure and stedfast . . . Jesus . . . an high priest for ever."

(Hebrews 6:18 – 20)

These are the blessings, certainties and everlasting hope of walking with God.

23

THE DISCIPLE AND THE WORLD

HOW does the disciple stand in relation to the world around him? Are the links and habits which he had before his belief and repentance affected by his new bond with God and the Lord Jesus Christ? What about his new life and his relationship with the State?

These and many questions like them have been asked for centuries. Answers and attitudes have varied among the various parts of Christendom. Some have felt that life goes on more or less as before, but that the principles of Christ's teaching should raise the standard of one's behaviour without necessarily producing radical changes in other respects. For example, a church which has strong links with the State, seems to expect to find its members in all branches of the Armed Forces and in politics. In contrast, there are those who belong to religious groups whose contact with the world around them is so deeply restricted as to regard other men and women as though they were totally alien.

What is the right procedure for the disciple to adopt? Or is it a matter of personal conscience and not general application? What does the Bible say? Let us adopt the practice followed throughout this book and set out a thoroughly representative selection of Scriptures. From these we should be able to find guidance for daily life for the true disciple of the Lord Jesus Christ. We surely cannot have been left without guidance. Here, then, are the words of the Bible:

"Behold the Lamb of God, which taketh away the sin of the world."
(John 1:29)

"God so loved the world, that he gave his only begotten Son, that whosoever believeth in him should not perish, but have everlasting life."
(John 3:16)

"If ye were of the world, the world would love his own: but because ye are not of the world, but I have chosen you out of the world, therefore the world hateth you." (John 15:19)

"Be of good cheer; I (Jesus) have overcome the world." (John 16:33)

"I pray not that thou shouldest take them out of the world, but that thou shouldest keep them from the evil. They are not of the world, even as I am not of the world." (John 17:15 – 16)

"If my kingdom were of this world, then would my servants fight, that I should not be delivered to the Jews." (John 18:36)

". . . all the world . . . guilty before God." (Romans 3:19)

"By one man sin entered into the world . . ." (Romans 5:12)

"Where is the wise? where is the scribe? where is the disputer of this world? hath not God made foolish the wisdom of this world?"
(1 Corinthians 1:20)

"But God hath chosen the foolish things of the world to confound the wise; and God hath chosen the weak things of the world to confound the things which are mighty; and base things of the world, and things which are despised, hath God chosen, yea, and things which are not, to bring to nought the things that are." (1 Corinthians 1:27 – 28)

"They that use the world, as not using it to the full: for the fashion of this world passeth away." (1 Corinthians 7:31, R.V. margin)

"(The) Lord Jesus Christ, who gave himself for our sins, that he might deliver us from this present evil world." (Galatians 1:3 – 4)

"But God forbid that I should glory, save in the cross of our Lord Jesus Christ, by whom the world is crucified unto me, and I unto the world."
(Galatians 6:14)

"That you may be blameless and innocent, children of God without blemish in the midst of a crooked and perverse generation, among whom you shine as lights in the world." (Philippians 2:15, R.S.V.)

"Pure religion and undefiled before God and the Father is this, To visit the fatherless and widows in their affliction, and to keep himself unspotted from the world." (James 1:27)

225

> *"You adulterous people, don't you know that friendship with the world is hatred towards God? Anyone who chooses to be a friend of the world becomes an enemy of God."* (James 4:4, N.I.V.)

> *"Love not the world, neither the things that are in the world. If any man love the world, the love of the Father is not in him. For all that is in the world, the lust of the flesh, and the lust of the eyes, and the pride of life, is not of the Father, but is of the world. And the world passeth away, and the lust thereof: but he that doeth the will of God abideth for ever."* (1 John 2:15 – 17)

> *"Who is he that overcometh the world, but he that believeth that Jesus is the Son of God? And we know that . . . the whole world lieth in wickedness."* (1 John 5:5,19)

This array of Scripture provides the divine comment, the divine perspective, on the world which otherwise would be a large, complex and bewildering subject for the disciple. In the first place, the world is not spoken of as the inhabited globe nor is it discussed as a mixture of immensely different activities, achievements and peoples. It is as though all of these make no difference to the divine assessment of what the Bible calls "the world".

Worldly Wisdom and God's Wisdom

Briefly put, the world, as the Bible sees it, is the sum total of human activity in which God is disregarded or disobeyed. It is the way of life without God. The world is man-centred. God sees the world lying in its own wickedness and sin, beguiled by its own wisdom and serving its own ends. The world resists the wisdom of God and His love revealed in the Lord Jesus Christ. The world does not want to know, because it thinks it knows already what is for its good.

The world resists the light from God in His purpose in Jesus Christ:

> *"For God, who commanded the light to shine out of darkness, hath shined in our hearts, to give the light of the knowledge of the glory of God in the face of Jesus Christ.*
> *The god of this world hath blinded the minds of them which believe not, lest the light of the glorious gospel of Christ, who is the image of God, should shine unto them."* (2 Corinthians 4:6,4)

> *"And this is the condemnation, that light is come into the world, and men loved darkness rather than light, because their deeds were evil."* (John 3:19)

226

Therefore the disciple lives in an alien world. He has been called out from the world (God hath visited the Gentiles *"to take out of them a people for his name"* — Acts 15:14) and the world seeks to recapture him. Does this mean that the disciple must isolate himself from the world by withdrawing from it to live in a commune or in some remote place where the world's influence is smaller? Or should he actively engage in opposition to the world by refusing to submit in any way to his surroundings, to government and all kinds of human law and order? At first sight, it may seem, in the light of the Scriptures which we have read, that parts of these choices should be adopted in the life of the disciple. What then of the words of Jesus when he prayed to his Father about his disciples?

> *"I pray not that thou shouldest take them out of the world, but that thou shouldest keep them from the evil."*   (John 17:15)

The disciple's place is in the world, but he must not belong to its way of life. He is himself to be an extension of Christ's own work and life in an alien world:

> *"Ye are the salt of the earth . . .*
> *Ye are the light of the world . . .*
> *Love your enemies, do good to them which hate you, bless them that curse you, and pray for them which despitefully use you."*
> (Matthew 5:13 – 14 & Luke 6:27 – 28)

The disciple is to be different from the world in which he lives. His whole life is to be founded on Christ. This world is not his true country: he is journeying through foreign territory towards the coming Kingdom of God on earth. He seeks to be like those great men of old who *"confessed that they were strangers and pilgrims on the earth"* (Hebrews 11:13).

All evil speech, evil deeds, lustful pleasures, violent attitudes and all covetousness and greediness are to be put away from his life. The basic and lifesaving principles of the Sermon on the Mount are to be his daily code of living. In his aims, objectives and behaviour he will be noticeably different from others, not arrogant or self-righteous. He is to seek for glory, honour and immortality by truly bearing the yoke of Christ:

> *"Rejoice in the Lord alway: and again I say, Rejoice. Let your moderation be known unto all men. The Lord is at hand. Be careful for nothing; but in every thing by prayer and supplication with thanksgiving*

227

let your requests be made known unto God. And the peace of God, which passeth all understanding, shall keep your hearts and minds through Christ Jesus. Finally, brethren, whatsoever things are true, whatsoever things are honest, whatsoever things are just, whatsoever things are pure, whatsoever things are lovely, whatsoever things are of good report; if there be any virtue, and if there be any praise, think on these things."

(Philippians 4:4 – 8)

Here are golden principles to govern the affairs of life, to rule our marriage, the upbringing of our children and the conduct of daily affairs. The disciple should be found not among the lawbreakers, the foul-mouthed, the dissolute, the marriage-breakers, the threatening and violent, the self-seekers and the pleasure seekers. This is not to be his way of life.

Politics and War

What, then, is to be the disciple's attitude towards the government of the country in which he lives, towards its politics and service in its Armed Forces? Is he to follow the dictates of his own conscience? Or are there any principles in these areas, too, which should direct his steps in a safe way?

The Bible has clear answers. In the first place, the disciple's thrust of life is in *"seeking first the kingdom of God and his righteousness"* (Matthew 6:33). He is not directed by Christ to be a great social reformer or a "Christian" political campaigner or a leader of protest movements of any kind. The New Testament steers the believer away from these things as not being appropriate or suitable for the life of the disciple. Disciples are scattered worldwide, live in all kinds of countries and under all kinds of governments, democratic and otherwise; and in social conditions which vary very widely. Is the disciple to choose the best of these and seek to bring about changes in the country in which he lives in order to achieve these things?

The Lord Jesus Christ and all the Jews in Palestine lived under the pagan rule of the Roman Empire. The Romans dominated everything and had put their stamp on civil and military matters. Their soldiers were in the streets and could command a civilian to carry their pack for a stated distance. The Romans tolerated, but often despised Jewish worship. There were Jewish terrorists who were avowed to oppose Rome, even at the cost of their own lives.

What did Jesus say and do? He made no comment about the politics of his land, sought no changes and stirred up no animosity or opposition. On the contrary he said: If the soldier asks you to carry his pack for a mile, carry it two miles!

It might at first be difficult to understand why Christ, and the apostles later on, took this line. The truth is both interesting and instructive. Christ was primarily concerned with showing the disciple how to live in the circumstances in which he finds himself. Christianity is not designed for this or that country, for this or that way of life; it is designed to survive everywhere, under all conditions. There are no Scriptural injunctions telling the disciple how to put the world right, or that he should be concerned in doing so. His concern is to live a Christlike life in his own country and under existing conditions. This is an important matter. Christ made no critical comments about individual governments. His comments about all governments were simple:

> "The kings of the Gentiles exercise lordship over them; and they that exercise authority upon them are called benefactors. But ye shall not be so: but he that is greatest among you, let him be as the younger; and he that is chief, as he that doth serve."　　　　(Luke 22:25)

The world has its way of life and the disciple has the Christ way. They are different and are serving different ends.

Let us consider the disciple's attitude to the government under which he lives. How should the true believer behave? In the first place, he knows that the government of his country is ordained of God, *whatever government that might be.* All governments are used by God in the furtherance of His final purpose. It is not that "good" governments are appointed by God, and the others by men. Bible teaching is plain: governments are ordained of God. Here are the Bible declarations on this subject:

> "Blessed be the name of God for ever and ever: for wisdom and might are his: and he changeth the times and the seasons: he removeth kings, and setteth up kings . . ."　　　　(Daniel 2:20 – 21)

> "The most High ruleth in the kingdom of men, and giveth it to whomsoever he will, and setteth up over it the basest . . ."
> 　　　　(Daniel 4:17)

> "Thus saith the Lord . . . I have made the earth, the man and the beast that are upon the ground, by my great power and by my outstretched arm,

and have given it unto whom it seemed meet unto me."

(Jeremiah 27:4 – 5)

"There is no power but of God: the powers that be are ordained of God. **Whosoever therefore resisteth the power, resisteth the ordinance of God.***"* (Romans 13:1 – 2)

God is at work in an evil world using "good" and "bad" governments to further His ultimate good will. We should take care not to read the situation wrongly. God is not approving or endorsing the political opinions and aims of the governments He makes use of. God has a purpose of which they are not aware and would not necessarily wish to accomplish. Nevertheless they are constrained to do so when seemingly following their own bent. They are the scaffolding which surrounds God's building. In due course they will be removed, but the building will remain.

These are fundamental principles. To be aware of them is to be safeguarded against mistaking the pursuit of human politics for Christian living. If the true distinction had been preserved in times past there would not have been the slaughter of millions of "Christians" by other "Christians" in time of war.

The prophets Jeremiah and Daniel carried out their work for God when the Babylonians were in the ascendancy and finally overran the kingdom of Judah and burned Jerusalem and its temple. Jeremiah declared: *"Now have I (God) given all these lands into the hands of Nebuchadnezzar the king of Babylon"* (Jeremiah 27:6). God's will and purpose reached beyond the mere nationalistic views of the king and his princes and people. Left to themselves they would have destroyed their nation and their hope. God's means preserved the people and in due course brought them back to the land of Israel to await the birth of Jesus.

When that time came we might have imagined that the last thing God would have wanted was a Roman government in Jerusalem where the King of the Jews was destined to reign. Had we been Jewish zealots and known that Christ was to be born in Bethlehem we might have been determined to rid that city of Roman feet by means of a resistance movement. And we would have been hopelessly wrong!

In the Christian era it is not for the disciple to seek to put the world right in the political sense. It is both a hopeless pursuit and it is a wrong one. The disciple is not "against" or "for" this government or that. He is grateful to be a disciple where he is.

Therefore he has to live his life in good times and bad, always guided by the same principles, the principles which work in all circumstances. If Christ could live under an alien government, an occupying power, who are we to seek to live by different standards? The disciple is commanded to submit to law and order:

> "*Remind the people to be subject to rulers and authorities, to be obedient, to be ready to do whatsoever is good, to slander no-one, to be peaceable and considerate, and to show true humility towards all men.*"
>
> (Titus 3:1 – 2, N.I.V.)

> "*Submit yourselves for the Lord's sake to every authority instituted among men: whether to the king, as the supreme authority, or to governors, who are sent by him to punish those who do wrong and to commend those who do right.*" (1 Peter 2:13 – 14, N.I.V.)

> "*Let every soul be subject unto the higher powers . . . for conscience sake. For this cause pay ye tribute also: for they are God's ministers, attending continually upon this very thing. Render therefore to all their dues: tribute to whom tribute is due; custom to whom custom; fear to whom fear; honour to whom honour.*" (Romans 13:1 – 7)

These admonitions are very clear. The disciple should not be found seeking to overthrow the authority of the government or bringing it into discredit. It is not a question of which shade of politics a man should adopt for the furtherance of whatever purpose he might have in mind. True Christianity is above politics and it is beyond them as a way of life. Disciples should not be divided among themselves by belonging to this party or that, and should not be nationally or internationally prejudiced.

"Render unto Caesar . . . and unto God"

True disciples are the minority wherever they are. They leave the government to the nation among whom they are privileged to reside, and they accept whatever comes as ordained of God. It is for these reasons that Christadelphians are law-abiding members of whatever community they live in, do not participate in politics, neither by nominating members of this party or that, nor by exercising their vote in local or national politics. They are thus never opposed to anyone in their own country or elsewhere. These principles have served to unify the Christadelphian community. At the same time, we are prompt payers of our taxes and dues and are willing observers of the law. We are not agitators or protesters,

231

nor are we members of "ginger" groups or parties designed to pull political strings. We heartily commend this way of the pilgrim life as being both consistent with the Word of God and conducive to the well-being of the believer and his fellows. Furthermore, it does not harm our neighbours.

Is the obedience to be rendered to rulers and authorities totally unquestioning? Suppose to obey would come into conflict with the clear commands of Christ, what should the disciple do? This is an old and a very real question and, as we have come to expect, the Bible provides guidance which is practical and sound. It so \ happens that the direct obligations of a disciple to the Lord and to government rarely come on a collision course. That would be much more likely to happen were the disciple to become involved in politics and the like.

But supposing the government commands us to do something which is contrary to our conscience in Christ? The Lord himself laid down a simple, guiding principle:

> "*Render therefore unto Caesar the things which are Caesar's; and unto God the things that are God's.*" /   (Matthew 22:21)

If there arises a circumstance in which Caesar demands that which is truly God's, there is only one answer for the disciple: I must serve God for conscience sake. We have an instance of this in the New Testament. At one point in the early development of the preaching of the Gospel the Jewish rulers instructed two of the apostles on the following lines:

> "*They called them, and commanded them not to speak at all nor teach in the name of Jesus.*"   (Acts 4:18)

This command was directly opposed to Christ's own commission to the apostles. They had been commanded to preach in Jerusalem. What were they to say to the authorities? Peter's answer was firm and reasonable:

> "*Whether it be right in the sight of God to hearken unto you more than unto God, judge ye. For we cannot but speak the things which we have seen and heard.*"   (Acts 4:19 – 20)

Accordingly, despite the warning, they prayed and then went out into the city of Jerusalem and made known the Gospel of the risen Christ. The result was that multitudes of people believed, and the good news spread like a bush fire throughout the city. The authorities were soon aware of it. The apostles were arrested and the rulers said:

> *"Did we not straitly command you that ye should not teach in this name? and, behold, ye have filled Jerusalem with your doctrine . . . Then Peter and the other apostles answered and said, We ought to obey God rather than men."* (Acts 5:28,29)

This unequivocal statement of their position and intent caused much private discussion among the members of the ruling Jewish council who, when they had reassembled, had the apostles beaten and afterwards warned them again. The outcome was that

> *"They departed from the presence of the council, rejoicing that they were counted worthy to suffer shame for his name. And daily in the temple, and in every house, they ceased not to teach and preach Jesus Christ."* (Acts 5:41 – 42)

When Caesar asks for what is God's, the answer must be, No. In modern times men and women are sometimes required to register for military service or to declare themselves to be conscientious objectors. It is a critical choice. On the one hand there is the need of the country to which one by birth belongs and under whose government one has been able to live; and on the other there are clear teachings of Scripture in respect of violence to one's fellow men, whether or not those men are good or evil:

> *"Ye have heard that it hath been said, An eye for an eye, and a tooth for a tooth: but I say unto you, That ye resist not evil: but whosoever shall smite thee on the right cheek, turn to him the other also.*
>
> *Ye have heard that it hath been said, Thou shalt love thy neighbour, and hate thine enemy. But I say unto you, Love your enemies, bless them that curse you, do good to them that hate you, and pray for them which despitefully use you, and persecute you."* (Matthew 5:38 – 39,43 – 44)

> *"Put up again thy sword into its place: for all they that take the sword shall perish with the sword."* (Matthew 26:52, R.V.)

> *"Dearly beloved, avenge not yourselves, but rather give place unto wrath: for it is written, Vengeance is mine; I will repay, saith the Lord."* (Romans 12:19)

> *"See that none render evil for evil unto any man; but ever follow that*

233

which is good, both among yourselves, and to all men."
(1 Thessalonians 5:15)

"For what glory is it, if, when ye be buffeted for your faults, ye take it patiently? but if, when ye do well, and suffer for it, ye shall take it patiently, this is acceptable with God."

For even hereunto were ye called: because Christ also suffered for us, leaving us an example, that ye should follow his steps: who did no sin, neither was guile found in his mouth: who, when he was reviled, reviled not again; when he suffered, he threatened not; but committed himself to him that judgeth righteously . . ."
(1 Peter 2:20 – 23)

"My kingdom is not of this world: if my kingdom were of this world, then would my servants fight, that I should not be delivered to the Jews: but now is my kingdom not from hence."
(John 18:36)

"And when they were come to the place . . . there they crucified him . . . then said Jesus, Father, forgive them . . ."
(Luke 23:33 – 34)

The life and teaching of the Lord Jesus Christ make it unthinkable that any of his disciples should be violent towards any man, whether in wartime or not. The disciple cannot defend principles by means which the Lord has condemned.

Peter's loyalty to Christ was totally misplaced when he drew his sword to defend his Lord — a righteous cause if ever there was one! He was rebuked. The disciple is instructed that violence and evil are not to be resisted by evil means. Christ's example is beyond doubt:

"Christ suffered . . . leaving you an example . . . when they hurled their insults at him, he did not retaliate; when he suffered, he made no threats . . ."
(1 Peter 2:21 – 23, N.I.V.)

Men and women will often acknowledge the wisdom and righteousness of these principles in everyday life, but plead extenuating circumstances when it comes to national conflict. Pacifism, they say, never stops evil aggressors. There is much truth in that. Wars never end wars. That also is true. That is the human dilemma.

Christadelphians are conscientious objectors in time of war (not pacifists in the accepted sense) because Christ has told us so to be. It follows naturally from our non-involvement in politics. We submit and do not complain. We believe that the removal of violence and all evil will have to await the coming of Christ. His

234

righteous rule will end wars among men. Meanwhile, we seek to live like Christ. We do not seek to defend by evil means our "rights" as individuals or nationally.

There is another force which moves men in time of war. There is a deep sense of allegiance and loyalty to the flag. The flag stands for honour and heritage. To fail to defend it is esteemed to be either treachery or cowardice. With this we would entirely agree, were it not for one other factor. Where does the disciple's primary allegiance lie? He belongs to a band of brothers world-wide and his allegiance is to Christ. Of course, he is deeply thankful for the shelter and privileges which come from his mother country. It is simply that he cannot kill to defend them. His honour and allegiance are first to the flag of Christ.

Citizens of God's Kingdom

The disciple is law-abiding in the country of his residence, not because of loyalty to his country, but on account of his allegiance to the commands of God. The disciple does not have two masters. He has One. Christ has given him the blueprint for living in all parts of his life. In this sense the disciple has but one allegiance, and one citizenship, that of the Kingdom of God. Therefore he has no doubts about what he should do when war looms and other men fight: humbly, he must refrain.

In fact, in most Western countries provision is made in time of war for those who truly have a conscientious objection to military service. In such lands, therefore, conscientious objection is itself law-abiding, and there is no conflict with government. At such times Christadelphians seek exemption from service in the Armed and associated Forces, and in peace time refrain from all employment in which violence is exercised; but, undertake willingly such other obligations as government lays upon them consistent with their service to Christ.

The disciple is commanded that he must "*must not strive: but be gentle unto all men*" (2 Timothy 2:24). Christadelphians are not aggressive for their "rights", and are not to be found taking personal grievances to courts of law. If other means of removing evil circumstances or injustice do not succeed, then the disciple must bear the evil, suffering himself rather to be defrauded than to violate his principles of life (compare 1 Corinthians 6:6 – 7).

There are times, of course, when the disciple may be summoned to court as a witness. This he cannot refuse to obey, and would not

235

wish to do so. However, he must not take the oath in a court of law. He must *always* be truthful, and should not require some special obligation to make him so. It is true that the oath places a solemn obligation on those who take it, "to tell the truth, the whole truth, and nothing but the truth". The obligation the Lord Jesus Christ laid upon the disciple is even more solemn and binding. The disciple must be truthful at all times:

> *"But now ye also put off all these; anger, wrath, malice, blasphemy, filthy communication out of your mouth: lie not one to another . . ."*
> (Colossians 3:8 – 9)

> *"Wherefore putting away lying, speak every man truth with his neighbour . . . let no corrupt communication proceed out of your mouth."*
> (Ephesians 4:25 – 29)

> *"Ye have heard that it hath been said by them of old time, Thou shalt not forswear thyself, but shalt perform unto the Lord thine oaths: but I say unto you, Swear not at all; neither by heaven; for it is God's throne: nor by the earth; for it is his footstool: neither by Jerusalem; for it is the city of the great King. Neither shalt thou swear by thy head, because thou canst not make one hair white or black. But let your communication be, Yea, yea; Nay, nay: for whatsoever is more than these cometh of evil."*
> (Matthew 5:33 – 37)

> *"But above all things, my brethren, swear not, neither by heaven, neither by the earth, neither by any other oath: but let your yea be yea; and your nay, nay; lest ye fall into condemnation."*
> (James 5:12)

It is the practice of Christadelphians to follow these principles and not to take the oath in courts of law or at any other times, but instead to read the Affirmation which is legally provided as an alternative method acceptable to all concerned.

Life in the modern world is very complex and the disciple is faced with many choices in what to do about everyday matters. Christ has not provided us with a set of rules by which we are to abide, as though being a disciple were to be a matter of law-keeping. Christ's principles are higher than law, and the disciple's response is one of love and willingness, reaching out beyond any obligations which laws could provide. His simple daily rule is: What would Jesus do? To a Bible-reading and prayerful disciple the answers to everyday problems are not usually difficult to find.

Developments in human affairs cause Christadelphians to

review their attitudes to them from time to time, and if necessary, to change course to meet the altered circumstances. Comparatively good things become contaminated in course of time, and the disciple may have to avoid what he once thought to be acceptable. The escalation of trade union power and action is a case in point. The disciple finds it difficult to square some of the things which unions stand for or demand with the principles of behaviour we have outlined earlier in connection with resisting evil. Christadelphians have never been politically or otherwise active in trade unions, but have been what others might term passive members of the unions appropriate to their occupation, at least in countries where this was the normal thing for workpeople to do. The current tendency among Christadelphians is to tread much more carefully and, if possible, to avoid union membership altogether.

Similarly jury service, always a matter of personal conscience among Christadelphians, is becoming increasingly unacceptable to members who feel that the nature of jury service has become much more difficult for them to bear with.

Christadelphians are, however, positive in life and not negative, as might wrongly be gathered from some of the attitudes we have been forced to adopt. We seek to be considerate folk, good neighbours, helpful to others, of a caring disposition and, in fact, the kind of people who give the authorities no cause for concern but rather the wish that more people would be equally law-abiding.

Despite all the signs of permanence, modern civilisation and the way of life of the world are transient and can offer no abiding hope. The Gospel of the Kingdom in Christ provides an anchor in the present life and unshakable hope of the life to come. There is no need for the disciple to be sucked into the vortex of despair and destruction which is opening up the world over, or to follow the fruitless path of materialism and self-satisfaction. If we heed the call of the truth, we shall have peace of mind in our present life, and hope of an inheritance in a world made glorious when the Lord Jesus Christ returns to make it so.

237

24

FELLOWSHIP

FELLOWSHIP is an important Bible word. It is particularly prominent in the New Testament. Fellowship means sharing, partaking and having in common. The word is translated in all of those ways as the following, fully representative selection of passages will indicate:

> "*Then they that gladly received his word were baptized . . . and they continued stedfastly in the apostles' doctrine and* **fellowship**, *and in breaking of bread, and in prayers.*" (Acts 2:41 – 42)

> "*That which we have seen and heard declare we unto you, that ye also may have* **fellowship** *with us: and truly our* **fellowship** *is with the Father, and with his Son Jesus Christ.*" (1 John 1:3)

> "*God is faithful, by whom ye were called unto the* **fellowship** *of his Son Jesus Christ our Lord.*" (1 Corinthians 1:9)

> "*The cup of blessing which we bless, is it not the* **communion** *of the blood of Christ? The bread which we break, is it not the* **communion** *of the body of Christ? for we being many are one bread and one body: for we are all partakers of that one bread.*" (1 Corinthians 10:16 – 17)

> "*If there is any . . .* **participation** *in the Spirit . . . complete my joy by being of the same mind, having the same love, being in full accord and of one mind.*" (Philippians 2:1, R.S.V.)

> "*Be ye not unequally yoked together with unbelievers: for what fellowship hath righteousness with unrighteousness? and what* **communion** *hath light with darkness?*" (2 Corinthians 6:14)

238

"If we say that we have **fellowship** *with him, and walk in darkness, we lie, and do not the truth: but if we walk in the light, we have* **fellowship** *one with another, and the blood of Jesus Christ his Son cleanseth us from all sin."* (1 John 1:6 – 7)

"That I may know him (Christ) and the power of his resurrection, and may **share** *his sufferings, becoming like him in his death, that if possible I may attain the resurrection from the dead."*
(Philippians 3:10,11, R.S.V.)

"And do not forget to do good and to **share** *with others, for with such sacrifices God is pleased ..."* (Hebrews 13:16, N.I.V.)

"Command those who are rich ... to do good, to be rich in good deeds, and to be generous and willing to **share**.*"*
(1 Timothy 6:17,18, N.I.V.)

"Our hope of you is stedfast, knowing that as ye are **partakers** *of the sufferings, so shall ye be also of the consolation."*
(2 Corinthians 1:7)

"I (Peter) ... am ... a witness of the sufferings of Christ, and also a **partaker** *of the glory that shall be revealed ..."* (1 Peter 5:1)

"He has granted to us his precious and very great promises, that through these you may escape from the corruption that is in the world because of passion, and become **partakers** *of the divine nature."*
(2 Peter 1:4, R.S.V.)

"The grace of the Lord Jesus Christ, and the love of God, and the **communion** *of the Holy Spirit, be with you all."*
(2 Corinthians 13:14, R.V.)

From the foregoing it will be seen that fellowship has many elements. Some parts seem to be the foundation for the others. Let us set out these different parts under the headings of foundations and life:

Foundations
  The apostles and their teaching
  The promises of God
  The forgiveness of sins and the blood of Jesus Christ

Life
   The Body of Believers
   The Breaking of Bread (Communion)
   The Unity of believers in love, purpose and mind
   The life of the individual believer in association with Christ
   Living close to the Father and the Son

In addition to these two parts, there is the promise of ultimately sharing the divine nature by being blessed with immortality.

Fellowship becomes a very practical and living thing when based on these principles. It embraces all that it means to be a disciple. *Discipleship is fellowship.*

Let us suppose that someone outside this fellowship came along and asked how he might share it. What would the answer be? We could at once assure him that such fellowship is possible for anyone, because the way has been made known for us in the Bible. We could say also that it is not a mysterious process by which we wait for God to impart something to us from heaven. Some people have burdened themselves with this latter notion, and have waited for God to act directly upon them. This is not the process described in any of the verses we have quoted. Fellowship is made possible through the Word of God.

To be specific, the way to fellowship is through the apostles' doctrine or teaching. This teaching is the challenge to our existing fellowship outside Christ. When we learn of the great and precious promises of God made certain by the sacrifice of Christ, the moment of choice comes along sooner or later. Am I to remain walking in darkness in fellowship with the world? Am I to stay in the fellowship of death? Or, shall I step into the light in response to the call of the Gospel, and come to the new fellowship in Christ? Fellowship comes by enlightenment and belief, by repentance and baptism, and by commitment to the new way of life. In this way the blood of Christ cleanses us from all sin and we enter into the fellowship of God and His Son. We share the apostles' doctrine and the hope which they proclaimed.

The believer's fellowship is both inclusive and exclusive. He does not choose his companions in the fellowship; they are chosen by the very process which brought him into a relationship with God. There can be no artificial barriers of sex, colour, race, class or caste. All who hold the same faith in truth and submit to its discipline by baptism share a common heritage. They are mem-

bers of the commonwealth of Israel and have a common hope. The
Lord makes believers one in him:

> "*There can be neither Jew nor Greek, there can be neither bond nor free,
> there can be no male and female: for ye all are one man in Christ Jesus.*"
> (Galatians 3:28, R.V.)

> "*There is one body and one Spirit, even as ye are called in one hope of
> your calling; one Lord, one faith, one baptism, one God and Father of
> all, who is above all, and through all, and in you all.*"
> (Ephesians 4:4 – 6)

From these declarations, it follows that there should be one united
Christian community throughout the world. Throughout history
this unity has suffered from the ravages of false doctrine and the
human lust for power over one's fellow men. This evil was already
at work or threatened in New Testament times:

> "*And they continued stedfastly in the apostles' doctrine and fellowship,
> and in breaking of bread, and in prayers . . . and all that believed were
> together, and had all things common . . . and they, continuing daily with
> one accord . . . did eat their meat with gladness and singleness of heart,
> praising God.*"
> (Acts 2:42 – 47)

> "*Now I beseech you, brethren, by the name of our Lord Jesus Christ, that
> ye all speak the same thing, and that there be no divisions among you; but
> that ye be perfectly joined together in the same mind and in the same
> judgement. For it hath been declared unto me . . . that there are
> contentions among you.*"
> (1 Corinthians 1:10 – 11)

> "*But if it is preached that Christ has been raised from the dead, how can
> some of you say that there is no resurrection of the dead?*"
> (1 Corinthians 15:12, N.I.V.)

> "*Do not be misled: 'Bad company corrupts good character.' Come back
> to your senses as you ought, and stop sinning; for there are some who are
> ignorant of God — I say this to your shame.*"
> (1 Corinthians 15:33 – 34, N.I.V.)

> "*For I (Paul) know this, that after my departing shall grievous wolves
> enter in among you, not sparing the flock. Also of your own selves shall
> men arise, speaking perverse things, to draw away disciples after them.*"
> (Acts 20:29 – 30)

> "*I marvel that ye are so quickly removing from him that called you in the*

241

grace of Christ unto a different gospel; which is not another gospel: only there are some that trouble you, and would pervert the gospel of Christ."
(Galatians 1:6 – 7, R.V.)

"For many walk, of whom I have told you often, and now tell you even weeping, that they are enemies of the cross of Christ . . . "
(Philippians 3:18)

"They went out from us, but they were not of us; for if they had been of us, they would no doubt have continued with us: but they went out, that they might be made manifest that they were not all of us."
(1 John 2:19)

The first happy community became distressed by heresies and by men who liked to have the pre-eminence over others. This resulted in schism and fragmentation. The apostles made every effort to rebuke and educate those in error, sometimes with success and sometimes not. We might ask what happened to those who refused to return to their former belief. Such persons had already broken the fellowship based on a common belief and, when the position became intolerable or entrenched, the apostles instructed the congregation in which it occurred to exclude the delinquent person from their company. This would apply particularly to the breaking of bread service which was one of the highest expressions of fellowship. In other words, whilst the brethren strove hard to recover those who had gone astray in a matter of the faith, they also had a responsibility for the integrity of the fellowship itself which they had to preserve when recovery of the wayward proved impossible. This was secured by excluding the heretic from their midst. Often, of course, the heretic would leave of his own accord. These verses illustrate the action taken:

"He that abideth in the doctrine of Christ, he hath both the Father and the Son. If there come any unto you, and bring not this doctrine; receive him not into your house, neither bid him God speed: for he that biddeth him God speed is a partaker of his evil deeds." (2 John 9,10)

"Warn a divisive person once, and then warn him a second time. After that have nothing to do with him." (Titus 3:10, N.I.V.)

However, as will be seen from the many verses quoted in this chapter, fellowship is not only a matter of common tenets of faith, it is also a common way of life. The word "doctrine" means teaching, and teaching concerns what we believe and what we do.

242

The apostles' doctrine therefore concerned a common faith *and* the life in Christ. Godliness is part of fellowship.

Unfortunately, all of us sin from time to time. What happens to the disciple when he sins? Does he leave the fellowship of Christ? Certainly, if he knowingly persists in his sin and remains unrepentant, his fellowship is deeply affected and severance occurs. In the mercy of God provision is made for the disciple to receive forgiveness by seeking it through the Lord Jesus Christ in prayer:

> "*If we confess our sins, he is faithful and just to forgive us our sins, and to cleanse us from all unrighteousness. If we say that we have not sinned, we make him a liar, and his word is not in us.*" (1 John 1:9 – 10)

There are, nevertheless, sins which, because they are grievous and bring the body of believers into disrepute, need more open treatment by the congregation. The elders should seek to restore the offender whilst also rejecting the sin which he has committed:

> "*Brethren, if a man be overtaken in a fault, ye which are spiritual, restore such an one in the spirit of meekness; considering thyself, lest thou also be tempted. Bear ye one another's burdens, and so fulfil the law of Christ.*" (Galatians 6:1 – 2)

> "*Brethren, if any of you do err from the truth, and one convert him; let him know that he which converteth the sinner from the error of his way shall save a soul from death, and shall hide a multitude of sins.*" (James 5:19 – 20)

> "*Them that sin rebuke before all, that others also may fear.*" (1 Timothy 5:20)

Compassion and renewal in the right way are the twin components of this path of understanding and restoration. Tolerance of deeply offensive unChristian conduct would do neither the offender nor the congregation any good whatsoever; bitter and immediate rejection of the offending disciple would itself be unlike the patient and cleansing restorative work of the Lord himself. Wisdom in the Word of God, a deep desire to uphold the godly standards of the Lord Jesus Christ whilst keeping the fallen from destruction, and an awareness of our common frailty, are essential elements in this work of recovery.

Compassion and Discipline

But suppose the sinner persists in his way or seeks to defend it so as to be injurious to the harmony of the whole assembly. What then? The counsel and commandment of the apostles are quite clear. The line is to be drawn in order to preserve the spirit and practice of the Lord Jesus in the congregation. In this connection, it is worthwhile remembering an Old Testament word which runs:

> "*These . . . things doth the Lord hate . . . a proud look . . . and he that soweth discord among brethren.*" (Proverbs 6:16 – 19)

Under the rule of Christ, as in Old Testament times, the time comes when the recalcitrant person must cease to be regarded as a member of the congregation. Fellowship cannot be sustained because, in effect, it has already been severed by the persistence in error of the person concerned. This is the final resort and a source of great sorrow. The Scripture which enjoins this action reads as follows:

> "*Now we command you, brethren, in the name of the Lord Jesus Christ, that ye withdraw yourselves from every brother that walketh disorderly, and not after the tradition which he received of us . . . and if any man obey not our word by this epistle, note that man, and have no company with him, that he may be ashamed. Yet count him not as an enemy, but admonish him as a brother.*" (2 Thessalonians 3:6 – 15)

> "*Now I have written unto you not to keep company, if any man that is called a brother be a fornicator, or covetous, or an idolater, or a railer, or a drunkard, or an extortioner; with such an one no not to eat.*" (1 Corinthians 5:11)

> "*If any man teach otherwise, and consent not to wholesome words, even the words of our Lord Jesus Christ, and to the doctrine which is according to godliness; he is proud, knowing nothing, but doting about questions and strifes of words, whereof cometh envy, strife, railings, evil surmisings, perverse disputings of men of corrupt minds, and destitute of the truth, supposing that gain is godliness: from such withdraw thyself.*" (1 Timothy 6:3 – 5)

The Ecclesia

Christadelphians adopt these principles by common consent in seeking to preserve their faith and way of life in each of their congregations (often called ecclesias — a word carried through from the Greek of the New Testament and meaning an assembly). The community is held together by the common consent of each congregation to the agreed fundamentals of belief and practice as found in the Scriptures. The Christadelphian community has no superintending body, no hierarchy or supra-authority other than the Word of God and the overlordship of Christ. By these means Christadelphians order their affairs in submission to God and His Son. Christadelphians believe that their arrangements are as nearly in accord with first century Christianity as they can achieve. The community has its own blemishes and has not been able to avoid schism over the years. Happily considerable healing of this has occurred in recent times.

Scripture teaches that preservation of unity is to be striven for and the tendency to fragmentation to be deplored. But unity must be upon sound principles. For this reason, ecumenism as a means of bringing together fundamentally different groups does not find favour with Christadelphians. In any case, our points of difference often make us unacceptable to others.

The weekly breaking of bread service in Christadelphian meetings is the centre of their expression of fellowship in Christ. Members regularly assemble in this way and meet in other Christadelphian ecclesias when they are on holiday or visiting in other places or other lands. The fellowship thus expressed is remarkably alive and there is a real family bond among Christadelphians wherever they go.

It is possible for the exclusiveness of the breaking of bread service to be regarded as unfriendly by non-Christadelphians, particularly those who like to have an open fellowship. As the reader will have gathered from what has gone before, Christadelphians base their fellowship on a common faith and a common way of life. We are heartily glad to welcome new members by belief and baptism, but we do not extend our breaking of bread service to any one who might care to come along irrespective of his belief or behaviour. We regard this as fundamental to our existence. Fellowship is not simply friendship. It is sharing all that is precious in the truest sense. We believe that to be worth preserving.

Bread and Wine

Despite the centrality of the breaking of bread service to the life of the community, Christadelphians do not ascribe any miraculous powers or holiness to the actual bread and wine which are used. We do not subscribe to the doctrine of transubstantiation or anything akin to it, or to any act or doctrine which would teach that the bread and wine are to be regarded as an offering to God, as though

245

Christ himself was present or could be present *in the simple elements themselves*. We believe that bread and wine are external tokens of inward remembrance, and hold no special virtue or strength in themselves.

Nevertheless the simple breaking of bread ceremony is a powerful means of support for the members. The ceremony was initiated by the Lord himself on the night before his death. It occurred at passover time when the Jews were remembering their deliverance from Egypt, more than a thousand years before. As the Jews in Egypt had taken a lamb in sacrifice and put the blood as a token upon their homes, so Christ was the passover lamb for his flock and they bear the token of remembrance upon their hearts.

As Egypt had held the Israelites captive in their iron furnace of affliction, so man had been held by Sin as taskmaster and Death as oppressor. Christ had come as deliverer:

> *"Christ our passover is sacrificed for us."*   (1 Corinthians 5:7)

Moreover, Christ regarded the cup of wine used at the service as a token of the new covenant in his blood. The new covenant, the everlasting covenant, is secured by his blood, and is the covenant which brings together all the promises made to Abraham and David of old:

> *"This is my body which is given for you: this do in remembrance of me . . . This cup is the new covenant in my blood, even that which is poured out for you."*   (Luke 22:19 – 20, R.V.)

> *"Let us draw near with a true heart in full assurance of faith, having our hearts sprinkled from an evil conscience, and our bodies washed with pure water . . . let us consider one another to provoke unto love and to good works: not forsaking the assembling of ourselves together . . . "*
> (Hebrews 10:22 – 25)

> *"Jesus the mediator of the new covenant . . . "*   (Hebrews 12:24)

> *"He is the mediator of a new covenant . . . that . . . they that have been called may receive the promise of the eternal inheritance."*
> (Hebrews 9:15, R.V.)

> *"Ye were redeemed . . . with precious blood, as of a lamb without blemish and without spot, even the blood of Christ."*
> (1 Peter 1:18 – 19, R.V.)

It follows that the people who share the remembrance are covenant people. This is why fellowship is precious and by its very nature exclusive, even though there is an open invitation to all men to become covenant men in the way determined by God.

There are two elements in the act of remembrance, bread and wine. Each tells its own part of the great act of redemption in Christ. The bread speaks of the victory of Christ by sharing our nature, that we might share his triumph; the wine is a token of life-giving, complete and free, that his cup of suffering and death might become the cup of joy and salvation for us:

> *"Then said I (Jesus), Lo, I am come . . . to do thy will, O God . . . by the which will we are sanctified through the offering of the body of Jesus Christ once for all."* (Hebrews 10:7 – 10, R.V.)

> *"You . . . hath he reconciled in the body of his flesh through death, to present you holy and unblameable and unreproveable in his sight, if ye continue in the faith."* (Colossians 1:21 – 23)

> *"He poured out his life unto death . . . he bore the sin of many, and made intercession for the transgressors."* (Isaiah 53:12, N.I.V.)

> *"Is not the cup of thanksgiving for which we give thanks a participation in the blood of Christ?"* (1 Corinthians 10:16, N.I.V.)

> *"Thou wast slain, and hast redeemed us to God by thy blood out of every kindred, and tongue, and people, and nation; and hast made us unto our God kings and priests: and we shall reign on the earth."* (Revelation 5:9 – 10)

It is remarkable that remembrance can be made so deeply effective by the use of everyday things of life at the time of Jesus, namely, bread and wine. There is no elaborate ritual, no question of ministration at the authorised hands of selected men and no holy place in which it is needful to conduct the ceremony. There is no such thing as holy bread or holy wine: holiness lies in the hearts of the believers remembering God's Holy One under His gracious blessing.

The bread and wine speak of the believers themselves. They are one in Christ, and this is shown in the One Loaf (the Greek word for bread is also the word for loaf). *"We being many are one loaf."* As the loaf is shared among many, so Christ's unity is to be made known in them because they are his body. The One Cup pictures their one life in Christ. He is the true Vine and they are the

247

branches. The life of the branches comes from the tree: the life of the believers comes from their life in him made effective by his death on their behalf.

So it is that the believer is part of the act of remembrance. He is one with Christ and with his brethren. Fellowship is unity.

In this way, past and present are united in the weekly breaking of bread service. It is held on the first day of the week, the day of the resurrection of the Lord from the dead, because that is the custom which the first century believers adopted:

> "*Upon the first day of the week, when the disciples came together to break bread . . .*"
> (Acts 20:7)

Much has been made of this service by various parts of Christendom, so that what takes place appears to bear very little resemblance to the simple, yet telling, things of which we have spoken. And there is often neglect. There is a part of the original Last Supper which appears often to be forgotten. It is an essential part; indeed, without it the rest loses its true meaning. The breaking of bread looks forward. It speaks powerfully of the future. This is what the Lord himself said at the Last Supper:

> "*And when the hour was come, he sat down, and the twelve apostles with him. And he said unto them, With desire I have desired to eat this passover with you before I suffer: for I say unto you, I will not any more eat thereof,* **until it be fulfilled in the kingdom of God** *. . . I will not drink of the fruit of the vine,* **until the kingdom of God shall come** *. . . and I appoint unto you a kingdom, as my Father hath appointed unto me; that ye may eat and drink at my table.*"
> (Luke 22:14 – 30)

The apostle Paul was not present at the Last Supper. He did not learn about it from any who were there. Jesus revealed directly to him what other apostles had gained by actual experience. What then did Jesus tell Paul about the last supper? Here are Paul's words from Jesus:

> "*For as often as ye eat this bread, and drink this cup, ye do shew the Lord's death* **till he come**.*"
> (1 Corinthians 11:26)

Compare the phrases from the Last Supper meal and the words of Jesus to Paul:

> "*Until it be fulfilled in the kingdom of God*"

"Until the kingdom of God shall come . . . "
"Till he come . . . "

The Second Coming is the completion of the meaning of the Last Supper. Jesus said: "Until it *be fulfilled* in the kingdom of God". The Bread and Wine were not simply tokens of the past, nor were they merely symbols of the present; they were prophecies of things to come. The Unity of Bread and Wine have hitherto been shown only in part. A great number of the saints are sleeping in dust and the time when all the saints will be gathered together in one place has yet to come. The Unity in Christ is now enjoyed imperfectly in our fellowship with him and with one another; the perfection is yet to come when, says the Word of God, *"He will gather together in one all things in Christ"* (Ephesians 1:10). That is the day of the Kingdom, the day of immortality, the day when the Shepherd will have gathered all his sheep unto himself. They will sit at his table in his Kingdom in the marriage supper of the Lamb. The Bride and the Lord will then be one for ever.

What a marvellous consummation! The sorrowful, dark night of the Last Supper, which filled the disciples with bewilderment and heaviness, will issue forth in the resplendent glory of the day of Christ.

No man who understands these things will want to be excluded in that day. The fellowship of the Kingdom will be exclusive. *"Many . . . will seek to enter in, and shall not be able. When once the Master of the house is risen up, and hath shut to the door . . . "* (Luke 13:24 – 25). Today the door is open wide. Wise men will enter in. Those within will not venture outside. In their acts of fellowship they will not make contracts with that darkness which endangers their hope of life eternal. In marriage, they will marry someone who shares their faith (1 Corinthians 7:39 and 2 Corinthians 6:14); in business, they will not pursue the ways of ungodly and doubtful gain; in daily life, they will show that they have been with Jesus; and, in all things they will live as men of faith waiting for the return of their Lord.

There is remembrance in heaven corresponding to true remembrance on earth, and it looks forward to the day when all things shall be fulfilled:

"And a book of remembrance was written before him (God) for them that feared the Lord, and that thought upon his name. And they shall be mine, saith the Lord of hosts, in that day when I make-up my jewels."

(Malachi 3:16 – 17)

249

25

THE ENIGMA OF ISRAEL

SOME readers may be surprised to find a whole chapter on the Jews in a book which purports to deal with the Gospel of the Lord Jesus Christ. The contrary should be the case. Were we to omit a proper treatment of this subject we would have failed to set forth the whole counsel of God. It is perhaps easy to forget that nearly all of the books of the Bible were written by inspired Jewish penmen; that Jesus himself was born of a Jewish mother and spent almost the whole of his life in the Jewish homeland; that the twelve apostles were Jews; and, most important of all, that Jesus said: *"Salvation is of the Jews"* (John 4:22). Christianity was nursed in a Jewish cradle and fed on Jewish scriptures.

"Salvation is of the Jews"

Christianity has an identity of hope and purpose with that of the Old Testament, it is the hope of Israel. This hope is centred in the promises which God made to Abraham and included both Jew and Gentile in their scope. They depended for their fulfilment on the coming of Messiah. In the same way, the royal promises made to king David relate to Christ who will be King on David's throne in Jerusalem. In other words, there is not a great gulf fixed between the Old and New Testaments as though they were entirely different and irreconcilable worlds. Men of faith in both eras share the same basis of hope as the following table clearly indicates.

Basic Teaching	*Old Testament Scriptures*	*New Testament Scriptures*
There is one God	Deuteronomy 6:4 Isaiah 44:6; 45:21 – 22 46:9 – 10	John 17:3 1 Corinthians 8:4,6 1 Timothy 2:5
The Scriptures came by the power of God's Holy Spirit	2 Samuel 23:1 – 2 Nehemiah 9:30	2 Timothy 3:16 2 Peter 1:21
Christ: the Son of God	1 Chronicles 17:13 Psalm 89:26 – 27	Luke 1:35; John 1:14 Romans 1:3 – 4
Christ of the seed of Abraham	Genesis 22:17 – 18	Matthew 1:1 Galatians 3:16
Christ of the seed of David	2 Samuel 7:12 – 16 Isaiah 11:1 Jeremiah 23:5	Matthew 1:1 Romans 1:3 Revelation 22:16
Christ to die for our sins	Isaiah 53:3,5 – 6,10	Matthew 20:28 1 Corinthians 15:3 1 Peter 2:24
Christ to be raised from the dead	Psalm 16:8 – 11	Matthew 16:21 1 Corinthians 15:4
Christ to ascend to heaven	Psalm 110:1	Acts 1:9; 2:33 – 35 Hebrews 1:3
Christ to return to earth	Psalm 96:13; 98:9 110:1 – 2	Acts 1:11; 3:21 1 Thessalonians 4:16 2 Thessalonians 1:7 – 8
There will be a resurrection	Job 19:25 – 27 Daniel 12:1 – 2	1 Corinthians 15:22 – 23 1 Thessalonians 4:16
There will be a judgement	Psalm 1:5	Matthew 16:27 John 12:48 Romans 15:10 – 12 2 Corinthians 5:10
The faithful will inherit life everlasting	Daniel 12:2	Luke 20:34 – 36 Philippians 3:20 – 21 Colossians 3:4
The unfaithful will be rejected and die	Daniel 12:2 Psalm 37:37 – 38 Malachi 3:18 – 4:3	John 5:29 Romans 6:23 2 Thessalonians 1:9
Man is sinful by nature	Genesis 8:21 Jeremiah 17:9	Mark 7:21 – 23 Romans 3:9,23
Man is mortal The dead are unconscious	Psalm 6:5; 89:48 115:17; 146:3 – 4 Ecclesiastes 3:19 – 20 Isaiah 38:18	John 11:11 – 14 1 Corinthians 15:17 – 18

Basic Teaching	Old Testament Scriptures	New Testament Scriptures
Salvation is the gift of God through the death of Christ	Psalm 49:15 Isaiah 53:12	Romans 5:17 – 21 Ephesians 2:8 1 Thessalonians 4:13 – 18 Titus 3:7 1 John 2:25
Salvation is by faith	Habakkuk 2:4	John 3:16; Romans 10:10
Salvation is by the promises made to Abraham	Micah 7:20	Galatians 3:7,9,26 – 29
The Kingdom of God will be established on earth	Daniel 2:44; 7:27 Psalm 72:8,11	Acts 17:31 2 Timothy 4:1 Revelation 11:15
The Capital City will be Jerusalem (Zion)	Psalm 2:6 – 7; 110:2 Isaiah 2:3 – 4 Jeremiah 3:17	Matthew 5:35 Luke 1:32 – 33 Matthew 25:31
The immortal faithful will reign with Christ and possess the whole earth with him	Psalm 37:9,11,18,22,29 Daniel 7:27	Matthew 5:5 Luke 22:28 – 30 Revelation 20:6

The great tragedy associated with the nation of Israel is that they rejected Christ as the Messiah promised to Abraham and to David. They had been disobedient many times before but this was their worst error. Christ foretold that they would be expelled from their own land. This work was accomplished by the Romans, and in due course Jews appeared in all countries of the world but with hardly a trace of them in their homeland.

There were however some Jews who responded to the Gospel and were often persecuted by their fellows who refused to depart from their formal worship according to the law of Moses. There were thus two kinds of Jews, the one unchanged and the other converted to Christ. The converts stood with the Gentile converts as the true spiritual descendants of Abraham because they believed the same faithful promises. Abraham lived in hope of the coming of Christ and the Christians in belief of Christ as the fulfilment of the promises. Indeed, the truly faithful men of the years before Christ came and those who sprang from Christ's coming are all one, they are the spiritual Israel of God:

> "For he (Christ) is our peace, who hath made both one, and hath broken down the middle wall of partition between us . . . that he might reconcile

both unto God in one body by the cross . . . and (he) came and preached peace to you which were afar off (the Gentiles) and to them that were nigh (the Jews)."   (Ephesians 2:14,16 – 17)

"There is neither Jew nor Greek, there is neither bond nor free, there is neither male nor female: for ye are all one in Christ Jesus."
(Galatians 3:28)

Does the constitution of spiritual Israel as the true Israel of God make an end of God's dealings with the Jewish nation as a nation? Many answers have been given to that question. Some assert that the wrath of God abides perpetually on the Jews and deprives them of any uniqueness they once possessed. Others have tried to identify some portion of the Jews with Britain and the United States in particular, and thereby have sought to identify them as the recipients of certain blessings. Neither of these positions will satisfy the extensive range of Scripture comment in both Old and New Testaments. The best way to arrive at the truth is, perhaps, to commence with a moment of anti-semitism in Jewish history when the following words were spoken:

"There is a certain people scattered abroad and dispersed among the people in all the provinces of thy kingdom; and their laws are diverse from all people; neither keep they the king's laws: therefore it is not for the king's profit to suffer them. If it please the king, let it be written that they may be destroyed."   (Esther 3:8 – 9)

Those words were spoken about the Jews in ancient Persia some two and a half thousand years ago. They are an almost timeless expression of the strange paradox of the Jews scattered throughout the world, and of the recurrent theme of anti-semitism. The words could have been spoken in the old kingdom of Egypt, in the Roman empire, in the countries of Europe, or in Russia.

The Eternal Jew

Almost everywhere this vagrant people have at some time or other been regarded as parasites to be exterminated. Harsh laws have oppressed them, governments have expelled them, the ghettos have contained them, unutterable tortures have been endured by them, the concentration camps have wasted them, and the gas chambers of the Third Reich have taken them to their deaths. Even in less hostile countries the Jew has been looked upon as strange, unlikable and a proper butt for scorn and execration.

253

Nevertheless the Jew remains, and persists, Generations of oppressors and conquerors have disappeared, the sun has set on the empires of their captors, and no measures of extermination have diminished their significance or removed them from being a factor in world affairs. In most fields of learning they have excelled in great disproportion to their numbers, and in some pursuits, such as music, they have constantly produced an excellence which is almost uncanny. The world's monetary systems owe much to their skills, and they exercise a significant degree of control in the financial centres of the world.

More than that, the whole shape of the modern world owes its origin to the Hebrew people for it is from their midst that Judaism and Christianity, and much that is Islamic, came into being. Were these to be removed or damaged, the structure of the western world would undergo a fundamental and radical change, and the Middle East would be thrown into turmoil. How did it come about that so small a nation could contribute to or produce such astonishing religious faiths?

Men have run out of adjectives in an effort to express their wonderment at the seeming indestructibility and undoubted genius of the Jews. But none of these descriptions, whether by Jews or by others, does anything to account for the unique nature of this people whose history is now almost four thousand years old.

In the second half of the twentieth century the fact of Israel has been placarded before the eyes of the world. Out of almost two millennia of dust they have resurrected nationhood, not obscurely or modestly but blatantly, and in the centre of world affairs. There is scarcely a man or woman anywhere on the face of the earth who is not aware of the existence, importance and awkwardness of this thrusting, unrelenting and seemingly insensitive modern nation. The world marvels at its exploits and is thrown into despair over its lack of regard for world opinion. How is it that this unloved people have managed to secure a toehold in an almost totally Islamic and hostile part of the world? How has it survived the repeated onslaughts of its enemies, and the endless vituperation of millions who have vowed to destroy it?

Everyone remembers that it was in Palestine, the home of the Jews, that Christ was executed at the instigation of the ruling Jews and at the hands of the Gentiles. Why has God allowed them to remain a people, distinct and for the most part non-Christian? Why should a nation who asked for Christ to be put to death succeed against fearful odds in its fight for existence? How does God regard them? Are they His favourites despite what they have done? If so, why is God biased in this way? If not, what accounts for their vitality, resilience and apparent permanence? Are there any truly satisfactory answers to all of these questions? Or, are the Jews simply a remarkable enigma without explanation?

The Bible answer is unequivocal and is sufficient to meet all of these intellectual, philosophical and religious questions, and to provide an explanation with good evidence of the past and present history of the Jews, and to outline their future with startling clarity.

Let us take the first fact: the Jews *are* indestructible as a people among the nations on earth. Here is what God has said:

> *"For I am the Lord, I change not;* **therefore** *ye sons of Jacob are not consumed."* (Malachi 3:6)

Those words were spoken when the Jews were detestable in God's sight because of their treachery toward Him and their widespread disregard for proper and sincere worship. The survival of the Jew does not depend on the Jews and it is irrespective of Gentile opinion or action; the Jews will stay on earth because God is permanent and consistent. The Jews are God's evidence that He exists:

> *"Let all the nations be gathered together . . . Let them bring forth their witnesses . . . or let them hear, and say, It is truth. Ye (Israel)* **are my witnesses***, saith the Lord . . .* **ye are my witnesses***, saith the Lord, that I am God."* (Isaiah 43:9 – 12)

> *"Thus saith the Lord, which giveth the sun for a light by day, and the ordinances of the moon and of the stars for a light by night, which divideth the sea when the waves thereof roar; The Lord of hosts is his name: If these ordinances depart from before me, saith the Lord, then the seed of Israel also shall cease from being a nation from before me for ever.*
> *Thus saith the Lord; If heaven above can be measured, and the foundations of the earth searched out beneath, I will also cast off all the seed of Israel for all that they have done, saith the Lord."* (Jeremiah 31:35 – 37)

> *"For I am with thee, saith the Lord, to save thee: though I make a full end of all nations whither I have scattered thee, yet will I not make a full end of thee: but I will correct thee in measure, and will not leave thee altogether unpunished."* (Jeremiah 30:11)

These words provide the explanation for the enduring nature of the

255

Israelitish nation. It will be seen that their survival is not a proof that they are inherently good, and is unaffected by their evident stubbornness and waywardness. Their permanence is due solely to the unfailing goodness of God who, despite man's forgetfulness or rebellion, causes the sun to rise, and the moon and the stars to appear. As the Lord Jesus Christ expressed it: *"He maketh his sun to rise on the evil and on the good, and sendeth the rain on the just and on the unjust"* (Matthew 5:45).

There is a rebuke for all of us in those words. Many men and women would like to criticize God for preserving the (in their opinion) unworthy and troublesome Jews, whilst at the same time not feeling any surprise that God sheds His sunshine and showers upon all men whatever their spiritual condition.

Israel's endurance is evidence to all men of the nature of the love of God, which remains undiminished even though men fail to recognize or respond to it. It is not that Israel is better than any other nation, or perhaps worse; rather is it that God loved them and His love is inextinguishable:

> *"The Lord did not set his love upon you, nor choose you, because ye were more in number than any people . . . but because the Lord loved you."*
> (Deuteronomy 7:7–8)

Their survival is not of works; it is by grace.

God has blazoned the evidence of His purpose with the Jews before the faces of all men. He has made them an uncomfortable factor politically and ideologically in world affairs. We are perhaps entitled to wonder why God's evidence has taken this particular form. Whereas we might consider that the influences of the sun, moon and stars are, for the most part, genial and beneficial, it is not easy for us to detect a similar kindness in the relationships between Israel and her neighbours, for example. The Bible tells us why it is so.

First, however, let us remember one thing, the most important thing for any man to know. The precious, undeniable and unforgettable truth is that Jesus Christ was born a Jew. Therefore, in all His dealings with this abrasive and self-willed people, God has worked and out of it has come the Saviour of the world:

> *"The book of the generation of Jesus Christ, the son of David, the son of Abraham."* (Matthew 1:1)

> *"His (God's) Son . . . was descended from David according to the flesh."* (Romans 1:3, R.S.V.)

> *"Remember Jesus Christ, risen from the dead, descended from David . . "*   (2 Timothy 2:8, R.S.V.)

Christ's earthly parentage is clearly Israelitish. He is in the direct line through king David back to Abraham. Therefore to all our other problem questions about the Jews, we have to add one more: Why was Jesus born a Jew? It may be that the answer to this latest of our questions will provide the answers to most of the others.

The Jews have a religious history and a religious heritage. About these things we read the following:

From Jesus: *"Salvation is of the Jews."*   (John 4:22)

From Paul: *"Israelites, to whom pertaineth the adoption, and the glory, and the covenants, and the giving of the law, and the service of God, and the promises; whose are the fathers, and of whom as concerning the flesh Christ came."*   (Romans 9:4 – 5)

Paradoxical as it may seem, Israel who rejected Christ were also the custodians of the Old Testament which contained God's promises concerning the coming Christ. Christ was laid in the lap of the Jews. It was therefore no casual selection which caused Christ to be born of a Jewish maid in Palestine: it was of God, and the prophets had said that thus it would be.

We are shortsighted if we look at the Jews merely in a political sense. We need to take the long range view and trace them back to the great patriarchs, to Abraham, Isaac and Jacob. Those three men were their forebears and it is because of God's purpose in them that the Jewish nation has been preserved. God's promises are indestructible and the Jews are God's evidence that this is so.

We have already considered the words:

> *"I will make of thee a great nation, and I will bless thee, and make thy name great; and thou shalt be a blessing: and I will bless them that bless thee, and curse him that curseth thee."*   (Genesis 12:2 – 3)

The nation of Israel is one of the results of this mighty promise made to Abraham, the father of the race. The existence of the Jews is God's evidence that His purpose is rolling forward and will not be overcome. Also we should note the warning signal:

> *"I will bless them that bless thee, and curse him that curseth thee."*

Those words account for a great deal of world history. Nations and

257

men have been blessed or cursed according to their treatment of the Jews. This is recorded in many parts of Scripture and in the pages of world history. It is *the* factor in the so-called fortunes of some nations.

When the first little family of Israelites went down into Egypt, in the time of Joseph, they multiplied greatly and were oppressed by their captors. Nevertheless, at the appointed time, according to God's word to Abraham, they came forth as a nation to inherit Canaan, and the Egyptians were punished for their cruelty and oppression. From that time forward the nations, large and small, have seen their own destiny determined by their attitude to this small and seemingly insignificant people. And it will happen again. The Third Reich made its greatest mistake when it made the Jews the scapegoats. The Third Reich is no more. Russia's own oppressiveness has marked her out for punishment, unless she relents.

But Israel herself is blessed or cursed according to her attitude to God. As a nation they were privileged above all peoples to become the custodians of a noble law. Think of the ten commandments, first given to the Jews, and how much better our own society would be were these basic rules to be observed more widely:

> "*Thou shalt have no other gods before me*
> *Thou shalt not make any graven image . . . thou shalt not bow down to them*
> *Thou shalt not take the name of the Lord thy God in vain*
> *Remember the sabbath day to keep it holy*
> *Honour thy father and thy mother*
> *Thou shalt not kill . . . not commit adultery . . . not steal*
> *Thou shalt not bear false witness . . . thou shalt not covet.*" (Exodus 20:3 – 17)

Those commandments touch upon the most profound instincts of man and upon his most personal relationships. They were intended to be a discipline of mind and conduct. Indeed, many of the commands are now part of the statutes of many countries. The moral decline of the West stands condemned by some of these basic precepts. Neglect or blasphemy of God, the breakdown of family life, corruption, violence and greed fly in the face of this charter of God. They provided for Israel a wonderful inheritance:

> "*What nation is there so great, that hath statutes and judgements so*

258

righteous as all this law, which I have set before you this day? Only take heed to thyself, and keep thy soul diligently, lest thou forget . . ."
(Deuteronomy 4:8 – 9)

But Israel were wayward and they refused to allow the good influences of God to fashion their hearts and their nationhood. They could have become wise, and noble, and good. Instead they were described repeatedly as "stiffnecked", unbowing to the word of God, and "hardhearted", unconverted to His good and holy ways. It was for this reason and for their faintheartedness that they remained 40 years in the wilderness on their way from Egypt to Canaan.

What then were the principles which determined the destiny of Israel when they defiled their precious land by idolatry, immorality and violence? To whom much is given, of them is much required. Israel had privileges beyond compare, and her responsibilities towards God were equally great. There are two chapters in the Bible which tell of what would happen to Israel were she to be obedient or disobedient towards God. These chapters (Leviticus 26 and Deuteronomy 28) read like Jewish history in advance. They are astonishing in their accuracy, and startling in their outworking:

> "**If ye walk in my statutes** and keep my commandments, and do them . . . I will give you rain . . . ye shall eat your bread to the full . . . dwell safely . . . and I will give peace in the land . . . and I will walk among you, and will be your God . . . **If ye will not hearken** . . . ye shall sow your seed in vain, for your enemies shall eat it . . . if ye will not yet for all this hearken . . . I will break the pride of your power . . . the land shall not yield her increase . . . I will bring . . . plagues . . . wild beasts . . . and if ye will not be reformed . . . I will bring a sword upon you . . . and pestilence . . . and if ye will not for all this hearken unto me . . . I will . . . bring your sanctuaries unto desolation . . . the land into desolation . . . I will scatter you among the heathen (nations) . . . and your land shall be desolate."   (Leviticus 26)

All these things came to pass, both the blessings and the cursings, until the land was rent in two and made into two kingdoms, and, later, each part went separately into captivity. The southern kingdom saw some respite, and the captives returned from Babylon after seventy long years, and the nation was in the land once more, though this time under the heel of Roman rule, when

the Lord Jesus Christ came to them. Their blindness and implaca-
bility were then manifested as never before. Despite the love, the
Gospel and the miracles of compassion; despite the resurrection of
the Lord from the dead, and the words and wonders through the
apostles, nationally they rejected their Messiah and his saving
grace. There was then no remedy. The last great overthrow took
place and, after Bar Kochba's revolt, in A.D.135 the Jews were
banished from the land, leaving no nationhood and but a few sorry
members behind. Their temple was in ruins, Jerusalem had been
sacked and their former mode of worship destroyed.

Dispersion

The Jews appeared everywhere, the world over, according to the
Word of God. Every country under the sun has its Abrahams,
Cohens, Isaacs, Jacobs and the like. Every reader has met them.
God has fulfilled His word in finally dispersing them. The centri-
fugal force of this dispersion is astonishing. God has put His
witnesses before the eyes of all men.

The story seemed to have ended. Despite the survival of the
nation amidst the overthrows or captivities by the Assyrians,
Babylonians, Medes and Persians, Greeks and Romans, the end
seemed to have come. The land lay desolate. Even Christendom
looked on with little more than a sigh. It looked as though the
Jewish nation was finished.

Meanwhile in every town where numbers of Jews were gathered
throughout the world, there sprang up synagogues and in the
synagogues was the treasury of the books of the Old Testament.
No nation on earth had anything like these wonderful books.

They contained the condemnation of the nation and the
promises of God. The Jews cherished these precious truths with
fanaticism and meticulous care. Somehow, despite all their
sorrows and desolating experiences, the Word of God remained at
the centre of their existence. The trembling hand of the persecuted
people clutched the sure Word of God and of prophecy. Their tears
ran in rivulets of hope. As a poet once said:

> "For in the background figures vague and vast,
> Of patriarchs and of prophets rose sublime,
> And all the great traditions of the Past
> They saw reflected in the Coming Time."

But what real hope could there be for this rebellious and unrepentant nation? Buried in countless parts of the world, it seemed that their nationhood was entombed, never to rise again. Each year they kept the Feast of the Passover, the memory of their coming out of Egypt, and expressed the hope that they would still be delivered from their dispersion. "Next year in Jerusalem" was their prayer. But only a miracle could save them after almost nineteen hundred years — and were they worth a miracle?

Amongst the embers of the ancient Word of God there glowed coals of living and inextinguishable fire. It was as though the savage winds of persecution and the cold air of dispersion had served only to preserve these fires of hope. In the chapter on the blessings and the cursings, we also read:

> "And yet for all that, when they be in the land of their enemies, I will not cast them away, neither will I abhor them, to destroy them utterly, and to break my covenant with them: for I am the Lord their God. But I will for their sakes remember the covenant of their ancestors, whom I brought forth out of the land of Egypt in the sight of the heathen, that I might be their God: I am the Lord."   (Leviticus 26:44 – 45)

God is unchanged and unchangeable. His covenant with Abraham remains, and He will honour it. Amidst the direst calamity and the deepest despair God has preserved Abraham's descendants in love, mercy and faithfulness. The truth of these things is evident to all men who have witnessed the survival of the Jewish people. But are the Jews preserved in this way merely to continue their existence in a largely dismembered condition? The Bible is emphatic that there are greater things to come, things which will affect the destiny of the whole world. Here are the beginnings from the Scripture:

> "For, lo, the days come, saith the Lord, that I will bring again the captivity of my people Israel and Judah, saith the Lord: and I will cause them to return to the land that I gave to their fathers, and they shall possess it . . . I will save thee from afar, and thy seed from the land of their captivity; and Jacob shall return, and shall be in rest, and be quiet, and none shall make him afraid . . . in the latter days ye shall consider it."
>
> (Jeremiah 30:3,10,24)

> "Hear the word of the Lord, O ye nations, and declare it in the isles afar off, and say, He that scattered Israel will gather him, and keep him, as a shepherd doth his flock."   (Jeremiah 31:10)

261

"I will cause the captivity of Judah and the captivity of Israel to return, and will build them, as at the first." (Jeremiah 33:7)

"I will deliver them out of all places where they have been scattered . . . and I will bring them out from the people, and gather them from the countries, and will bring them to their own land."
(Ezekiel 34:12 – 13)

"I will take you from among the heathen, and gather you out of all countries, and will bring you into your own land." (Ezekiel 36:24)

"Behold I will take the children of Israel from among the heathen, whither they be gone, and will gather them on every side, and bring them into their own land." (Ezekiel 37:21)

It is from these and many similar Scriptures that the Christadelphians have been heralding the return of the Jews to Israel for about one hundred and fifty years.

When we first started to make these Scriptures known the land of Palestine (as it was then called) lay within the Turkish empire and was desolate. Jews languished the world over, but there was no return to the land. A few visionaries arose among the people and eventually the Zionist movement took root.

It was in the First World War however, that, as a result of a service rendered by a Jew to the British people in their hour of need, the famous Balfour Declaration was published:

"His Majesty's Government view with favour the establishment in Palestine of a national home for the Jewish people, and will use their best endeavours to facilitate the achievement of this object . . ."

Regathering

With the defeat of the Turks and the coming of the British mandate over the land, the Zionist dream began to be realised, but always under considerable restraint and difficulty. It was not until the Holocaust of the Second World War that the real return began with a spirit of earnestness and longing. Wave after wave of immigrants from many places broke upon the shores of Palestine where Britain was trying to exercise some kind of quota system. This resulted in many scarcely seaworthy vessels being turned away and made to take their place in the queue, the lengthening queue.

262

The Arabs were naturally apprehensive and increasingly resistant. The Jews were fanatically determined, and there were Jewish terrorists at work among the British troops. The pressures on the mandate and the failure of world powers to produce a practical solution to the Palestine problem, caused Britain to withdraw from the land and leave its inhabitants to their own devices. Many believed that this would spell the end of the Israeli return. Their people were pathetically ill-equipped, while the Arabs were numerous and some of them had well-trained and fully armed units. That was in May 1948.

But everyone counted without God. Out of the seemingly inevitable destruction arose the State of Israel, and the Arabs suffered their first defeat. Ever since that time the State of Israel has taken her place among the nations, and her voice and position have affected the politics of the whole world. The Palestine Liberation Organisation, well-financed and determined, has carried on a ceaseless campaign of violence against Israel both in Israel itself and in many places in the world. Major Arab efforts were made in 1967 and 1973 to destroy the State of Israel, but always with greater worries for the assailants and more territory for the Israelis. The struggle still goes on and the Israelis, admired in their exploits, are losing more and more the sympathy which nations felt for them after their terrible experiences of the Second World War.

All of this is political in content and, superficially, purely political in intention. Christadelphians have no interest in politics and are not associated in any way with the nationalistic, military and political aspirations of the State of Israel. But it is impossible to look at Israel and at the prophets of God without having to declare that what is taking place is what was foretold. That conclusion is inescapable, unless we wilfully blind ourselves to the facts.

What will the outcome be? Has God brought the Jews back to the land to live in a state of military alertness and of strife? Are they to be in constant jeopardy? What does the Bible say?

Israel's troubles are by no means over. Her land and her capital city are to become the focus of world tensions and military movements on a scale never seen there in all history. But before we examine that prospect and its outcome, we must face another and very intriguing fact.

The Jewish nation is non-Christian. Apart from a very small

minority, the Jews have no time for Christ. He is not accepted as their Messiah. The orthodox Jews remain deeply traditional in their faith and practice. The liberal Jews look upon their religion more as a way of life than as a devotional faith. A lot of Jews are frankly agnostic or atheistic. All of this accords badly with what should be. In fact it raises a very serious question. If God scattered Israel at the time of their disbelief in Jesus Christ as the promised Messiah, why has He regathered them when they are still in a state of disbelief and, moreover, are even less religious than they were at the time of their dispersal?

Israel is to become Christian! Astounding as this may seem, it is what the Bible foretells. She is to repent of her blindness and acknowledge Christ as the promised Anointed One. This change of heart is perhaps more difficult for us to believe than any of the other facts and prophecies which we have considered. We had occasion earlier to remind ourselves of a question which God posed in the Old Testament: Is anything too hard for Me? The answer is that nothing consistent with God's holy name is impossible with Him. He has said that the Jews will repent, and there is no doubt that it will come to pass:

> *"For in mine holy mountain, in the mountain of the height of Israel . . . there shall all the house of Israel, all of them in the land, serve me: there will I accept them . . . when I bring you out from the people, and gather you out of the countries wherein ye have been scattered . . . and there shall ye remember your ways, and all your doings, wherein ye have been defiled; and ye shall lothe yourselves."* (Ezekiel 20:40 – 43)

> *"For I will take you . . . into your own land. Then will I sprinkle clean water upon you, and ye shall be clean . . . a new heart also will I give you, and a new spirit will I put within you."* (Ezekiel 36:24 – 26)

> *"I will cleanse them: so shall they be my people, and I will be their God."* (Ezekiel 37:23)

That this repentance involves also their belief in Christ as Messiah is made plain in the New Testament, where these or similar passages are taken up and used as the means of proclaiming the Gospel in Christ (see Hebrews 8:8 – 13; 10:16 – 18 and Romans 11:25 – 27).

But how shall this be? How could so radical a change take place in a people whose firmness of heart in their present commitment has been made known to the whole world? It is evident from the

Scriptures we have quoted that this complete change of heart will be brought about by God. The God who said He would cause them to return to their desolate land and has done so, is the God who has said that He will cause them to repent. The Bible gives us the story.

The Lord will touch Israel upon her weakest, yet strongest point. She is undoubtedly arrogant (with an arrogance born of adversity and the struggle for survival, certainly) and by virtue of prevailing circumstances she is confessedly self-reliant. Indeed, her experiences since 1948 have deeply reinforced this spirit and filled Israel with an alarming degree of self-justification. It is this characteristic, renowned throughout the world, which the Lord God will shatter by experiences which will humble the nation and bring her to the dust.

At that time it will seem that all that Israel has built and rebuilt will be in irrevocable ruin. The people gathered from afar and the children born to them in the land will have their self-dreams destroyed, and an intense disillusionment will arise among them. Israel is to be overwhelmingly invaded, and the invaders will swallow up the land. Jerusalem will be under siege, and all will seem to be on the brink of total disaster. Every indication from Scripture, and the one followed by students for a long time, is that the confederacy of invaders (for there will be many) will be Russian led, supported by Iran, Libya and Ethiopia. Although the invasion will not go unchallenged, the challenge will be too late and ineffective. The size and rapidity of the attack will leave any defenders helpless. The Suez canal will be cut off because the Bible tells us that the invaders will also occupy Egypt.

Israel will be in despair (one can imagine that the world will be in turmoil). Their fighting skills and astounding bravery will be ineffective, even though they were to make a stand such as took place against the Romans in Masada.

Contrition and Conversion

Out of this ruin there will arise a new Israel, repentant and humble. They will discover that there is another Power and another Leader. He who died under the superscription, This is Jesus of Nazareth the King of the Jews, will, unknown to the invaders and to the Jews, already be in the earth; and he will come to deliver Jerusalem, and bring about the destruction of the northern invaders and their associates. Cataclysmic happenings, including an earthquake which will rend the Mount of Olives to the east of Jerusalem, will engulf the foreign armies. A variety of measures will ensure their complete defeat and destruction.

All of these things can be found out by reading Ezekiel 38 and 39, Daniel 11 and Zechariah 12 – 14, as well as other Scriptures. Here are some extracts:

> *"On that day I will set out to destroy all the nations that attack Jerusalem. And I will pour out on the house of David and the inhabitants of Jerusalem a spirit of grace and supplication. They will look on me, the one they have pierced, and mourn for him as one mourns for an only child . . ."* (Zechariah 12:9 – 10, N.I.V.)

> *"On that day a fountain will be opened to the house of David and the inhabitants of Jerusalem, to cleanse them from sin and impurity."* (Zechariah 13:1, N.I.V.)

Israel, all her self-confidence gone, cries to God and in doing so is reduced to sorrow and contrition. It is then that Christ is made known to them. They learn the dreadful truth that, *"He came unto his own, and his own received him not"* (John 1:11). The chosen people had put their appointed Messiah to death. Their sorrow and repentance will be unrestrained, and they will be accepted by their God whose ways will have brought about the impossible!

Israel's return to favour and blessing begins at this time. She is then used to chastise the nations and to lead them to the God of Israel whose temple, in due time, will be built in Jerusalem. Scattered Jews over the rest of the earth will be escorted to the land when they have passed through a period of repentance similar to that displayed by their companions already there. The fully regathered Jews will have a service to render in temple worship when the Gentile nations come, year by year in turn, to worship in Jerusalem.

Mortal Israel will live in cantons in the land of Israel during the millennium, right at the heart of the Kingdom of God on earth. Their rulers will be the twelve apostles (Luke 22:30). This period of time will be their opportunity to demonstrate by faith and love that they belong to God. If they prove individually faithful at heart, they will receive the gift of immortality at the end of the millennium.

Thus will draw to its climax the history of this people. God's witnesses will have been there to the end of mortal history, and God's faithfulness to them and to all mankind will have been made known. Into the eternity beyond, faithful Jews and Gentiles without distinction, will, as Abraham's truer seed, give everlasting praise to the God who keepeth covenant and mercy:

> *"And so all Israel shall be saved . . . O the depth of the riches both of the wisdom and knowledge of God! how unsearchable are his judgements, and his ways past finding out!"*   (Romans 11:26,33)

26

SIGNS OF CHRIST'S RETURN

THIS is an absorbing subject. For some individuals it becomes an obsession. At various times they declare that Christ will return on a particular day, and perhaps even at a certain time of day and to a named spot on earth. Devoted followers of such forecasters have sold up their possessions and, on the eve of the day selected, have waited with complete confidence that Christ would come. The sun rose, reached its zenith and sank again to rest; and the moon rose and the stars came out, but the Lord had not come. What then?

Sometimes it has been sad disillusionment; sometimes the leader has explained his error, and on at least one occasion the leader said that, although Christ had not appeared to anyone, he had in fact returned in spirit. Unbelievers have taken the opportunity to mock or pity those concerned, and to scoff even more loudly at the belief in the Second Coming.

There is, of course, no doubt that the Lord Jesus Christ will come back, personally, bodily, in glory and with the holy angels. There are hundreds of verses in the New Testament where this is plainly taught. It was the hope of the early believers and is still the hope which Christadelphians cherish. Without the return of Christ there would be no resurrection from the dead, no blessing of immortality for the faithful and no Kingdom of God on earth. God's purpose would be lost. The certainty of the return of Jesus is clear in this selection of verses:

"*This same Jesus, which is taken up from you into heaven,* **shall so**

268

come in like manner as ye have seen him go into heaven."
(Acts 1:11)

"He (God) **shall send Jesus Christ**, *which before was preached unto you: whom the heaven must receive until the times of restitution of all things, which God hath spoken by the mouth of all his holy prophets since the world began."* (Acts 3:20 – 21)

"For **the Son of man shall come** *in the glory of his Father with his angels."* (Matthew 16:27)

"When the Son of man shall come in his glory, and all the holy angels with him, then shall he sit upon the throne of his glory."
(Matthew 25:31)

"Then shall they see the Son of man coming in a cloud with power and great glory." (Luke 21:27)

"Wait for his Son from heaven ..." (1 Thessalonians 1:10)

"At the coming of our Lord Jesus Christ." (1 Thessalonians 3:13)

"The Lord himself shall descend from heaven ..."
(1 Thessalonians 4:16)

"He shall come to be glorified in his saints ..."
(2 Thessalonians 1:10)

"The Lord Jesus Christ ... shall judge the quick and the dead at his appearing and his kingdom." (2 Timothy 4:1)

"A crown of righteousness ... the Lord ... shall give ... unto all them also that love his appearing ..." (2 Timothy 4:8)

"Looking for that blessed hope, and the glorious appearing of the great God and our Saviour Jesus Christ." (Titus 2:13)

"Surely I come quickly. Amen.
Even so, come, Lord Jesus." (Revelation 22:20)

These verses are conclusive in their teaching that Christ will come again. This is the belief of Christadelphians, and it is the reason for their being interested in the signs of the times. We have always had an interest in this sphere, and although there have been occasional enthusiasts who have ventured to suggest a date or a period of time, we do not dogmatise about when the Lord will come. We believe that dogmatism and lurid scaremongering are notoriously

269

unreliable, and are no substitute for sober and serious Bible reading. We believe that we are living in what the Bible calls, "the last days", and we seek to take heed to the warnings of the Lord Jesus Christ:

> *"Therefore be ye also ready: for in such an hour as ye think not the Son of man cometh."* (Matthew 24:44)

> *"Take ye heed, watch and pray: for ye know not when the time is."* (Mark 13:33)

Whether or not, therefore, we think that we have arrived at a reasonable conclusion in deciding that the return of the Lord Jesus is upon us, the Lord is telling us that we shall not truly know when the time will be. Moreover, the return will be "in such an hour as ye think not". There is something very instructive in all of this. We might be skilful in times and seasons, as though it were an art or science, and yet be totally unprepared in heart for the Lord himself. It may be for this reason that we cannot pinpoint the precise time, so that we may always be watching and praying.

The Pharisees in the days of Jesus were regarded as the contemporary experts and they were supposedly looking for signs of Christ's first coming. But they failed to recognise Jesus as the promised Messiah:

> *"When it is evening, ye say, It will be fair weather: for the sky is red. And in the morning, It will be foul weather to day: for the sky is red and lowring. O ye hypocrites, ye can discern the face of the sky; but can ye not discern the signs of the times?"* (Matthew 16:2 – 3)

So eaten up were they in asking for and seeking to interpret signs that they failed completely to recognise that Christ was amongst them. Wrongly, they were hoping for observable things, miraculous perhaps, which they could see on demand before committing themselves. Jesus reproved them:

> *"The kingdom of God is not coming with signs to be observed; nor will they say, 'Lo, here it is!' or 'There!' for behold, the kingdom of God is in the midst of you."* (Luke 17:20,21, R.S.V.)

Christ the appointed King and Saviour, stood in their very midst, and they had not discerned him! It is not that signs were absent — there were many at Christ's birth and in his miracles, for example — but the Pharisees were altogether wrong in their spiritual discernment. A man must be ready for the Kingdom of God, else he will never be allowed ultimate entrance into it when the Lord comes.

Therefore in our further observations in this chapter, we must remember that first and foremost for the disciple is to be ready for Christ — always. One of the ways to examine the signs of the times is to see what the Bible says about the time of the end, and determine how the world looks in comparison with the Bible description. We have broken the subject down into general headings and given the analysis under each of them.

World Morality

The Bible tells us that decent standards will have broken down to the extent that the fabric of society will be threatened; even the communities of believers will be affected by the decline:

> *"But mark this: There will be terrible times in the last days. People will be lovers of themselves, lovers of money, boastful, proud, abusive, disobedient to their parents, ungrateful, unholy, without love, unforgiving, slanderous, without self-control, brutal, not lovers of the good, treacherous, rash, conceited, lovers of pleasure rather than lovers of God . . ."* (2 Timothy 3:1–4, N.I.V.)

> *"Just as it was in the days of Noah, so also will it be in the days of the Son of man. People were eating, drinking, marrying and being given in marriage up to the day that Noah entered the ark. Then the flood came and destroyed them all."* (Luke 17:26–27, N.I.V.)

> *"Take heed to yourselves, lest haply your hearts be overcharged with surfeiting, and drunkenness, and cares of this life, and that day come upon you suddenly as a snare: for so shall it come upon all them that dwell on the face of all the earth."* (Luke 21:34–35, R.V.)

Materialism, disregard for common decencies, self-indulgence of all kinds and a deliberate choice of pleasure rather than of God is the theme of these verses, and it is characteristic of our society. These things are not unique to this present age; decadent societies, such as the Roman empire at its end, have shared similar things. By itself, this sign would not be in any way conclusive. The sign fits our times, but does not of itself declare that we are in the last days.

The State of Christianity

In the early part of the twentieth century it was not uncommon for

271

people to believe that enlightenment, improved social conditions, and the removal of some of the evil effects of the industrial revolution would bring about the golden era and spread what they called the Kingdom of God on earth. These were sincerely held convictions shared by deeply committed social reformers, politicians and religious leaders. Their drive and devotion succeeded in bringing about many changes which swept away some of the worst abuses and bad conditions of the under-privileged in society. Poverty of the desperate and hopeless kind was largely eradicated and the social conscience was aroused to care for the sick and the unfortunates. Disease was contained and medical science effected widespread improvements. Infant mortality and the loss of mothers in childbirth were greatly reduced.

It looked for a while as though the sails were set for the fair haven. But a new phenomenon revealed itself: full stomachs did not produce thankful hearts. Social welfare did not necessarily engender good consciences. Improved living standards did not mean living better lives. It was as though Christianity of whatever shade had been left in a backwater or, at best, given but polite respect. The social gospel had been born, but the true Gospel was stunted.

Can we hope for something better? Will it be possible to produce a society in which the teachings of the Lord Jesus Christ are respected and used for daily living? Can the Kingdom of God come about by the sincere efforts of devoted people? What will be the state of Christianity at the time of the return of the Lord Jesus Christ? Here are the Scriptures:

> "*I charge thee therefore before God, and the Lord Jesus Christ, who shall judge the quick and the dead at his appearing and his kingdom . . . for the time will come when they will not endure sound doctrine; but after their own lusts shall they heap to themselves teachers, having itching ears; and they shall turn away their ears from the truth, and shall be turned unto fables.*" (2 Timothy 4:1 – 3)

> "*But evil men and seducers shall wax worse and worse, deceiving, and being deceived.*" (2 Timothy 3:13)

> "*But the Spirit saith expressly, that in later times some shall fall away from the faith, giving heed to seducing spirits and doctrines of devils, through the hypocrisy of men that speak lies, branded in their own conscience as with a hot iron; forbidding to marry, and commanding to*

abstain from meats, which God created to be received with thanksgiving
by them that believe and know the truth."

(1 Timothy 4:1 – 3, R.V.)

"Now we beseech you, brethren, by the coming of our Lord Jesus Christ,
and by our gathering together unto him, that ye be not soon shaken in your
mind, or be troubled . . . let no man deceive you by any means: for that
day shall not come, except there come a falling away first . . ."

(2 Thessalonians 2:1 – 3)

There have been heresies and new religions from the earliest days of Christianity. This book has demonstrated how some of the more popular heresies have taken root. But the verses we have quoted make it plain that we cannot look for their removal from the scene. The troubles will remain. Ecumenism is not being sought on the basis of original Christianity and therefore it will not succeed.

Therefore impure Christianity, deteriorating at that, will be here when the Lord returns. The Kingdom of God will not come by preaching, although there will be faithful men and women who will become heirs of the Kingdom despite the world around them and the decadence of Christendom.

War or Peace?

Whatever men and women the world over think of religion, we know that they yearn for peace. It is the common longing, especially in those places where war has decimated the ranks of the young, destroyed towns and villages, and ravaged the countryside. It is a sad comment on human history that it is heavily scarred by warfare. Millions of human beings have died at the hands of their fellows in all kinds of conflict throughout the ages. Worst of all, some of the most appalling bloodshed has occurred in strife between countries considered to be part of Christendom.

The art of warfare has developed from the days of hand to hand combat to the time of inter-continental ballistic missiles, multiple nuclear-headed at that. There are also chemical, nerve gas and disease-bearing weapons. The man in the street finds it impossible to understand what the effect of this wide range of weapons would be in a major war. He is helpless. Moreover world rulers are in no better case because they are now caught up in the 'defence and peace-by-arms' planning and budgeting.

Of course, it is argued, and with some truth, that the nuclear deterrent has prevented war between the major powers for the longest time this century. The question to be decided is whether these weapons are the ultimate deterrent, that is, whether they can abolish major war. What does the Bible have to say? Will a quiet earth welcome the return of the Prince of Peace?

Whatever aspirations and hopes men may have, and however successful their peace efforts from time to time, the Bible teaches us that world turmoil and distress will herald the return of the Lord Jesus Christ:

> "*There shall be a time of trouble, such as never was since there was a nation . . .*" (Daniel 12:1)

> "*Proclaim ye this among the nations; prepare war: stir up the mighty men; let all the men of war draw near . . .*" (Joel 3:9, R.V.)

> "*Upon the earth distress of nations, with perplexity; the sea and the waves roaring; men's hearts failing them for fear, and for looking after those things which are coming on the earth . . . then shall they see the Son of man coming in a cloud with power and great glory.*" (Luke 21:25 – 27)

> "*And the nations were angry, and thy wrath is come, and the time of the dead, that they should be judged . . . and that thou shouldest . . . destroy them which destroy the earth.*" (Revelation 11:18)

Amidst the great decline in moral standards and of true Christianity will arise untold troubles throughout the world, nations coming into conflict, and the people of the world being distressed beyond measure. It is at such a time that Christ will be revealed. The Prince of Peace will come, not because the earth will welcome him in peace, but because without Christ mankind would face annihilation.

Where will the major conflict take place?

Post-war society has been nurtured on the doctrine that the worst threat facing mankind arises from the East-West tension. East and West have reacted accordingly. Europe is divided and the barrier between the two ideologies and powers runs through that continent. European countries are afraid of becoming the cauldron around which the powers will unleash themselves one on the other. Peace movements in Europe, when not stimulated by purely political agitators, are the efforts of some of the people who are afraid to have a voice before it is too late.

Will the conflict, the final major conflict, take place across Europe? Is that the final battle ground? What does the Bible say?

The Bible draws the axis at right angles to the east-west line through Europe, and makes it pass through Jerusalem. The Middle East, particularly the land of Israel, is the final focus, the place of decision.

The Bible teaches that the land of Israel will be invaded, suddenly and successfully, by a confederacy of nations coming down from "the uttermost parts of the north". The leader of the confederacy, if one draws a north-south line through Jerusalem, will be either Turkey or Russia. The north-south line passes through no other countries. The *uttermost* parts of the north would indicate Russia rather than Turkey. Indeed, there is nothing to exclude the view that both powers will be involved. It may be that the two countries will be in league or, as some Bible expositors have expected, Turkey will be occupied by Russia in due course. The view that Russia is the chief aggressor has been held for a long time, certainly from the middle of last century when Russia had nothing like the influence or military might she wields today.

Two whole chapters (Ezekiel 38 and 39) are devoted to this world-shattering event. Three of the allies of the leader are mentioned by name: Persia (Iran), Ethiopia and Libya. As conditions are at present, it would not be in the least surprising to see those powers confederate with the invader. Persia is avowedly anti-Israeli; Ethiopia is communist and a natural ally, if Russia is the leader; and Libya is fanatically against the State of Israel, and greatly admires the Russian military system. Of course, political scenes change rapidly and what we have in those three countries today may not be the final picture. But the Bible has mapped out for them the course they are sure to follow.

The invasion will straddle the Suez Canal because Egypt will be occupied as the powers sweep south. Not that the invasion is unchallenged, but the challenge is too late and ineffective. It is only the intervention of God through the Lord Jesus Christ that brings desolation to those who have dared to desecrate the land of promise.

Perhaps, a word should be said about another confederacy mentioned in Revelation 17. This confederacy, seemingly under a religious head, opposes Christ and the saints. Clearly, this event takes place after the return of Jesus and after the saints have been blessed with immortality. For reasons which it is not convenient to

275

develop here, it has been thought by many Christadelphians that the religious authority could well be Roman Catholic. The political alliance is more difficult to define and we may have to await further developments in the European scene before things become wholly clear. The rebellion is extinguished and the religious power obliterated.

From all that has been written in the foregoing paragraphs, it is evident that the nations are going to be very active in warlike ways. Let us look further at what the Bible has to say.

The Nations

The Bible has comments about the nations generally at the time of the end. It might be expected that the smaller nations would be absorbed by larger ones, and that the weak would go to the wall in the game of power politics. However, this is not to be the general drift. In fact, the Bible gives a picture of nations flowering at a time when the nation of Israel would come once again on the world scene:

> *"Behold the fig tree, and all the trees; when they now shoot forth, ye see and know of your own selves that summer is now nigh at hand. So likewise ye, when ye see these things come to pass, know ye that the kingdom of God is nigh at hand."* (Luke 21:29 – 31)

Obviously this little parable draws the simple lesson that we can detect the coming of summer by the leaves of the trees. Therefore we should be ready for the coming of Christ when the signs of the times blossom forth. Since, however, the fig tree is one of God's symbols for Israel (Jeremiah 24:1 – 3; Hosea 9:10; Joel 1:7), it may be that the parable tells us a little more than appears at first sight. It may well point to the fact that at the time when the nation of Israel is once more established in the land of Israel, there will also be an upspringing of nationhood among other peoples too.

It is remarkable that since the Second World War there has been a considerable increase in the number of nations represented in the United Nations Organisation. This is due to the independence achieved by former colonies and by the rising up of powers in under-developed lands.

The resultant mix of strong and weak nations is clearly indicated in the Bible (in the toes of the Image in Daniel 2, for example, where clay and iron appear together), and the weak nations make their voice heard:

"Proclaim ye this among the Gentiles; Prepare war, wake up the mighty men, let all the men of war draw near; let them come up: beat your plowshares into swords, and your pruninghooks into spears: let the weak say, I am strong." (Joel 3:9 – 11)

At the time of the end the nations will be arming for war, and will be diverting into military expenditure monies which could have been spent on more peaceful pursuits such as agriculture.

Amongst other nations mentioned by name, Egypt is singled out by the Word of God for a prophecy concerning her future. She does not appear among the invaders. She is at present separately at peace with Israel and this is not at odds with what the Word of God has to say. In the end she will receive a special blessing from the Lord God, after she has suffered the chastisement of invasion (Isaiah 19:16 – 24 and Daniel 11:42 – 43).

Though not so clearly defined, there is probably a reference to Saudi Arabia under the names of two places which lie within the borders of that country (Sheba and Dedan). They too will not be with the invaders; in fact, they are part of the challenge to them (Ezekiel 38:13). From these indicators it seems unlikely that Saudi Arabia will break her present links with the West whose commercial interests and strategic concern are probably indicated by the expression "the merchants of Tarshish" in Ezekiel 38.

Certain it is that the Gulf is of major concern to the West, and it will be a devastating blow to them when the invaders sweep south to Egypt and stand also within a short distance of the oil states.

The Sign above all Others

This is the sign of Israel, and we have dealt in some detail with the matter in the preceding chapter. We stress it again at this point because the coincidence of the other signs with the sign of Israel renders the age in which we live quite unique. It removes any ambiguity from our thinking. Never before in world history have all these factors been operative together with the return of the Jew to his Homeland. Ever since the Declaration of the State of Israel in 1948, we have had placarded before our eyes God's greatest visible evidence that He is at work, and that Christ is coming back.

This sign was mentioned by the Lord Jesus Christ in his prophecy concerning the last days:

"And they (the Jews) shall fall by the edge of the sword, and shall be led

277

away captive into all nations: and Jerusalem shall be trodden down of the Gentiles, **until the times of the Gentiles be fulfilled**."

(Luke 21:24)

This brief prophecy has four elements to it:

The Jews would be conquered
The Jews would be dispersed among the nations
Jerusalem would be occupied by non-Jewish powers
The occupation would come to an end

The strands cover the period of history from A.D.70 until the present time. The Romans broke the power of Judah, destroyed the city and its temple, and the Jews were driven out of the land into captivity. Jerusalem was thenceforth occupied by non-Jewish powers right up to the Six-Day War in 1967 when, for the first time, the city of Jerusalem passed into wholly Jewish hands. We must observe, however, that the re-occupation of Jerusalem would be at that time in history which is described by the Lord Jesus as when "the times of the Gentiles are fulfilled".

The "times of the Gentiles" are most easily understood as the times of Gentile domination over the land of Israel. They may, however, also indicate the time allotted to the Gentiles by God following the end of the Jewish kingdom. As the Jews had their opportunity to be godly and failed, so the Gentiles have had the opportunity to be sincerely Christian. They too have failed. As the Jews reaped the judgement of God, so the Gentiles will reap theirs. This is signified in Daniel 2:44; 7:27 and Revelation 11:15 – 18.

Meanwhile God works out His purpose with Israel and will bring the Gentiles to the day of judgement for them politically when Israel is invaded:

"For there will I sit to judge all the nations round about . . . multitudes, multitudes in the valley of decision! for the day of the Lord is near in the valley of decision." (Joel 3:12,14, R.V.)

Christ's return, the desolating rebuke of the invaders and the establishment of the Kingdom of God on earth with Jerusalem as the capital city are the means ordained by God for the world's deliverance from its misery and wickedness.

Conclusion

More could be written to tell of the rise of Communism and the welding of nations together under that ideology; the scourge of

Islam; the power of oil and the importance of the Middle East in this respect. But sufficient has been said to show how all the signs of the Second Coming are coming into line.

There remains a significant change to take place before the land of Israel is ready for invasion. The prophet Ezekiel declared that the invasion would take place when the land was "at rest" and the people "dwelt safely". It cannot be said that those conditions obtain at the present time (1986). Israel is always under tension and military alertness. This has to change. Precisely how this will be is not explained for us in Scripture. Whether it will come about because Israel will persuade the Arab nations into quietness or whether it will be a development which will take place under God's hand between the time of Christ's return to judge the dead and the appearance of the invader in the land, we do not know.

Suffice it to say that as God dried up the power of Turkey and made way for the beginnings of the return of the Jews to the land, so will He bring about the quietness and rest which He has promised. Nothing is impossible with Him.

279

27

FAREWELL

THE reader who has come thus far will have travelled a long way through the pages of the Bible in learning about the faith of the Christadelphians. We would earnestly commend these things to the heart and mind of those who are seeking a purpose for life and a hope which does not end in death.

As the reader will have gathered, Christadelphians are a world-wide community which has existed for almost a century and a half, though the faith they hold they believe to be first century Christianity and right for us today.

Christadelphians believe that there is one God and one person in the Godhead. He is the God of Abraham, the God of Isaac and the God of Jacob, and the God and Father of the Lord Jesus Christ. Christ is the only begotten Son of God, born of the virgin Mary by the personal power of God, His Holy Spirit. Christ was all God's promises and intention made flesh. Sharing fully our nature, he revealed to us what God is like, not in form or feature, but in sublime holiness, absolute righteousness and boundless love, all of which qualities run through every word, every purpose, every act of compassion, every part of the whole life lived by the Saviour.

Christadelphians believe that man is mortal and sinful, in need of salvation and unable to save himself. When man dies his existence ceases and he has no hope except by resurrection from the dead.

God's grace and desire to save were made known in the gracious promises revealed to man of which the greatest are those given to Abraham, as well as those subsequently made to David. These promises make known God's coming Kingdom on earth with Christ as King, and the way in which man can share the glory of that age in life eternal by the saving grace of God in Jesus. His perfect life, sacrificial death and resurrection to glory and immortality are the guarantee that man's twin enemies, his sinfulness known as the devil, and his mortality known as death, have been altogether conquered by Jesus who, though the only begotten Son of God, shared our nature in everything, but without sin.

Every believer must acknowledge his faith in the things concerning the Kingdom of God and the name of Jesus Christ. He must acknowledge his need of help, of forgiveness, and of deliverance from death. This he shows when, believing the truth of the Gospel, he asks for God's pardon and help, and is baptized by immersion in water, confessing his sins. He then belongs to God, and is in the new covenant through the blood of the Lord Jesus Christ. As an heir of the promises made to Abraham, he waits in patience for the coming Kingdom of God.

His new life in Christ is a life of fellowship with fellow believers through fellowship with God and the Lord Jesus Christ. His life of discipleship must be free from personal selfishness, unsullied by politics and violence, and based upon the love for God and for his neighbour. The life of the believer is one of prayerful confidence in God and His purpose, and in His providential care. Week by week, in the breaking of bread, he remembers the saving work of God in Christ, and "shows forth" the Lord's death by associating himself with it. He is convinced that Jesus will personally return to the earth to bring peace to a troubled world and to establish God's Kingdom with Jerusalem at its centre. The regathered Jews are God's witnesses that God will fulfil this purpose.

Death has no final sting for the true servant of God. Life's fitful fever over, he sleeps in peace, knowing nothing of the passing years, until, as though it were but a moment after death, his Lord, returned from heaven, awakens him from death for the day of resurrection and judgement. Then the responsible among men, living and dead, will stand forth to receive the due reward of their deeds: eternal life and endless joy in the kingdom of God for the faithful; and shameful dismissal and oblivion in the second death for those who have been unfaithful to the Word of God or knowingly have rejected its call.

These things we believe because we find them clearly taught in the Bible, and we are glad to have them as the common bond in

Christ for our community. World wide we seek to hold our faith without distinction as to race or class; and without bishops or clergy, we worship and witness in a simple and consistent way. We do not observe any days or feasts other than the breaking of bread on the first day of the week.

We are glad to make our Faith known by talking about it to others, by the literature we issue which is available free, and through our Sunday Schools and Youth Groups; and at our regular, advertised Gospel talks, mostly on Sunday evenings, but often on other days, when we examine some facet of Bible teaching, always with an open Bible as our basis. Our message goes from land to land and is known in all parts of the world. It is often taken to fresh countries by some of our members who go and settle there for a time, obtain normal employment when they can, and preach from God's Word those things which Christadelphians everywhere believe.

We would sincerely urge our readers to get to know at first hand the things we stand for and the kind of people we are. You are earnestly invited to make contact with us.

SUBJECT INDEX

SCRIPTURE INDEX

OLD TESTAMENT